Praise  Here

"Trish Williams, as a responsible and dutiful daughter, weaves an engaging story of the struggles and painful moments in caring for her aging parents. But she doesn't stop there. With humor and insight, she gives the reader a clear and compassionate view of their lives, including those sweet moments that make them more lovable in spite of themselves. She also shares her difficulties and frustrations in her role as 'the responsible one.' Of course, the irresponsible child would never have written the book!"

—ROSALIE THOMAS, RN, PhD

"The emotional roller coaster of caring for an aging parent is not an easy ride. Baby boomers—the population riding that train right now—often find themselves trying to balance respect for a parent's intelligence and independence with providing for his or her safety and security. It is a juggling act of epic proportions. In *While They're Still Here*, that juggling act is an emotional tribute to self-sacrifice and a daughter's unfailing love for her parents. To the author's credit, it also glimpses the depth of understanding of her family and self that Williams achieved during this formidable experience. This book is written with honesty, humility, and love, and will remind anyone involved in caring for an elderly parent that you are not alone in your labor of love."

—SANDRA BULLOCK SMITH, award-winning author of *Trading Places: Becoming My Mother's Mother*

"A refreshingly candid, poignant memoir that lays bare the physical and emotional costs of care, *While They're Still Here* powerfully demonstrates the lengths we go to ensure the health and safety of our aging parents. Williams' writing is stark and lucid, her well-crafted anecdotes filled with compassion even as her life is upended and her caregiving duties mount. Her book reminds us of the ability we all have to redefine our lives and our relationship with our parents—and to savor the time we have left with them."

—JANA PANARITES, author of *Scattered: My Year As An Accidental Caregiver*

"In her new memoir, *While They're Still Here,* author Patricia Williams writes about the ultimate role reversal. Her role as a loving daughter is slowly upended as she becomes a lifeline and caregiver for her aging parents as they try to negotiate the daily challenges that overturn their lives and hers. The role of caregiver is one many of us must face. Williams candidly shares the intimate and rewarding moments along with the fears and unexpected burdens that go along with this complex relationship. The reader will empathize and learn from her experience and will take away familiar themes they can learn from and that will stay with them."

—IRIS WAICHLER, MSW, LCSW, patient advocate and award-winning author of *Role Reversal: How to Take Care of Yourself and Your Aging Parents*

While They're Still Here

While They're Still Here

A Memoir

Patricia Williams

SHE WRITES PRESS

Published 2017
Printed in the United States of America
Print ISBN: 978-1-63152-240-6
E-ISBN: 978-1-63152-241-3
Library of Congress Control Number: 2017943955

For information, address:
She Writes Press
1563 Solano Ave #546
Berkeley, CA 94707

Cover design © Julie Metz, Ltd./metzdesign.com
Interior design by Tabitha Lahr

She Writes Press is a division of SparkPoint Studio, LLC.

Names and identifying characteristics have been changed to protect the
privacy of certain individuals.

Dedication

To my mother, and all the neighbors, friends, relatives, and caregivers who have graced her life, especially my father and our two beloved redheads—my grandfather and my brother.

Chapter 1

....

The driver hadn't required much more than a grunt or a single-word contribution from me to maintain his prattle for an hour.

"What time you leave home this morning?" he asked, his battered toothpick waving like a bandleader's baton in time with his words.

"Four," I answered.

"Long day. Almost there now. You're so lucky you can do this. I wish I coulda had the chance."

"Um," I answered uncertainly.

"Once they're gone, it's forever too late." He coughed out the last word, and I looked to see if I should begin first aid for a swallowed toothpick. From the way he was shaking his head, I decided he was only choking on a sliver of regret. I had no remedy for that.

"Yeah" was all I could muster, but I knew his taxicab wisdom held truth. I'd heard this same comment several times in the last few days from friends and relatives.

He yanked out the toothpick after it tangled in his scraggly mustache, then fondled a pack of cigarettes under the dash.

That explained the reek of pine air freshener from dangling cardboard trees.

"Here we are," he announced, as if I didn't know. "Do you want me to wait until you get in the house?" An unlit cigarette swayed from his lips now.

"No, you go on ahead. Thanks." I didn't want to hurry my fate just so he could smoke.

His airport van sputtered away, leaving me alone in the dark driveway with only my suitcases and my dread. I stood there, unable to move, my new job description stiffening me like a nurse's starched white uniform. The rain-soaked concrete was still steaming at eleven o'clock at night, with that indelibly acrid stench of simmering road grime. I was starting to sweat and steam, too, but I rolled my sleeves down against the mosquitoes reconnoitering for the only available flesh.

I had kissed my partner and my dogs good-bye in the opposite corner of the country before breakfast, zigzagged and layovered in an exhausting and inefficient short-notice flight plan to arrive in Englewood, Florida, but I was reluctant to undertake the last thirty feet to my destination.

Bad travel plans symbolized the end of my well-ordered life. When I had signed on for this job two weeks before, I had known I was relinquishing my nutritionally balanced, organic meals, eight hours of sleep, short to-do lists with each task crossed off at the end of the day, and regular exercise. My career as a dental hygienist had abruptly screeched to an end after a shoulder injury, so I couldn't use work as an excuse to turn down this assignment.

Straightening my invisible caregiver's uniform, I zipped up my courage, tucked in my compassion, and pasted on my smile. I could do this. I had to do this. I had trained my whole life to do this. I marched up the driveway to the front porch of this familiar stucco ranch-style house, crunching through oily seeds and dried leaves from the witch hazel tree. I swatted its prickly branches out of my face, wondering if I should prune it or cut it down, already initiating a new to-do list.

When I tiptoed into the house, the boiled-cabbage fumes of old age foreshadowed my future. No chicken soup simmering on the stove, no lingering cinnamon from a fresh apple pie to welcome me back. My mother was sick in bed, and my father was asleep, gasping and rattling in his threadbare recliner in the living room. Where was his apnea equipment? I pulled a notebook from my back pocket and jotted down *witch hazel tree* and *snoring*.

The memorabilia of my parents' lives, our lives, burgeoned wall to wall: inlaid end tables my dad's father built while out on strike from the railroad; pen-and-ink drawings by my mother's artistic sister; glassware from a great-aunt's estate auction forty years before; and afghans crocheted by each of my grandmothers. My mother's only concession to new decor when they had retired here from Maryland fourteen years ago had been to leave behind her early-American couch and chair and buy a pastel floral set more in keeping with Florida's ambience. She still lamented that choice, as if she'd deserted an old friend.

My parents had bought this new, contemporary house in a rural, coastal neighborhood and packed it snug with their living museum, reincarnating our childhood nest. Although moderately sized, with three bedrooms and two baths, it was smaller than their last home and half the size of the house in Ohio where I wilded through my teens. Mom and Dad never scaled down their belongings when they downsized their homes, just pushed and shoved and squeezed it all in, although the effect felt more cozy than cluttered.

I crept through the stagnant house, toward the guest room, inventorying symptoms of my parents' decline: kitchen sink overflowing with spaghetti-smeared plates; cat hair upholstering every surface; baskets of ripe laundry. In my fifty-some years, I had never known my mother to go to bed without washing, drying, and putting away the dishes. I rinsed the plates, threw a sour sponge out the back door with a grimace, and tossed a load of laundry in the washer.

My blood pressure was rising as quickly as my blood sugar was plummeting. Maybe a piece of toast and a glass of milk would help. No bread. No milk. No cheese. No fruit. No food that wasn't fuzzy and blue.

The most shocking sight was the dining room table, littered with a jumble of rolled-up newspapers, mail, medicines, paper plates, and coffee cups. This round, four-foot slab of old oak, the center of my mother's universe, had always been orderly and always strictly her domain. I knew my brother and father weren't sure what the boundaries for intervention were when Mom was sick, and were afraid to trespass even to tidy it.

Under normal circumstances, every morning my father set the newspaper by Mom's spot at the table, where she read it cover to cover with her coffee. He couldn't see fine print anymore, so she shared snippets of news and stories with him over his breakfast, then folded the paper right into a recycling bag by her chair. After lunch, Dad carried in the mail, sat at the table with her, sliced each envelope open with his pocketknife, and waited while she sorted through things. She read anything of interest to him, filed bills and papers in the cabinet behind her chair, and recycled the junk. Her last act of each day was a survey of the table for cups and crumbs, refilling the napkin holder on the lazy Susan, and straightening the place mats.

I stacked the newspapers, sorted the mail, cleared the dishes, and wiped off the tablecloth. Traipsing into the bathroom, I hung up a musty towel, splashed cold water on my face in the stained sink, and peed. The toilet didn't flush. I added *plumber* and *bigger notebook* to my list.

Chapter 2

....

Looking for moral support, I headed for my brother's lair in the garage. He had recently moved back home for temporary financial relief while establishing a career in photography and graphic arts. I knocked lightly. "Chip, it's me."

He opened his door and stepped aside to let me squeeze past his full-bodied, six-foot frame, acknowledging me with a casual "hi"—an unemotional, nonphysical, typical family greeting after a three-thousand-mile trip.

"Hi, honey. How are you?" I responded in the same flat tone, my uniform intact, no distress leaking out around the seams. The lack of emotion in greeting this "chip off the old block" was no indication of our relationship. Although he was named Thomas, after our father, Chip had earned his nickname by being the spitting image of our mother's beloved Irish father. I had adored my grandfather, and I cherished my brother beyond words.

The computer monitor and two televisions lit his face, highlighting his cobalt-blue eyes, dimples, and freckles. He was a cute baby when my mother handed off her wailing newborn to me and cradled her wine bottle instead, and he was a striking forty-something man now.

"Okaaay," he sighed, his always-answer in a sweet sing-song, which could mean anything.

My eyes adjusted to the dark as I wedged myself between the cats on the futon.

He turned to face me, his red Irish curls backlit now by the strobing screens, and asked, "How was your flight?"

"Greeaaat," rang out my standard answer, in a ridiculously energetic voice.

That done, we could talk.

His words poured out: "Jeez, I'm glad you're here. They shouldn't have released Dad from the hospital today; he's panting and pale. I'm too busy with work and packing to take care of him. I have some photos in a show next weekend, and I'm not ready."

The trembling voice in my head was trying to categorize *panting* and *pale*. What was I doing? I was only a dental hygienist.

My calm caretaker's voice asked, "Did they diagnose anything? It sounds like the hospital ran every test in the book for three days."

Chip answered, "Panic attacks. He has a new prescription to fill tomorrow. I think he's upset that the eye surgery didn't work."

Behind my brother, Jay Leno was chatting up Ringo Starr while Peter Jennings cross-examined General Tommy Franks. Was it mere irony or karmic gravity that had pulled me into my mother's orbit at this precise time, March 2003, during a second-edition George Bush war? The first Gulf War had seared a landmark divide in our mother-daughter relationship.

I didn't want to hear the answer to my next question: "How's Mom?"

"I don't know. She's been in bed for three days and hasn't said what's wrong."

My family practiced and perfected "don't ask, don't tell." I needed to pose one more question before I covered my ears and started braying, *Lalalalala*. "Do you think they're serious about moving to Washington?" I couldn't hide the trepidation in my voice.

He flipped through channels, checked his e-mail, and answered me simultaneously. "They have to go. They can't stay here alone, and I'm moving in three weeks. Dad can't manage the outside, and Mom can't take care of the inside. I help them with appointments and prescriptions, but they won't let me do anything else. They say they don't want to bother me, but I think they haven't wanted to admit they can't manage things on their own. They can't afford the house; insurance and taxes have tripled in Florida since they moved here."

Okay. So I really was here to pack up my parents and move them to Olympia, where I'd lived for nearly thirty years. I accepted my fate and chuckled sarcastically. "I actually dropped the phone when Linda called and said how happy she was that Mom and Dad were moving to Washington. That's how I found out. I felt like I was rehearsing for our personal family TV sitcom."

My brother scoffed, "Typical. Don't discuss anything with the ones who need to know. I didn't find out until you called me."

Our half sister, Linda, who also lived in Washington State, was older and more like a doting aunt to us. Our mother confided in her, and they shared a secret past to which we were not privy. I was not informed Linda was my half sister until I was twelve and realized some dates for marriages and births didn't add up. After a brief, confusing explanation, that subject fell permanently into my family's "don't ask, don't tell" category.

Had it really been just two weeks earlier when every fiber of my life had frayed after Linda's phone call? I had squeaked out a feeble agreement with her about this being good news before I went flat, all the air out of my tires. Not usually theatrical, I collapsed on our living room floor and stared at the ceiling while my dogs stood stock-still over me, hanging their cocked heads in a question.

I *was* genuinely happy about my parents' decision—I wanted them to move—but I had intended to ease gently into the idea when the time came by gradually repositioning the pieces of our lives. This was too much all at once for a methodical person like me to organize. When I extracted myself from my emotional muck on the floor, I forced myself to think. *Moving. Sell their house. Pack. Find a place for them to live.*

When? I stared at the calendar while waiting for blood to flow back to my brain. I chided myself to think positively: no more grueling flights back and forth to Florida, no more diagnosing obscure medical symptoms over the phone. *Good. Breathe. Plan.*

It might have been easier to arrange their exodus if there hadn't been a sense of urgency, but when I spoke with Chip after my sister called, he fine-tuned the gloomy picture. He was moving to live with his girlfriend, and both Mom and Dad appeared near nursing home–caliber sick. Chip could hold down the fort until I got there, but he was balancing that with a new full-time photography job, his own art exhibits, and his ongoing work as an animal communicator.

He advised me to hurry, and I knew he wasn't one for melodrama. I needed to act quickly. Plane reservations. Instructions for the dogs while I was away. My prescriptions. My medical appointments. A haircut. Lists and lists.

My partner of twenty years, Katy, understood my daughterly mandate. She had readily agreed to assume my responsibilities for running our household, but I knew she didn't perceive the extent of the commission. She managed her own thriving small business as a counselor, which consumed most of her waking hours, while I handled our home life. I didn't have time to worry about it, though. If she couldn't start the mower or find the dog food, she could call me.

I couldn't answer her question, "How long will you be gone?" and I couldn't answer my question, "How long will they live?"

Chapter 3

....

Saying good night to Chip after midnight, I dragged my bags to my parents' guest room and wondered why the carpet was swaying. I plopped down on my suitcase and lowered my head between my knees, figuring I was fainting. As my head dangled closer to the floor, I realized either the carpet really was undulating or I was hallucinating. I didn't have time to be sick. How could I take care of them if I couldn't take care of myself? And what kind of illness was preceded by acute eye squiggliness?

Not to worry. It was just bugs—millions of tiny insects stampeding in waves to escape my fatal footsteps.

Chip walked by the room while I was still hunched over the carpet, then came in, asking nervously if I was okay. Looking down where I pointed, he said, "Damn termites. They erupt like volcanoes after every rainstorm."

He pulled a portrait of our grandfather away from the wall and peeked behind it. "They're even in the drywall and the cardboard behind the pictures. I'll go change my clothes; you get the vacuum. We have a long night ahead of us."

I wrote *exterminator* in my notebook and sneaked past my reverberating father to smuggle the vacuum cleaner from the front-hall closet. I definitely did not want to wake him and then cope with both him and the termites. He would have been embarrassed and determined to help, and that, predictably, would have sparked an angina attack. My father never considered that his limitations were less than those of the sailor he'd been sixty years earlier, and I didn't have the energy to triage his self-esteem and the vermin.

Clandestine cleaners, my brother and I quietly stripped every piece of cat hair–covered fabric in the guest room and laundered everything twice. Chip skulked down the hall to make sure Dad was still asleep; then we lugged the mattress and box spring to another room so we could vacuum the entire termite-laden rug, the inside and outside of every piece of furniture, all the drawers and all their contents, and the walls behind the infested pictures.

My brother left me with "I don't think we should tell them any of this."

I knew he was right. I'd need a pest inspection to sell the house, so the bugs would be dealt with anyway. But was not telling them perpetuating the "don't tell the ones who need to know" family creed or genuinely protecting them? It didn't matter—I couldn't bear to tell them.

My parents had devoted their life energy to cultivating their tidy homes, always fixing, painting, improving. Now that they were approaching eighty, their infirmities and stress had catapulted the house downhill with lightning speed. My perspective of the house had changed, too, since I had assumed the task of preparing it for sale. I was now scrutinizing it through the lens of a potential homebuyer.

By then, at five in the morning, I should have been tired, but adrenaline had fully charged my battery. This morning I would begin setting the stage for my parents' rite of passage: having a child take care of them. I had maintained a fairly consistent relationship with them throughout my life, so the whole idea wasn't completely unthinkable. I couldn't qualify our relationship as good, bad, or indifferent. It ran the full gamut of adjectives, just as most relationships do. What would this next phase render?

Over the last three years, as their health had declined and my father had lost most of his sight, I had traveled back and forth from Washington to Florida with increasing frequency. Based on my undeniable history as a caregiver, I didn't even question my role. From the beginning, I dressed my Tiny Tears doll in a warm coat to go outside and in snuggly pajamas for bed. I bathed, brushed, and tucked Bluey and Sugarfoot, my stuffed dogs, under the covers with their muzzles peeking out just enough to sniff fresh air. I still have them.

I indulged my pets with every comfort. I had cared for my dental hygiene patients with my full heart and soul. After fifty years of nurturing anything in my proximity, politically correct or not, I had conceded that I was a caregiver. I didn't analyze or defend it; it was the character card I'd been dealt, and I played it when it was my turn.

During the previous years of my cross-country geriatric nursing, I had assured both of my parents that if they decided to move to Washington, I would make it happen. Dad had been ready to pack up years before, but Mom wouldn't budge. She clung to her bottle in Florida and knew it wouldn't survive the trip. Even though her on-and-off alcoholism was at the very top of the "don't ask, don't tell" list, I had somehow managed to make it clear that drinking was not a way of life in my West Coast land of clean air and healthy habits.

Now here I was, dropped from the sky into Florida, at boot camp for eldercare training. I was up and at 'em for my first day on the job when Dad shuffled into the kitchen for breakfast.

"Hi, Dad," I said quietly. "I got here all safe and sound." That would clarify who I was and my location in the room without startling him. He could see well enough to know someone was nearby, but he required a minute or so to line up his remaining speck of eyesight to identify people. In the last two years, he had undergone several eye surgeries to battle macular degeneration and ocular blood clots. He now had no vision in his left eye and a tiny dot of peripheral vision in his right eye.

"Oh, good. How are you?" he wheezed, then collapsed in a chair to catch his breath.

"Greeeaaat. How are you?" Silly, cheery voice for someone who'd had no sleep.

"Terrrific," he coughed out, trying for his Tony the Tiger voice for his always-answer.

What a bunch of liars we were.

He was not terrific. I was not great. He was too weak to go to his grocery-bagging job with his buddies, his shoulders were hunched to his ears as he struggled to draw a breath, and he was stuck at home unless a neighbor or Chip drove him somewhere. He couldn't drive anymore because of his vision loss, and Mom hadn't driven in years. We didn't know why she wouldn't drive, but no one pushed her, since her drinking was unpredictable.

"Didya sleep okay last night, Dad?"

"I guess so. I sleep better sitting up, so I'm sleeping in my chair."

"That's good. Let's move your apnea equipment out there, then." I tried to make it sound like a great idea.

"I don't need it," he grumbled.

"I heard you kinda gasping last night in your chair," I said, hoping I wasn't going to alienate him this soon.

"Okay. I'll move the machine."

I crossed *snoring* off my list and added *hospital bed*, so his head could be elevated.

"What are we going to do today?" he asked, his voice tinged with hope.

"Let's go to the grocery store. We can get your new prescription, too."

He heard it as "let's go to Coney Island." He perked right up and recited a list. "I'll open the car doors to cool it off, see if your mother wants anything at the store, shave, and be ready in a half hour."

We were going out! In the car! To his store! To see his friends! Out out out. It was a dose of medicine for him, and a caregiver's reward.

Mom heard the magic words *grocery store* and crawled out of her cave. The raving beauty we all remembered now lugged an extra one hundred pounds, distending a faded, flowered muumuu. Her stooped, barefooted cargo was capped by stringy hair and swollen eyelids.

"Hi, Mom. How are you?"

Leaning on a chair, she cocked her head, squeezed one eye closed, kinked her upper lip, and shrugged. In the "don't ask, don't tell" playbook, that meant, *How the hell do you think I am?* Nevertheless, she rattled off a grocery list before she hobbled back to bed. I told myself things would get better because they couldn't get much worse. Could they?

Chapter 4

....

Those first few days, I devoted as much time to worrying as possible. I tried to excuse it as planning, but my heart rate belied the truth. I decided the most pressing problem was my parents' stress levels. My own tension was not resolvable. Mom remained in bed and was not forthcoming with any information regarding her condition. Dad had never been much of a talker. I would need to decipher their anxiety by reading between the unspoken lines.

Aware that I was erecting the scaffolding for our relationship in this new era, I knew I had to be my best self. I ran errands, did light cleaning, and ostensibly kept them company while I was conducting my research and planning. I didn't ask any hard questions or require decisions of them, just casually mentioned possibilities suggesting a rosy future in Washington. They began to trust that they would be taken care of but still have choices. All of our shoulders slipped down a few notches, although they remained up around earlobe level.

Mom showered on the fourth day and asked me to cut her hair, even though the only hair I had ever cut grew on my standard poodle. I realized it was the least of the tasks I was unqualified to perform and plowed ahead. She plopped her busted and bursting body in a chair and began directing me in haircut protocol. Handing me a worn bedsheet with frayed edges and a cigarette burn, she instructed me, "Drape this sheet around me, and then fasten it in the back with this pin. Here are Uncle Shorty's barber shears. This side goes toward your thumb. You can use this spray bottle if you want."

I was baffled at the explicit directions, since no one had ever cut her hair at home. Then I recognized this was the way she had trimmed our bangs when we were kids, maybe the way her mother had cut her bangs, too.

Dad stuck his head in and said he was walking next door to see his friend Carroll. Once Mom had me to herself, her worries gushed out: "I cut up all our credit cards, but we owe thousands more than we can ever pay. Don't tell your father. He would just worry." She shifted uncomfortably and groaned.

I wasn't sure if the familiar refrain "don't tell your father" was for her sake or his, but I knew I wouldn't violate her trust or add to his stress. "Do you need a different chair?" I asked while I combed and snipped.

"No, my hip replacement is loose, and the only specialist willing to redo it is three hours away. It's complicated because of the Paget's disease. Don't tell your father." She paused to weigh my reaction. My invisible caregiver's uniform was evidently on straight, so she continued, "I don't want any more medical bills anyway. The insurance won't cover Dad's Sarasota hospital stay because they say it wasn't preauthorized. How could I have gotten it preauthorized? He had a grand mal seizure in our hospital and fell out of bed in the middle of the night. They had to race him by ambulance sixty miles to the Sarasota hospital for emergency surgery. They just sent the bill to collections. Don't tell your father."

I wondered if I should wait to see if more overflowed or try to dam it there. She paused, so I plunged: "You can give me whatever jobs and bills need to be looked into, and I'll see what

I can do. Your expenses will be much lower in Washington, so you'll catch up financially. We have well-respected orthopedic surgeons in Olympia; when you're ready, you can have your hip evaluated."

Did I get it all? Did I get it right?

She sat up straighter and turned to face me, saying, "Thank you so much for everything. You are a lifesaver. I think I'll go get dressed and curl my hair. Thanks for the trim." She swirled her head back and forth to feel her new length, just like my dog shook after a haircut.

I unveiled her from the tattered sheet, and she located her handholds on the arms of the chair. She rocked backward a bit, to build up velocity for her trajectory, then hurled herself forward, hoisting her pain-filled prow out of the chair. She reeled toward her bedroom, a decrepit shuffle-hobble-grunt of decaying carapace.

My eyes tracked her, but my brain featured a video of her signature exits in younger days: One arm up in the air, her fingers snapping a rhythm, one hand on her abdomen, swaying her shapely hips, she would hum and swoosh out of the room in a beguiling rumba flourish. As a teenager, I burned with embarrassment at her exhibition; now, I ached for a trace of sashay.

How did she manage these mounting medical tragedies? In the last ten years, she'd had a knee replacement shatter, a malignant kidney removed, breast cancer, Paget's disease diagnosed as the source of her bone degeneration and pain, and my father's continuing cardiac saga and vision loss. Maybe it was no wonder that she had started drinking again after a decade of sobriety.

Although he didn't drink, Dad bought wine for her, rather than suffer the consequences of her ire. No one blamed him. When crossed, Mom could slam her face shut and keep it locked for months. Privately, my father berated himself for not having dealt with her alcoholism in their younger years. My frequent reply to him and abiding life philosophy was, "You did what you thought was right at the time."

The next day, my father spilled his worries via show-and-tell in the backyard, his transplanted Midwestern terrain. Unlike the adjacent yards of swimming pools and palms, ours had a forty-foot spreading oak tree. We sat in its shade, watched birds at the log cabin–style feeders, and admired the baskets of geraniums hanging on the laundry-line posts. The previous year, Dad had grown sweet corn, calling his patch an ear of Ohio.

I thought we were resting, but his fret timer went off. He nodded at the storage building he had installed for my brother's excess possessions and said, with a tight throat, "That storage shed is too close to the house to pass inspection, so we need to get rid of it." He pointed up to a gable vent, squinting his eyes and furrowing his forehead because he couldn't see that far, and asked, "Is there still a TV cable running up there into the attic? It's disconnected but needs to come out. What should we do about the broken glass on these windows? Can you see the roof? Is it in good shape?" I scribbled in my ever-present pocket notebook.

I found a ladder and climbed up onto the roof, knowing that my inspection was the only way he, and now I, would feel reassured. The condition of the roof hadn't bleeped on my radar screen of repairs yet, but now it hit me with gale force. With relief, I hollered down, "We just need to repair this one spot where Chip's satellite dish was, and then it's perfect."

After I came down, he rushed on to his next concern. "This irrigation system is really going to bring down the price of the house." We walked over to the main control box. He had fretted about this a few times, but I didn't understand the problem. My father had designed and installed an irrigation system for the entire piece of property. It was a large corner lot, and he'd dug all the trenches by hand and laid the pipe himself when he'd retired here in his late sixties. The flourishing flowerbeds, fruit trees bursting with buds, fragrant ornamental shrubs, and lush grass proved the irrigation system's success. What was wrong with it?

He pointed to the control box and pipes. "The water filters need to be changed, and I can't see in there. Could you try to do it?"

He leaned on the house and lowered himself onto his rickety knees. I knelt beside him.

He lifted the cover and instructed me from memory. "First, put your left hand on the green knob way in the back and hold it tight; then turn the blue one clockwise with your right hand. It will turn hard, but it'll go."

He directed me through six more steps with precise instructions, then said, "I asked Mr. Bigshot to change them the last time, and he said the system was crude and needed to be upgraded."

Aha! Now I knew the problem: Mr. Bigshot was Mom's nickname for a puffed-up neighbor with fancy cars, an Olympic-size pool, and corrosive commentary.

"This is a great system, Dad. It allows you a lot of individual control with a minimum amount of expensive equipment to maintain." He knew I had a professionally installed system at home, so my opinion had credibility with him.

Between the roof's being in good repair and the first-rate irrigation system, he'd received a double dose of medicine. Dad went indoors and took a restful nap. I went in and organized lists and sublists.

Even though I was so stressed that I couldn't fully unclench my teeth, I didn't feel resentful toward my parents. I knew the headlines, if not the details, of the ebb and flow of the eight decades that were bringing them under my care, and I viewed their lives more compassionately through this lens of hindsight. I knew they needed to be able to depend on me, regardless of our stormy past.

When I was growing up in the Midwest in the 1950s, we were the essence of a postwar, blue-collar American family. Mom happily wore her freshly ironed aprons, and Dad came straight home from work every night at five thirty sharp, depositing a kiss on her cheek while she stirred something on the stove. Unlike the happy TV families, though, we lived in tornado country, literally and figuratively. Unpredictably, the emotional winds would shift and send my two siblings and me swirling. I can only sift through those tumultuous times with my adult understanding of the potential undercurrents brewing. The slamming doors, sharp silences, and stilted conversations were never explained. We weren't supposed to notice.

As a headstrong, manipulative child, I plotted my course during those blackened skies and maneuvered my way around my mother's prevailing winds. As a strong-willed teen, I did as I pleased, defying my parents to enter the eye of the storm to control me. As an adult, I mostly bobbed my head in wonderment at my parents' idiosyncrasies and hoped it looked like agreement. They probably did the same. It just wasn't worth fighting about anything anymore.

Even the difficult times had been interspersed with happy interludes, though, and I had maintained a connection with each of my parents through thick and thin. The only hiatus in our relationship was in 1990, when my mother, an "I like Ike" Republican, hung up on me, a Vietnam-era "make love, not war" Democrat, because I disagreed with her about the first Gulf War. Just a week before, she had been charming, witty, thoughtful, gracious, and bright. She had chatted, "How are the dogs? Did you try that recipe? Did you get the book I sent?" By the next week, she had downshifted into bitterness and spat at me, "If you can't support our country, you should just leave it. See how you like it in Russia." She slapped the phone down and cut the cord of our relationship.

In my teens, I blamed my mother's dramatic mood swings on her Gemini birth sign, the twin. In time I realized that alcohol and a caustic reservoir of entitlement invoked her churlish counterpart, fueling a mean drunk who could suddenly take up residence for a few hours or a few years. No matter which twin manifested, she reflected some of the vanity and physical remnants of Mom's former life as a 1940s nightclub starlet.

A month after she'd hung up on me, we'd still had no contact. I cautiously composed a letter to her, pleading for her to stop drinking. A year slid by, with no response and no communication, until my boss planned a trip for our entire staff to Disney World. Jiminy Cricket on my shoulder would not allow me to vacation within sixty miles of my parents' home without visiting them. I called, and we reconciled in our traditional family way: Everyone pretended nothing had ever happened.

My intention now was not to confront my mother's bad moments or bad years. My father had his, too, of a different sort. Let's call him overly flirtatious and leave it at that. He was my mother's Cary Grant, tall, dark, and handsome, and she was outwardly madly in love and inwardly just plain mad about the attention he paid to other women. My parents each had kept a bitter, private balance sheet of personal infractions throughout their lives but seemingly now had thrown away the scorecards. I could, too.

By their subtle comments, I gathered that they fully grasped the complexities of putting all their eggs in my basket. When they asked me if I would ever want to leave Olympia, I knew it meant, *Are you going to leave us high and dry in a strange city?* In my heart and mind, I had accepted the responsibility of caring for them for the rest of their lives, and I reassured them of that with my words and actions. They asked if I was tired, if it was all too much, how they could help me. They wondered how they would get to the doctor or the grocery store. I answered each worry and coated my words with kindness. We were all on our best behavior, a community pulling together after a twister called aging cut a swath through our lives.

Chapter 5

···························

I was cautious about the number of problems I presented to
them each day, but I had to talk to them about where they
were hoping to live and how and when they were going to get
there. Planning for travel had never been part of their résumé.
The only big trip we had ever taken when I was a kid was a
spontaneous two-week vacation to Florida with no motel reservations. Most of our sightseeing consisted of driving around,
looking for affordable lodging and cheap food.

Did they think I'd load them up, we'd drive off, towing a
U-Haul, and then they'd cram in with Katy and me until we
found a place for them? Pack up a three-bedroom house myself
and drive across the country with ailing oldsters and their cat? I
resolved to bring it up at the next available calm spot.

We were all seated at the dining room table for lunch, and
no one was hyperventilating or squirming, so I casually floated
a test balloon: "I was thinking about getting some estimates
from moving companies."

Dad, ever the twenty-year-old seaman, proposed, "Do you
think we could just take a U-Haul?"

I hoped I sounded like I was seriously considering the idea
when I replied, "Maybe, but let's just get an estimate." They
reluctantly okayed the idea.

"When do you want to go?" I asked, like it was a trip to the zoo.

My mother was fidgeting now, smoothing the tablecloth and straightening napkins. Dad was hunching over to fill his lungs. Mom's lips quivered and her eyes filled up as she spurted, "I figured you wanted to get home as soon as possible, so we'd just pack up and go next week."

Instead of pointing out how ridiculously unrealistic that was, I said, "Well, I thought I'd be here a couple months to pack and get the house ready." Their joint sighs of relief calculated the degree of my information failure. Why had I waited to talk about this?

Dad cleared the table and started putting the food away. He'd probably had enough, but I wanted to get this settled. "Where do you want to live?" I asked, in the tone of "What would you do if you won the lottery?" A few months earlier, I had asked this same question hypothetically when Mom had first hinted that they could no longer afford the house. At that time, she had pursed her lips and spat out, "I will not live in an apartment. I don't want to stare at a slumlord's peeling wallpaper or hear the baby next door crying. I will *never* live in an apartment again. And don't even think about a retirement complex. *Never.*"

This time, before Mom could rev up steadfast refusals about renting, Dad asked, "Do you think we should rent a house?"

"You could," I answered, "but it would be pretty expensive, and you'd still have to worry about taking care of a yard." Then I swiftly got on a roll before Mom could lead her charge. "I did some research before I left home, and I think I found a good option; at least, you could live there temporarily. Do you remember the apartments across the street from us? There are twelve apartments there, hidden by the trees, right on the lake."

I could see Mom cocking her stink-eye at the word *apartment*, preparing to shoot me with a lethal glare. I had to talk fast so her negativity couldn't find a gap and derail my presentation. "Here's the floor plan, and here are some photos I took inside one of the apartments." I told them the price, which was surprisingly affordable because of its rural location, proximity to railroad tracks, and outdated appliances and fixtures.

My parents had visited Olympia several times in the past, staying with us for a month each time. They loved our rustic setting near the lake and woods and enjoyed our neighbors and friends. Mom studied the photos I spread out on the table, and a promising reality quickly replaced her inchoate fears. Necessity, persuasion, a secluded lake, affordability, and a clean apartment changed her mind. I signed and faxed the lease. I wasn't sure they would both survive a full year, but at least I had a place to deposit them. We were all on track. Dad said, "Let's go get boxes and start packing. I have stuff to take to the Goodwill."

The movers estimated our load and showed us the giant-size truck we'd need. That resolved the U-Haul issue but presented a new one: The cost was much more than we anticipated, and my parents had no savings. I downplayed the dilemma and assured them I could front the money. Gulp. I hoped they would make a profit on the house. The mover had suggested we could reduce moving expenses by paring down their belongings and by packing all the nonbreakables ourselves.

To that end, Dad picked up whatever object he walked past and carried it to the garage to pack. Gardening shears with photo albums. Cat toys with hot-water bottles. I went to the grocery store every morning at six and jammed the car with boxes. At night I repacked Dad's cartons in sensible categories, labeling and inventorying as I went along. We gave things away to neighbors; we set flowerpots, fertilizers, and cleaning supplies out front with a FREE sign; we hauled a dozen loads to the dump; we donated to Goodwill every time we went into town.

Proportionately, though, not much went to Goodwill or the curb. Mom clung to their possessions as a tether to a formerly full life, not a lower-class apartment life. I packed and labeled, telling myself my only goal was to transport them and their belongings to Washington in relatively good condition. I could deal with sorting their stuff in Pacific Standard Time just as well, and sleep in my own bed during the process.

At least we were moving forward together. We weren't in a cold war, and no one was in the hospital.

On day ten, I strolled into the kitchen with my make-believe caregiver's uniform refreshed and my to-do list ready. I was humming and happy with our progress. Mom smacked shut a cupboard door and growled, "Where's my measuring cup?" She warehoused a dozen measuring cups, so I didn't take her too seriously and just kept moving as if I were only passing through.

She snapped, "The two-cup glass one with the big spout."

I couldn't pretend I hadn't heard her and replied, "I don't know. Maybe I put it in the wrong cupboard."

Snarling and slamming, she screamed, "Did you take it to the Goodwill? Ask your brother if he has it. Why does everyone think they can throw away my things? I'm taking everything to Washington. Don't get rid of anything." She banged door after door, punctuating her wrath. "I want everybody to stay the hell out of my stuff."

Admittedly, I had been cleaning, sorting, and tidying, but I knew better than to decide the fate of any of her belongings. "Mom, I'm sorry," I said, hoping I sounded apologetic, not sarcastic. "I thought I was helping, but I can go home and just come back when you're ready to go. The movers can pack everything."

Her rapid and panicked "no!" told me I was misinterpreting her tantrum, but I didn't have a clue about her behavior. Obeying our family code, I knew it was unreasonable to expect her to explain herself or for me to request an explanation.

I phoned Katy to bemoan my fate and described my mother's eruption. Katy, a psychotherapist with a specialty in treating addictions and trauma, asked several questions and promptly diagnosed alcohol withdrawal. My mother had likely squeezed out her last drop of wine and had no hope of procuring any more while I drove the grocery cart. Nor could she count on acquiring contraband from her former grocery runners, including Dad. She knew he could feel safe teaming up with me in banning alcohol, and she couldn't requisition a neighbor for supplies when I was obviously managing the shopping. I didn't know all the details of how she had formerly obtained her stash, but I knew my presence blockaded it.

The next morning, I slithered around, avoiding her as long as possible, trying to take the temperature of our world before I slid in—a skill I had mastered in childhood. By midmorning, too hungry to avoid her anymore, I edged into the kitchen.

Hair combed, apron tied, and voice soft, my mother cooed, "I'm going to bake some cookies this morning before it gets hot. Why don't you call that place down the street and get a massage? I'll pay for it. You're working so hard."

This was as close to an admission of "I'm sorry, I'll try harder" as she ever came, and more than I expected. I never dared to hope that this was the version of my mother I would take to Washington. Maybe she did have a reserve of the courage she'd draped on like a fur coat so many times in her past. Maybe she was still the person who, if she didn't go to bed with a bottle, woke up grateful and gracious.

Chapter 6

A s the alcohol drained out of Mom's bloodstream, her metamorphosis continued. A few days later, she timidly asked, "Do you think you could take me shopping for clothes?" A simple question, but so many layers of her life fabric were sewn into it. She hated being overweight. She had no patience for shopping and felt intimidated by every other body in the store. She wanted to be the svelte, blue-eyed vixen who had wowed nightclub audiences in her twenties, and nothing less would do.

"I'd love to," I said. "You have great stores here. I can shop for a birthday present for Katy. When do you want to go?"

"Not tomorrow. I called the handyman to fix the leak in my toilet, and he's coming in the morning at eight o'clock."

She knows a handyman? Those were magic words for me and my list.

I didn't know there was a leak. That bathroom was inexplicably off-limits to anyone but her, so I had no idea of its condition. Not wanting her to be embarrassed in front of the handyman, I asked if there were things she'd like me to do in there before he arrived.

"No. I'll clean the toilet," she answered adamantly. I saw a struggle in her eyes that I interpreted as her not wanting to make more work for me.

"I could wash the floor. That's easy for me," I offered.

"Oh, all right. It probably needs it. Let me tidy things up in there first." As she turned away, I heard a muffled "damn it."

After she reluctantly granted access, I charged into her bathroom with gloves and cleaners and spent several hours scrubbing. As I wiped out under the sink on my hands and knees, the odor of sloshed, fermented fruit defined the room: It was her bar. Prohibition had just shut it down, and I was preparing it for reopening to the public for its traditional use. I couldn't begin to think about what my mother was going through. I just hung on to my gratitude for her not drinking, no matter how it came about. Maybe someday we'd talk about it. Probably not.

The next morning, I answered the doorbell when it rang precisely at eight, but it wasn't the handyman. It was a tanned, handsome, typical Florida retiree, dressed in pressed khakis and a polo shirt, ready for the golf course.

"Hi. Can I help you?" I asked, thinking he might be a realtor who'd caught a whiff of our plans.

"I'm Alex," he announced.

That elicited a blank stare from me, so he continued, "Margaret called about a leaky toilet?"

This was the handyman? He excused himself as he passed me and said hi to Mom. She pointed. "In there."

He came out before I gathered my wits and said he'd be back in twenty minutes with the parts he needed. He returned in that time frame, fixed the toilet, and charged fifteen dollars. While he was chitchatting with Mom, she asked him about painting the walls.

"Oh, sure," he replied. "The whole inside? I'm going to be away for three or four days, but I could start Monday at eight. Probably take four days. Get twelve gallons of eggshell and three gallons of semigloss. See you Monday."

I filed his proposal in the *pretty unlikely* category because it seemed too good to be true. The cost of his labor was too cheap, the plan too easy. I bought paint and started rolling the walls.

At seven thirty Monday morning, he arrived dressed for eighteen holes with paint tarps in tow. It didn't take long for my skepticism about him to turn into admiration. Alex painted like wildfire, without a splatter or a drip. He didn't need the paint tarps he so carefully smoothed over the carpets. He was gracious and spoke engagingly about his life. He had been a vice president of a large corporation and consulted for them occasionally but mostly kept his schedule open for his grandchildren. Mom had told me he lived on a golf course in a high-end neighborhood, but he gave no allusion to that. He worked as a handyman to keep busy.

Our painting and chatting were interspersed with companionable quiet. I studied him. He was so confident and comfortable; I wanted to be like him when I grew up. But why didn't I feel grown-up? I was over fifty, I owned a house, I had a retirement account and a stable long-term relationship. I just wasn't prepared to be in charge of my parents.

We finished painting in three days, and Alex went to the garage to say good-bye to Dad, who was touching up paint on the wood lap siding of his handmade three-story dollhouse. I knew Dad had wanted to paint with us but couldn't; instead, he had scaled it down to a manageable project by painting the dollhouse.

Alex couldn't help admiring the realistic construction of the large, nine-room miniature house. "Where did you get this? It's huge! Look at all that gingerbread and Victorian window trim! Do the lights work? It even has a cedar shake roof! This is a real work of art."

Dad's chest swelled like a cartoon character's as he turned on the tiny lights with the flip of a switch, saying, "I built it from scratch. Marg hung the wallpaper and made the curtains. We've sold quite a few of them."

Alex asked, "How are you going to move it?"

We gave him blank stares.

He didn't wait for us to come up with an answer. "I have a huge box from a big-screen TV that will be just right. I'll be gone for a few days, but then I'll bring it over." I should have trusted him by then but put *build crate* on my list anyway, ever the doubter.

A few days later, Alex showed up in a linen suit, looking like the CEO of a Fortune 500 corporation, but with a huge reinforced-cardboard crate tied to the roof of his sporty little silver car. It was the ideal size box, sturdy, and had plenty of room for packing material to cushion the clapboards, trim, windowpanes, and shingles—packing material Alex also provided. Problem solved.

Maybe moving would go smoothly after all. Maybe I'd learn to relax and trust that things would work out.

Chapter 7

....

After Alex left, I headed to the kitchen for a lemonade break.
I should have been relieved the painting was finished but
instead felt myself amping up to review the dreaded job list.
Mom sat ensconced on her throne, an antique captain's chair
at the dining room table, a setup affectionately called the Command Post. She picked up a newspaper clipping from the lazy
Susan in the middle of her grandmother's table and handed me
the daily word puzzle.

"Can you get that one?" she asked, in a motherly challenge.

I wanted to say, *No. I don't have time. You're sitting here
reading the paper while I'm hauling ass twenty-three hours a day. If
you lost weight and took care of yourself, you could help, too.*

Instead, I answered, "Wiener schnitzel," the solution to
the puzzle, while I worked on the next one. She twirled the lazy
Susan and handed me a pencil from her great-aunt's cut-glass
sugar bowl and a napkin for my dripping glass from the napkin
holder Dad had made in high school shop class.

"By the way," she said, "my friend Barb is a realtor. I called
her, and she said to let her know when we're ready for a walk-
through. She'll tell us if we need to fix up or upgrade or whatever."

She has a friend who's a realtor? She called her? I tried to look
happy, rather than flabbergasted. She swiveled around to the file

cabinet within reach behind her and said, "Look at these pictures I found. We were at Catawba Island. You must have been about three. Weren't you cute? You loved those bunny slippers."

The phone interrupted our reminiscing. From Mom's station, she tapped the remote to turn down the volume on the *Leave It to Beaver* rerun, answered the call, and grabbed a tablet and pen. She pulled a prescription bottle out of the bottom drawer of the buffet, also within her stretch. "Yes, that's the one. Thanks. Bye."

She hung up and said, "That was the drugstore. My thyroid prescription is ready. No hurry—I have plenty."

I went back to work, breathing a little more slowly, my muscles a little looser. She knew exactly what she was doing. She had distracted me, relaxed me, and shown me she could take care of things. My mother was blooming.

As the number of Mom's days of sobriety increased, so did her role in running the household from her post. When we were young, she was generally in perpetual motion, sitting at the table only for meals or for coffee with one of her frequent visitors. Her degenerating joints trapped her in her chair more and more each year, but she still kept her finger on the pulse of the world from her perch. Now, each day further from the bottle, she regained a piece of herself, recovering her humor, helpfulness, and charm around that table.

Her improvement energized me during the daylight hours as I cleaned, painted, repaired, grocery-shopped, and shepherded Dad to medical appointments. Left to myself at night, though, I worried, made lists, and tried to relax. I lay in bed a stiffened mass, forcing myself to focus on breathing exercises, systematically trying to thaw muscles head to toe. I downed soothing natural medicines and drank chamomile tea.

When it became apparent that there was no hope of sleep, I saved certain tasks that I wanted to attempt alone and completed them under the cover of night. In the part of the house where I wouldn't wake Mom or Dad, I cleaned, packed, and repaired. I felt guilty knowing my father would enjoy helping, but it felt good to work unencumbered by his limitations.

One night, while lying in bed trying to untangle my shoulder muscles, I heard rustling up and down the exterior walls of my room. My nerves on edge, I calmed myself, remembering the house was constructed of hurricane-proof cinder block; whatever lurked, it wasn't inside the walls and probably couldn't get into my room. I didn't dare go outside to investigate, knowing a battalion of mosquitoes was ready and armed.

The next morning, I searched for the source of the noise and discovered a huge mouse nest in the downspout. First I wanted to cry, rip off my job title, and go home; then I laughed at my reaction. Mice were the straw to break the camel's back? Each problem by itself was relatively simple, so why was I so darn stressed? I had accomplished much more complex tasks in my life than packing and moving. I decided then that I didn't have the time or energy to process or rationalize or whatever it would take to explain my stress to myself. It was just plain hard. I didn't even want to call home and talk about how I felt because I didn't have the energy to discuss it. This dose of adulthood was simply exhausting me.

My friends already knew my parents had presented me with many challenges during my life. They'd probably heard all too often about the time I flew from Washington to Maryland for a visit during a semester break from dental hygiene school and found my mother in bed, barely conscious and soaked in urine. She didn't recognize me, but I didn't recognize her, either. She was only fifty-five at the time, but her swollen, yellow-gray skin distorted her face and aged her twenty years. She had forbidden my father to call 911, but I didn't ask permission. The paramedics located only a thready pulse and were not certain of her survival.

At the hospital, the nurses were callous and rude to my mother; she was just a drunk to them. I pulled them aside with fire in my eyes and tersely rebuked them, "This may be a drunk to you, but she is my mother. You will treat her with kindness and respect." To their credit, they did. Eventually, Mom's room became the gathering place for the nurses to gab and laugh on their breaks. My mother's good side was always very good.

As Mom grew more coherent all those years ago in the hospital, she started biting her lip and looking worried. Working the edge of the blanket like a rosary, she asked me what all the tests were for and what was wrong with her. Stunned that she didn't know, I lied about routine tests. By the next day, I had organized my courage and asked, "Mom, have the nurses told you why you're having all these tests?"

"No," she said, with a tremor in her voice.

"Your liver has shut down from alcoholism."

Her face stricken and wordless, she locked eyes with me, waiting for the other shoe to drop. I gaped back, realizing I hadn't thought through the explanation of her problem any further than the diagnosis. Was she hoping or terrified that I might recommend options for treatment? Mercifully, a nurse came in with pills and broke our stare-down. As far as I know, that was the one and only mention of alcohol, but she didn't drink for the next decade. A very good decade.

After ten years of sobriety, my mother suffered enough losses, sorrows, and physical pains to send her back to her bottle. Problems developed between my parents but were never discussed, except for snippets revealed to me. They confided separately in me, trusting my support without having to spell out the painful details each time. "Your mother is at it again" was a chapter title, and I knew how all the pages read. "Does he think I don't know what's going on when he comes home late?" was a song title, and I knew all the words and all the verses.

Although I was a lifelong confidant to each of them, by the time they were approaching their eighties, it didn't matter anymore. They had selectively rewritten their history, editing out the bad parts.

I pondered my parents' abilities to recover and rebound from their traumas while I stared out my open bedroom window, fascinated by the thundering crashes and lightning strobing my parents' backyard. We don't experience many thunderstorms in the Pacific Northwest, and I stood mesmerized, until I realized part of the clamor was garbled bellowing from the living room. I slammed my window shut and reached Dad in the living room at the same time Mom did.

Chapter 8

....

Every part of my father was quaking in his chair. There was so much commotion between the flashing storm, his flailing body, and my pounding heart that I couldn't figure out what was happening.

My mother instructed me, in a controlled but quivering voice, "He's having a seizure. He's had three since his last stroke. The cardiologist said to call 911 every time. You stay with him. I'll call. Your brother isn't home."

I pushed away the end table containing breakables and sharp corners and stood guard, ready to prevent Dad from falling out of his chair. He began regaining consciousness as the medic van arrived a few minutes later.

Three paramedics wheeled in a gurney, asked Mom a few questions, and started prepping for transport. I could see Dad's increasing distress in the tightening of his jaw.

I attempted a friendly yet authoritative voice: "Let's slow down here and just see how he is before we make any decisions." I had no idea whether he needed sirens and a race to the ER or a glass of warm milk, but I sensed he wanted to stay home.

A medic scowled at me while wrapping her blood pressure cuff around Dad's arm, declaring that his cardiac history required evaluation at the ER.

I ignored her. "How're ya doin', Dad?"

He stammered, "What happened? I had a bad nightmare."

"You had a seizure. But it's over. We called the paramedics only because the doctor said to."

He was fully conscious now and sheepishly smiled at the medic, saying, "I'm sorry to have bothered you. You can go now if you're busy."

"No, we'll stay here out of the rain for a while. You had a bad dream?"

"I was on the deck of the *Mascoma* in a terrible storm, a typhoon, and our boiler went out, so we had only half power. We were refueling a ship, and it was attacked. It exploded in flames and sank. I could smell the fire in my dream. I was so scared."

She raised her eyebrows at the other paramedic, and he responded by unwrapping the belts on the gurney. I waved her into the next room and explained, "My father has a seizure disorder caused by a stroke, and PTSD from World War II, with recurring nightmares. I'll watch him carefully and call his doctor first thing in the morning. I'm a dental hygienist, so I know a tiny bit of medical care."

"Okay. Are you sure? I was afraid he was hallucinating from a medication overdose. Do you have a blood pressure cuff? Do you know how to evaluate for stroke?"

I pulled the blood pressure cuff out of Mom's desk drawer and recited stroke symptoms from my first-aid training. By the time we returned to Dad, he had tucked his terror back into its box, saying, "I'm fine now. It must have been the storm that made me think of it. Thanks for everything."

The crew monitored him while his blood pressure stabilized and the storm passed, then left for another emergency, assuring us it was okay to call again if we needed them.

Mom proposed taking shifts to keep an eye on Dad, assigning me first watch.

"Do you want the TV on, Dad?" I thought a distraction might be useful.

"It was so real. I was right back on the ship," he said, now more amazed than afraid.

"That was the most intense thunder and lightning I've ever seen," I said. "It *was* like bombs bursting. No wonder it reminded you of the war."

He shook his head, then said, "I saw it all happen again, just like the first time. I was on deck in Ulithi just before dawn. We were refueling a sister ship, and it was hit by a Kaiten torpedo. There was a huge explosion, and the ship, the *Mississinewa*, caught fire and sank right before our eyes. Flaming oil and pieces of metal landed at our feet. I saw guys jumping off the burning boat, buddies of mine. They were burned so bad I grabbed the blanket from my cot and laid it in the basket we were using to pull them out of the water. We rescued only a few because we were on half power and the waves were unbelievable. Our captain got us back to shore on one boiler during that typhoon. He was a great guy."

I was speechless. I knew Dad endured recurring nightmares about the war, but I'd never heard the details. He had never mentioned Ulithi, *Mascoma*, Kaiten, or *Mississinewa*. I didn't know what they were. I couldn't really even describe the World Wars. When I was young, no one wanted to talk about them because the pain was too recent and raw. How could this have been so important to my father and I knew nothing about it?

He continued, "A few months ago, a guy at the VA gave me a website that tells the story of each Navy ship until it's decommissioned. I tried to get it, but the computer froze up. Could you try? My ship was the USS *Mascoma*. We left from Sausalito in May and went to Portland to get the guns and equipment installed."

"Sure. I'll do that tomorrow," I said, hoping he'd forget the request by then.

He seemed to settle down, and I thought he was asleep, when he asked, "Did you ever have a premonition?"

"I have," I acknowledged. "The day before the nuclear accident at Chernobyl, I looked at my garden and wondered what it would look like with radioactive fallout on it. It was so strange and real that I told Katy about it. But better than that was when I imagined a big, beautiful black dog in my yard, and a few months later we adopted Dakota."

"Okay," he said, "then I'll tell you something I've never told anyone. Before I left for the service, I was in my bedroom, looking at everything one last time. I was sitting on my own bed, on the fancy bedspread my mother had made, looking out my own window through the drapes she'd made that matched the bedspread, but instead of the cherry tree, I saw ocean waves crashing and a ship burning and sinking. I thought it meant I was going to die at sea. I've never forgotten that. I can still see it."

"Jeez, that must have been terrifying," I said, wondering if I could find a class or a self-help book on appropriate empathetic responses to disturbing geriatric revelations.

I knew fatality and war were going to merge and plummet into another sad topic, the death of his brother, Nelson, at Iwo Jima, so I searched for another subject. I remembered that when my parents had visited me in Olympia, Dad had mentioned that he loved Portland. I tried it: "Where were you located in Portland?"

"We were stationed at the Swan Island shipyard on the Columbia River. People drove out from Portland, picked us up, and took us home for dinners or into town for a movie. Everybody took care of sailors and soldiers during the war. Then, when we were finally leaving for San Francisco, we ran aground in the river and had to go back to the shipyard for repairs. The crew was pretty embarrassed, but lots of ships crashed and grounded there. See what you can find out on that website."

"Sure. I'll look it up. That's a great idea." My brother had set up Internet access and e-mail for Mom and Dad before Dad had lost his sight. By feel and memory, my father could still retrieve and print e-mail for Mom to read, but he couldn't search.

I tried to continue with happier events: "You were in Portland a long time?"

"A few months. They installed the guns and equipment on the *Mascoma*, and we had to learn how to use and maintain it all. We spent days wiping all the Cosmoline off the metal parts. It was beautiful there. But that river was impossible. It has tides, you know. Whole islands disappear during high tide."

"No, I didn't know that," I answered. And I didn't know he knew that. It also fascinated me that *Cosmoline* rolled off his tongue as if he said it every day, since he generally had a little trouble finding unusual or unused words. I didn't know what Cosmoline was, but I didn't want to interrupt his flow to find out. He typically didn't talk this much about anything.

He went on, "It's a long river with a huge amount of water that ends up right in the ocean. No lake in between. You know . . . what do you call it?"

"I don't know," I said.

"Delta." He answered his own question. "There's no delta to slow the water down. It just rushes right into the ocean over one of the world's most dangerous sandbars. The wind blew hard all the time. That water changed from smooth to rough in minutes. A lot of spaghetti and meatballs had to be swabbed off our ship's deck, but I was never seasick. The river and cliffs were so beautiful." He nodded off, I hoped with sweeter dreams.

The computer was in my room, and the next morning I searched online and found photos and descriptions, and even 16 mm film, of the *Mississinewa*. Mom came in, saying she had checked Dad's prescription bottles and that the VA doctor had discontinued his seizure medicine. Dad's Medicare supplement had no prescription coverage, so he used the regional VA for that but saw local doctors for his care.

She turned and saw the burning-ship video on the screen and gasped, "Oh my Lord, where is that?"

"This is Dad's nightmare from the war. Did he ever tell you about it?"

"Never. He just says he has bad dreams about the war. He yells and thrashes in his sleep all night. I assumed it was about Nelson and Iwo Jima."

She closed the door, sat on the edge of the bed, and stared in horror at the computer screen. The flames shot into the air as the ship sank in the sepia tones of the old film.

I said, "After you went to bed last night, Dad told me that he was on watch when this happened. He saw the periscope of the manned suicide torpedo go by his ship right before it hit the *Mississinewa*."

"This is an actual home movie of it? Where did this happen?" she asked.

"In the South Pacific—the Ulithi atoll. November 20, 1944."

"Oh, I've heard him ask other veterans if they were at Ulithi," she said, as she pieced the history together. "I thought something bad happened there when they just shook their heads and looked sad. What caused so much fire?"

"The USS *Mississinewa* carried fuel for planes and other ships, and the fuel exploded like bombs. The crew jumped into the water, but even the water was covered with fire because of all the oil spilling out. Dad's ship saved twenty-one men; most were rescued by other ships, but sixty died."

"Your dad rescued guys?"

"Yes. He said he watched them jump and helped pull them out of the water. He had friends on that ship."

She took a moment to digest that, then said, "He told the paramedics it happened during a typhoon, but the ocean in that video was smooth. Does the article mention a typhoon? He's always been terrified of storms."

I typed in *typhoon, South Pacific, 1944, USS Mascoma*.

"Listen to this. Whole books were written about the typhoon of December 1944 and its impact on the war. This says it was one of the worst storms in recorded history. Three destroyers capsized and sank, dozens of ships were damaged, around a hundred and fifty planes were lost, and almost eight hundred sailors died. Dad's ship, the USS *Mascoma*, was in the eye of the storm, lost power for nine hours, then limped to shore with only one boiler powering the engines."

"Good grief. No wonder he's so afraid of tornadoes and hurricanes," she said.

"I think he braided the separate terrifying events into one horrifying recurring nightmare," I said, and she agreed with a slow nod of her head. I wondered if I should tell him what I had found out or leave the monster in its hiding place.

She answered my unasked question: "I don't think we should tell him about this. It might make it worse. I think I'm going to have nightmares now, too."

Chapter 9

....

I called Dad's local doctor to report the seizure. The nurse informed me in a reprimanding tone that Dad's blood level for the seizure medication hadn't been checked in months, according to both her records and the recent records forwarded from the hospital. She was unforgiving about my explanation that the VA doctor had discontinued the prescription. I hung up and nonchalantly told Dad that the doctor had ordered a blood test, and maybe it was a good idea to get it over with. He was happy to go out for a ride.

He didn't realize it felt like I was at the wheel of an ambulance and wanted to turn on the flashing lights. I drove him to the lab, then to the doctor's office to await the results. I didn't know how many seizures his weakened heart could handle, and I wanted to reduce the chances quickly.

The grouchy nurse said we'd have a long wait for the lab to fax the results, so we settled in. When we were the only ones left in the waiting room, Dad said, "Last night I wanted to think about something good that happened in the Navy so I wouldn't keep remembering just the bad stuff, and I remembered becoming a shellback after crossing the equator."

He started giggling and expected me to join him, but I had no idea what he was talking about.

"You know," he insisted, "my fancy certificate on the wall in your bedroom from King Neptune's Court. The Crossing the Line ceremony. Everyone in the Navy does it when they cross the equator."

"I just don't know anything about this, Dad. Start at the beginning." But why didn't I know anything about it? What kind of daughter was I?

"Okay, well, anyone onboard who hadn't crossed the equator yet was called a pollywog, even if he was an officer. The guys who had already crossed were named shellbacks. Just before crossing the equator, the shellbacks took over the ship and started a sort of playful torturing of the pollywogs. The shellbacks dressed in silly costumes and formed the Royal Court of Neptune. It was their duty to prepare the pollywogs to become shellbacks. It was all a joke, you know, like joining a fraternity. What's that called?"

"Hazing?" I suggested.

"Right. A lot of these guys had been in the war for years and needed to have some fun. They spent hours thinking up the worst things for us pollywogs."

He drifted into his memory, so I asked, "What did they make you do?"

"We had to crawl through a long chute, probably fifty feet long, filled with stinky old garbage, while they paddled our butts. Then we had to walk across a greased deck without falling, kiss the fat cook's slimy belly, eat raw eggs, and . . . well, you get the idea. As soon as you finished, you were a shellback and you joined the paddling-and-punishing end of things."

"Was it fun or torture?"

"It was a riot. I have pictures of it somewhere. I figured out one thing right away. I thought, *Why wait for all these pollywogs to become shellbacks and add to my pain and humiliation?* So I volunteered for the first group, to get it over with as fast as possible. I was pretty happy about that decision as the shellback line got longer and longer, torturing the poor pollywogs."

His whole story riveted me with his principles and examples, something I hadn't ever thought about as lessons or how they shaped my character. Doing the hardest thing first to get it over with and trying to find some iota of good in every bad were gifts from him that he didn't realize he had given me. Here he was, still unknowingly teaching me by example, his memories and brain sharp in his withering body.

The doctor motioned us into an exam room, even though we had no appointment. Dad's blood level of antiseizure medication was zero, and the doctor demanded to know why. I had no answer beyond a weak explanation of a VA mix-up, to the doctor's dismay and mine. Dad just downed whatever pills Mom set out for him. With a look of futility, the doctor handed me a prescription and a lab slip for another test in one week. He ordered me to get a list of all Dad's medications from the nurse and make sure the VA filled them with no alterations. Externally, I played the low blood level of the medicine as a good thing, telling Dad it meant he wouldn't ordinarily have seizures once he was back on it. Internally, I wondered how I was ever going to keep all this medical care straight. How could I not have known he was supposed to be on seizure medication and have regular blood tests to monitor it? What else didn't I know?

Realizing I had to stabilize my father's health and educate myself before we traveled, I requested copies of all his medical records and scheduled consultation appointments with his doctor, cardiologist, eye specialists, and VA doctors. I believed I was getting a handle on his general health issues, but his eye problems confused and terrified me.

The eye surgeon always focused our visits on how well Dad was functioning, saying he was managing much better than expected, given the amount of vision loss he had suffered. Dad moved slowly, maneuvering more by touch than by sight. He had worked with his hands all his life, repairing cash registers and building dollhouses, cultivating the tactile sensitivity that was now his primary navigator. He possessed a tenacious memory for the location of everything from a broken piece of a lamp placed in a drawer years ago to batteries at the hardware store, and clambered along relatively well in his circumscribed world.

But what ongoing care would he need, and what would I do if he lost the rest of his vision?

On our last visit, the eye surgeon had not adequately answered these questions or quelled my worries. I had spotted a brochure titled "Visual Therapy" and asked the doctor about it. He offhandedly remarked that it might be a good idea for my father's condition and said he would write a prescription for it. I wondered why he hadn't recommended it earlier and why I knew nothing about it. The word *therapy* gave me hope of help on the horizon.

Almost a month now since my arrival in Florida, Mom, Dad, and I positioned ourselves in our customary seats at the dining room table to await the doorbell. We still had no idea what *visual therapy* meant, but the first session was about to unfold. The house smelled clean and fresh from the gardenia blooming outside the door. My parents were combed and scrubbed, and fragrant with Old Spice and Emeraude. They sat alert and hovering on the edges of their chairs; a lot had improved in one month.

The doorbell chimed, and Dad snapped to attention like it was reveille. Mom signaled me with a "just let him go" wave of her hand, so I restrained myself in my chair. He hadn't answered the door in months because he couldn't see who was there. He was quivering with excitement by the time he escorted an attractive young woman to the table and introduced us to Olivia.

Mom complimented her elegant long black hair and dancing dark eyes and engaged Olivia in conversation about her Italian heritage and lasagna. I fidgeted, telegraphing, *Get on with it.*

Olivia assumed authority. "You sit over here, where the light is best," she instructed Dad. We rearranged our seats, and she asked, "Do you have a high-intensity light?" I found one and set it up. Why hadn't I thought of that?

Olivia unloaded her briefcase of magnifiers, pages of large type, and paper lined for kindergarteners or first-graders. "What do you like to do, Tom?" she asked.

We knew it was just an interview question, but it baffled him. "Do?" he muttered.

Mom, his lifelong medical interpreter, translated, "He putters in the gardens, fixes things, watches football on TV. He can't read the newspaper anymore."

Olivia placed Dad's hand on a lighted magnifier over a large-print book. "Can you see that, Tom?"

He struggled to aim his dot of vision on the target. "No." He dropped the tool and slumped back in the chair, defeated. The test was over, and he had failed.

"Okay," she said, as if he'd given the right answer. "Now, let's try this. Hold this paper and point where you can see something." He painstakingly circled his eyes around and haltingly tapped his index finger on a letter.

"Great. So you need to move your eyes down to see straight in front of you. Let's try it. Look at this paper, but roll your eyes down."

He laboriously read through the magnifier, "The . . . quick . . . brown . . . fox . . ." He hadn't read a word in over a year, and Mom and I silently choked on tears running down our cheeks.

Olivia stayed for three hours, teaching Dad to use lighted magnifiers to read the newspaper and determining the size of print he could read and write without magnification. The most important and hardest lesson was learning to move his whole head to catch an object in his minuscule visual field. To see a face, he focused on the person's waist, which felt creepy to him.

He asked her if we could tell where he was looking or if he looked odd. We couldn't and he didn't.

He was an eager and determined student. The next morning, he arranged his homework on the dining room table, ready to practice. Mom and I nonchalantly cleaned out the refrigerator, pretending we weren't hanging on his every nuance. We heard *splat-splat-slat* on the paper, and Dad sobbed, "I can't see anything."

I sat next to him and suggested, "Try moving the paper all around until you see the letters. It will take time to train your eyes." He found the words, but his bubble had burst. He scuffled out to his workshop to grieve and regroup.

"Do you think he can do it?" Mom asked warily. "He misses reading so much. He likes to study. He loved his NCR classes."

I remembered how he had gone away for a couple weeks each year for training on new cash registers and had always returned home happy and bearing gifts.

I started fretting and feeling even sadder about his challenge and the potential for failure as she continued, "Remember when he took all those electronics correspondence courses from DeVry? He even studied the Dale Carnegie courses on communication skills and self-improvement after he became a manager. He loved those accomplishments. I just don't want him to try to do something that's impossible."

I was sinking more deeply into worrying I'd made a big mistake.

So was she, as she continued, "He was really enjoying learning to use the computer before his eyes went bad. He was so frustrated about that. Maybe this is just not realistic."

"I don't know what to do, Mom. I don't want him to fail, but maybe he'll succeed."

"Maybe you should talk to Olivia and find a way for him to bow out gracefully."

When Olivia arrived the next day, she asked him how he was doing. "Terrrific," he roared, in his big Tony the Tiger voice.

I covertly flagged her attention and pointed toward the front door. Without missing a beat, she told Dad she needed to get her appointment book out of the car. I left by the garage door and joined her in the driveway, where I recounted Dad's disappointing efforts. When she went back in and worked with him, she clarified that this process was more like building muscle than like memorization, and that he would build a little muscle each day.

He grasped that concept and diligently worked on his exercises three times a day, slowly broadening his perception and confidence. Even at his ripe age, his discipline shone through. He studied at set times every day and never missed a session with Olivia. He was so dedicated to improving that she increased her visits to twice a week. He practiced writing everything he could: messages for Carroll, reminders for Chip, lists for the hardware store. He said the kindergarten paper embarrassed him, but it "just had to be"—an expression of acceptance I was hearing more and more from him.

Learning to use his single pinhole of vision was arduous, and changes in his eyesight weren't steady or measurable to him. Some days, the practice made him more aware of his limitations; other days, he was aware of his progress. He never complained out loud; Mom and I just read the cues and delivered our lines to encourage him: "Wow, Dad, you couldn't do that last week." "Thanks for picking that up. It's amazing you can see that now." "Would you make a list for that? Use Olivia's paper." "Thanks for labeling those boxes. Your writing is perfect."

Mom and I noticed the improvement in his sight and in his general outlook on life. Every time Olivia coached him, he gained a little radiance; she directed positive energy toward a vast, negatively charged field. Despite my questioning, the doctors and nurses wouldn't declare a long-term prognosis for Dad's vision. He'd had multiple surgeries and invasive tests, but his doctor had only recently hinted that there might be no improvement. Visual therapy built a bridge to that new landscape.

I worried about the stress of adding this therapy on top of everything else Dad needed to manage. I monitored his attitude about it, and even though it was challenging, it nourished him. Like so much of our agenda, the difficulties were buoyed by hope and faith. Both my parents were intentionally squinting hard to imagine a glass half full when it looked darn near empty to me.

Olivia arrived for her last session with a salesman in tow, wheeling a big, closed-circuit TV system. "Tom, sit here," she directed. "Put the newspaper here. Okay. Now look at the TV screen." The newspaper was visible on the screen.

"Blank. Nothing there. It doesn't work for me." His despair shrouded the room.

She picked up his hand and wrapped his fingers around a dial. "Keep looking at the screen, and turn this dial clockwise."

He turned the dial, enlarging the print, then drew toward the screen, reading, "Sunny and hot, high near ninety-eight." He moved the paper around, checking other stories. The sales rep hinted about another appointment he had scheduled in twenty minutes, but Dad didn't budge. He saw a lifeline, and he was hanging on.

Eventually Dad leaned back from the machine and returned to our world just in time to hear the price. He shriveled in his seat, saying, "I don't need it. Marg reads the paper to me." He wouldn't have dreamed of spending several thousand dollars on himself.

"Dad, this is a medical expense, not a luxury item. I think you should have one." He trusted me for medical decisions and changed his mind immediately. The rep gave me all the information for buying it in Washington because it seemed foolish to risk moving expensive equipment cross-country. Olivia suggested we check out the VA's visual therapy programs on the West Coast, adding that there weren't many of them but they were the best in the country. I put it on my "Maybe When Everything Is Settled" list. I imagined the closest facility would be Denver or San Francisco and thought since Dad had already received visual therapy, what more could he learn?

I was pre-overwhelmed with our impending lives in Washington and didn't like adding one more thing to that ever-growing list. My to-do list seemed to be mutating into a to-worry-about list. My mother was beginning to tease me about what I had gotten myself into, and although I laughed, it wasn't very funny to me. What *had* I gotten myself into? Our three-thousand-mile geographical buffer had worked so well for our relationship, why wreck it? It didn't matter now—there was no turning back. My heart was in this, lock, stock, and barrel.

I had not lived near my parents for my entire adult life, and I had not expected to feel such a part of them. I had imagined our relationship now would be more like the ones I had with my dental hygiene patients. Instead, I felt like I had just adopted two children and was starting to care for them like a mother bear. Every day we were smoothing the sharp edges of our rearranged relationship and gaining respect for one another. Our puzzle pieces were melding together in our new roles, forging an interdependence with comfortable boundaries.

Chapter 10

....

Aware that I was the conductor of this rite of passage, I was determined to keep the wheels on the tracks. But every bend we rounded tempted me onto rails from earlier journeys, enticing me to explore well-traveled paths of our past from this new vantage point of caretaker. My brother had sparked many of my divergences into my parents' past. He was leaving soon, and their entwined history was complicated from conception.

In the late 1950s, when my mother arrived home from her long hospital stay after Chip's difficult birth, she bent forward to embrace my sister and me but stiffened when she saw our hair. "Who cut your hair?" she demanded.

In all our preadolescent years, our hair had never been cut and had trailed, long and lush, down our backs. Mom routinely trimmed our bangs and brushed us into braids and ponytails. Now it was sheared off in pageboys.

Not waiting for our responses, she laid into Dad: "How could you? Their beautiful hair! Now I have to fuss with it and curl it, instead of pulling it back. Damn you."

Dad knew where to hide when a tornado hit and headed for the basement. This was the first time we had ever seen our parents fight, and Linda and I froze in our shoes.

"Who did this to you?" Mom interrogated us, her blue eyes blazing molten metal.

"A lady downtown. Dad said she was a friend," I defended.

"Downtown where? What was her name? What did she look like?"

Someone needed to answer, and my sister's body was there, but the rest of her had evaporated.

Dad was my pal, and I wanted to get him out of this mess. When he ran the lawn mower, I used the grass shears. If he had a hammer in his hand, I carried the nails. I attempted a rescue by explaining to Mom, in my most grown-up, seven-year-old voice, "It was upstairs from the restaurant where we get milkshakes. She had a big dog. A dobie man pincher. We weren't allowed to pet it. Her name was Molly."

Mom didn't ask if that was the dog's name or the lady's name. I didn't add that Dad had greeted the lady, "How's my sweetheart?" or that she had fawned over us too familiarly. I also was now remembering his kiss on her cheek and a pat on her rear, and hoped my sister didn't remember, or at least didn't blurt out those details.

Mom shoved the baby into my arms and ordered, "Put him in the crib and go to your room." Even then, we knew that meant, *Don't ever talk about this again.*

A contingent of women relatives and neighbors streamed in unexpectedly a few hours later, explaining, "Your mom doesn't feel good, so we're going to help out for a few days."

None of us felt very good. I don't know where my mother went—maybe just to her bedroom—and I had to take care of a baby.

Over the next few days, Mom's friends and relatives showed me how to warm up formula and feed my brother and let me help bathe him in the shallow baby tub on the kitchen counter. We practiced everything from rocking him to sleep to checking and changing diapers. I didn't know I was in training;

I was just having fun playing house with a living, breathing baby doll.

My sister was involved in her own activities and friends, but I readily accepted caring for him. I thought of it as babysitting, a normal job for an older sister, but it was much more. I dressed, fed, and played with him. In my early teens, I took him everywhere I went. After I left home, he lived with me whenever things got rough with my parents. By the time I fled to the West Coast, he was out on his own, but our hearts were permanently welded together.

In the years between my birth and Chip's, my mother had suffered two miscarriages and the loss of a baby who had survived only eight days, so it was quite possible she was afraid Chip would die, too. But what had tipped my mother over the edge into the wine bottle: the lost babies, Chip's difficult birth, or the possible transgression by my father? What really happened with the haircut lady? What did Mom suspect? How much did she know?

Every heart holds its own definition of infidelity, somewhere between a wink and a weekend in Paris. What was my mother's? Eventually she climbed halfway out of her abyss and performed housewife tasks, but she didn't bond with my brother until he was grown, and didn't show the same joie de vivre. That's not to say our lives were a wreck from that point on— we still had good times—but there was a lack of genuineness in her, and impenetrable walls. She would anticipate a holiday celebration in high spirits, cleaning, decorating, and preparing food, but when we were all finally assembled for the event, she would suddenly wear an unexplained, distant melancholy, as if she could no longer keep up the facade.

That fateful homecoming after Chip's birth might have been my father's first lesson in surviving my mother's abrupt and bewildering conversion into her wrath-filled counterpart. He shut up and shut down. He deferred every decision to her and allowed her to humiliate him at every opportunity, even as he continued to test the waters of infidelity.

My brother's upbringing had nothing of the predictable, carefree 1950s that I remembered. In his childhood, during the turbulent '60s, he had weathered our disintegrated family, yet he harbored absolutely no ill will about it. He developed a deep bond with my parents as an adult and occasionally lived with them. They loved him unconditionally, with indescribable depth.

We knew Chip was happy to be moving to Sarasota to live with his girlfriend, but we were worried how he might take this cross-country separation. He was very emotional and sensitive, perceiving and feeling things deeply. To the world, he was talented, accomplished, witty, and bright; to us, he was still the youngest child. We were determined to do our best to make the transition a happy one.

Now, as moving day nudged closer, my parents faced the impending separation from their home and from Chip by injecting us with optimism, their homemade vaccine against tears. Dad slouched into the kitchen. "Chip thinks he'll be ready to leave in three days."

Mom administered a dose of antigrief vaccine: "I told him they'll have so much fun fixing up their first apartment together. He said he would e-mail us lots of pictures."

Dad returned the remedy with his own inoculation: "I am so happy for him. Jonquil is a great girl. They get along so well."

The potential for unbridled sorrow hung viscous in the Florida humidity. I was exhausted and edgy. I needed to accomplish a mammoth project in a short time and manage these emotional currents all the while. My parents were doing their best, but I knew it could turn the tide if I showed irritation or let them know how overwhelmed I felt.

I imagined they pictured a desolate future of fending for themselves in a distant state if our arrangement went sour. I knew I had to remain steady. There was no dress rehearsal. My mother could read me from cover to cover in twenty seconds flat just by the tone of my voice or the look on my face. She was never wrong. My graciousness must be heartfelt or we would revert to tornado-watch behavior, nervous and guarded.

I pondered all this while slicing an apple that slipped away and rolled across the floor. Mom used a cowboy voice to issue her standard comment for anything out of control: "Hold 'er, Newt—she's gonna rear." I laughed, thinking that fit my whole approach to this scene: holding all our emotions steady so we wouldn't buck and rear.

I added a booster shot to my parents' grief-prevention program: "Won't it be fun to have Christmas with Linda and Michelle?" My sister had blessed the family with the only grandchild, now in her early twenties.

Mom supplemented the treatment: "I know! And we'll have snow. I can't wait to see snow!" As was her custom anytime the word *snow* was mentioned, she began singing "Snow," our favorite family anthem from Irving Berlin's *White Christmas*.

Chip came in and harmonized with her, continuing the lyrics. He got a little teary, saying, "I want to see snow, too!"

Mom injected us all with a strong dose of tear protection: "You come visit as often as you can. We'll pay your airfare. I can't wait to go to the farmers' market. Fresh apples right off the trees. Washington cherries. Walk out the door and pick blackberries. I'm going to bake a pie every day."

She didn't voice the ache of leaving their own trees, especially the fruit trees that she and Dad had nurtured from twigs. My father pruned, watered, fertilized, and harvested the fruit from those trees, caring for them like pets. Mom had nicknamed each tree as they planted it with a moniker linked to its actual name. Every day she waved a greeting to Tommy, the Thomson orange, and hummed a samba for Swing and Sway, the palm tree pair. The temple orange tree was Shirley, the gum tree was Bubbles, the magnolia was Maggie, and the maple was Aunt

Jemima. My parents were silently leaving their cherished property's care to its next owners, and their son to his girlfriend, as they bravely turned their hopes toward their future.

A future that depended on me, and I wasn't feeling nearly as brave.

Chapter 11

....

Every day, Dad and I sorted, packed, and hauled. I knew keeping him busy kept his mind off worrying, and I worked hard at planning tasks he could accomplish successfully. It was partly self-preservation, because I could be more productive when he was occupied. One day, I was several hours into my list by midmorning, and the hot, sticky weather was already making everything prickly, especially my nerves, when Dad reported for his day's assignment with his usual sunny disposition.

"Isn't that Carroll just something?" he asked, as he made his way into the garage.

"He is. He seems to show up right when we need him. I barely had time to worry about what we'd do without a car if it needed a big repair or how much it would cost." Carroll lived right next door, and the day before, when he had seen the tow truck by Mom and Dad's car, he had come right over, looked under the hood, removed a huge, disgusting mouse nest, dismissed the tow truck, and bought and installed the main battery cable the mice had eaten through—and all for fifteen dollars.

After we amused ourselves with details of the mouse episode, Dad asked what he should do. I didn't answer fast enough, so he proposed, "All these shelves need to be torn apart. I'll do that. It would be too hard on your bad shoulder."

We were hauling to Washington the eight metal racks from his workshop, although where they would fit in a two-bedroom apartment was a mystery. Each one was six feet tall and had five or six shelves. I doubted Dad could manage the disassembly, but he already held a screwdriver in his hand, so I just kept packing dollhouse furniture. A moment later, I heard *scritch-scritch-scratch* but no sounds of shelves separating.

"How's it goin', Dad?"

"The bolts are rusted. I think I need a wrench on the inside to hold the nut."

I grabbed a wrench and anchored the nut, but he couldn't aim the screwdriver into the slot of the bolt head. I reached over and lined it up. Was he going to start crying? Was I?

I said, "These bolts are really rusty. How about if we loosen them together, then you can take them out by hand?"

"Terrrific."

How did he tolerate the loss of his titles of repairman and maintenance man? What enabled him to accept his diminishing abilities so graciously? My heart was breaking.

I positioned the tip of his screwdriver while I held the nut with the wrench in my other hand. He twisted the bolt until it was just loose. I reset his screwdriver every few turns when it slipped out of the slot. We loosened all the bolts for one shelf, he took it apart, then we loosened the next ones. I worked close by so I could ease over whenever he was ready for the next shelf without his asking.

Neither of us was a chatter, so we were comfortably quiet and made only occasional comments. Then he surprised me: "I can't read the bank statements anymore, and your mother just tells me not to worry about it. Do you think you could sneak a look at them?" He glanced toward the door to make sure we weren't overheard. He was nearing a line he had never crossed, nor had he ever had a potential financial ally against my mother.

"Sure," I answered. "I probably need to deal with closing your accounts here, so I'll let you know how everything stands. Is there something in particular you're worried about?"

He hesitated, considering how wide to open the floodgate. He cracked it, and the current carried him. "I think we're in bad shape. Your mother always spent every penny I ever earned, sometimes before I earned it. We don't have any savings, and I don't know how deep we're in debt. I think she took out loans on my life insurance policies, and we've refinanced the house twice. I don't know what to do."

"Okay, Dad. I'll see what I can find out. But no matter how bad it is, it will get better soon. You will only have to pay rent, instead of repairs and insurance on a house. You have plenty of income to cover that."

The word *income* increased his anguish, and he chastised himself, "I never should have picked the retirement option I did. That was the worst mistake of my life."

I needed to divert this surge. He didn't remember his original pension choices; he just had it branded on his brain that he had picked the wrong plan for his monthly distribution. When he had retired from the National Cash Register Company, he had simply chosen the option that paid him the most money every month, without understanding the fine print. He had discovered later that Mom's income would be severely reduced if he died first, which had seemed likely and imminent to everyone but him. The pension selection was a one-time, irrevocable option.

I attempted to console and convince him: "It ended up being the right choice, Dad. It would have been bad only if you had died young. The really good thing about your pension is that you receive a set amount that doesn't depend on the stock market." I didn't add that the really bad thing about it was it had no cost-of-living adjustment, so what had sustained them originally didn't stretch very far now.

He twisted around, trying to orient his view to my face. All the creases and ridges were tight around his mouth and forehead when he said, "But what happens to her if I die first? Will she have enough? I should have gone to college, like my mother wanted me to. She wanted me to be a doctor."

We'd been here before, too. I needed to put a positive spin on his monthly reward for forty years of working six days a week. I said definitively, "Mom would absolutely have enough money to live on. She could afford the apartment on her part of your retirement. Your medical insurance from NCR would continue to cover her."

This line of reasoning was incomprehensible to him. He didn't think of himself or Mom as old. He thought he could still leave Mom in long-term poverty if he died before she did. He didn't consider that the actuarial charts were swiftly shrinking the number of years she might outlive him.

Thankfully, I had not been involved in his original pension dispersal choice, because I would have studied all the options and guided him toward the wrong one, based on his life expectancy—or, rather, unexpectancy. He'd accumulated so many heart problems starting in his early forties that no one anticipated his reaching his next birthday each time we celebrated one. Every Christmas was framed with the morbid sentimentality of potentially being his last. When we put the big 5 and 6 candles on his birthday cake for his fifty-sixth birthday, he said, with his usual optimism, "Look, we can use these again when I turn sixty-five." I firmly believed he would never reuse those candles.

He wasn't denying his health conditions; he simply had complete faith in doctors to keep him alive. But by the time he had turned fifty-six, Mom had nursed him through a debilitating stroke and several heart attacks, and we'd witnessed the surprise in doctors' eyes each time Dad recovered. No one had shared Dad's optimism about his life span.

We continued dismantling the shelves, each adrift in our own thoughts. Whenever Dad and I were working, the parallel with my childhood was palpable. When I was six, he built a workbench for me right next to his and always had a project for me to work on that was within my capability. He cut wood that I glued together for jewelry boxes, or I nailed together scraps for doll furniture. I held pieces of wood he was gluing, painted his building projects, and retrieved tools for him.

I'm sure he thought about this comparison, too, but it remained unspoken. It was too potent with emotion in the midst of our current trials. I decided to file it in the "pleasant memory" category, rather than the "so this is what it's come to" one. Somehow, we both seemed to be able to enjoy our role reversals, despite the bittersweetness around the edges.

I'd finished packing miniatures and was scouting around the garage for another project near Dad's shelf disassembly. I studied the big box Alex had delivered for the dollhouse and said, "I think I'll cut down this crate. It's too tall."

He must already have been considering this task because he jumped right in: "What are you going to use? Chip has the jigsaw at his new apartment to cut some shelves. I'd better do it. You can't use a handsaw with your bum shoulder."

At home I had a selection of power tools, but here we were limited to hand tools; Chip had "needed" the power tools because they were just too dangerous and too tempting for Dad.

"Well, just let me give it a try," I said. I measured the dollhouse, laid the huge box on its side, drew a line around it, and attempted to cut it with a utility knife in my left hand while stabilizing the box with my right. After quickly demonstrating that a utility knife in one's nonpreferred hand was a dangerous enterprise, I switched to a handsaw, but I wasn't strong enough left-handed to engage the teeth in a back-and-forth motion.

Groping through shelf parts, Dad came over to the box and commanded, "Give me the saw."

I hesitated but obeyed with a silent *aye, aye, matey,* not knowing whether his heart could take the activity, even if he could figure out how to cut something he couldn't see.

"Put the saw on the line," he ordered. I set the teeth on the mark.

He slowly sawed around the entire crate, which was about the size of a big desk, while I said, "A little more left," "A little more right," or, "Two inches to go." It took over an hour, and when he was finished he was ecstatic and exhausted. His only frustrations had been my not very cleverly disguised rest stops for bathroom breaks, drinks, and phone calls anytime I'd noticed he was out of breath. The whole episode made a great story, and we got a lot of mileage out of "he can't see and I can't saw." It was a landmark of his emotional well-being. Probably of mine, too. I'd take every one I could get at this point.

I knew I needed help, but, not knowing where to turn, I simply kept my wheels in motion, adding to and subtracting from my list. The long column of minor tasks included spackling the shower ceiling, calling the exterminator, steam-cleaning carpets, and selling a bedroom set. It was the major column that was jangling my nerves to the edge of my skin: schedule the mover, make plane reservations, sell the car, call the realtor.

From each of those items flowed a sublist. *What will the airline require to permit the cat to travel? Where do we stay once the house is packed? How do we get to the airport? Where do I house Mom, Dad, and an antisocial cat when we arrive in Washington, five days ahead of the moving van?* It was a tenuous line of dominoes with multiple places for crashes, each step dependent on the prior.

Don't anybody sneeze.

Chapter 12

························

I placed phone calls and began piecing together our departure schedule, anxiously sequencing every item on the checklist. I really wanted the house sold before we left, and it wasn't ready for viewing. I steam-cleaned the carpets for two days, steeping my skin in the soggy Florida heat. I washed and mended all the drapes, repaired window screens, replaced broken glass panes, and weeded the gardens. A clean-and-tidy facade unfurled.

The exterminator did his thing, the realtor scheduled her initial inspection, and I finalized airline reservations. Although my plan was progressing, I still wasn't sleeping. In my wired, weary attempt at it one night, dreamlike images of my beloved but dead relatives and friends appeared. Dancing in a chorus line, they cheered me on from above. They clapped and sang and kicked like the Rockettes, then waved pompoms in choreographed cheerleading routines. They offered themselves as guardian angels.

All my life, my mother had "seen" helpers when something suddenly went better than expected. If a piece of furniture we were trying to move became hopelessly wedged in a doorframe and then, inexplicably, we were able to push it through, she'd look up, blow a kiss, and say "thank you" to the spirit she felt. Often she'd say it was Richard, my father's father, but there was a good assortment.

Now there were ten or twelve of them who visited me nightly, and I beseeched them to aid me in general and specific causes. I asked my mother's father for humor, my father's mother for strength. She was the matriarch of the celestial group, although I never knew if they or I had decided that. Maybe she did; during her life she had reigned with an iron will. Some nights, when I was too tired to plead my case, I asked her ghost to assign the right angel for the task at hand. That group never let me down; problems were solved, helpers materialized, and improbable resolutions appeared out of thin air.

After a tiring day of phone calls, appointments, and cleaning, I called on my heavenly helpers near midnight as my body stiffened into a rigid slab on my bed. That evening, my brother had hauled away his last load of belongings with no fanfare and had said he'd see us in two or three days. He was peeling the Band-Aid off slowly.

Now that Chip had moved out completely, I threw myself into a full fret about tearing down his room. With two-by-fours, drywall, and a false ceiling, he had cordoned off a large, private living space in the garage that violated building codes and had to disappear before the realtor's appraisal. I turned it over to my troupe of guardians and fell into a restless sleep.

The angels complied forthwith. The next morning, Dad stood gabbing in the garage with a neighbor, a big, brawny guy named Ted whom I hadn't met. I labeled boxes while they caught up. Dad asked him how things were going.

"It's been tough," Ted replied. "I got laid off, and my wife had breast cancer. She's okay now, though. The kids are fine. Growing like weeds. How are you?"

Dad sympathized with their hardships, then said, "We're coming along. Chip moved to Sarasota with his girlfriend, so we need to tear down this room now. I don't think we can do it ourselves."

"I can do it for you," Ted offered, and they started scoping out the job. Dad was saying "we," implying he would help.

I stepped in to negotiate. "That would be great. When can you do it?"

"Probably next week."

"The sooner, the better," I urged. "You can do it whenever it works for you. We don't need any prior notice. But are you sure you can do it?" I wanted to sound grateful, not pushy, but my clock was ticking toward airplanes and moving vans. I needed time to patch and paint the garage walls and ceiling and repair the floor.

"It'll be easy. It's just wood and plaster," Ted said casually.

"Do you have an idea what it will cost?" I asked.

He pointed to the freezer. "I'll swap you for that if you aren't moving it." I considered his proposal the steal of the century but referred him to Mom, since all things food-related were her department.

Ted headed to the Command Post, chatted with Mom for an hour, and closed the deal. She traded the freezer, all its contents, and a cake she had just baked and urged him to take it all right then. He emptied the freezer, thrust it into his pickup as if it were a small cooler, and packed the food back into it while thanking us for each item.

My parents loved to help neighbors; as they aged, they had less to offer others, so each opportunity carried more emotional weight. They were thrilled about this whole freezer-for-work arrangement. I was skeptical, especially of the paid-in-advance part. As Ted left, I implored, "Any time at all works for us."

At seven the next morning, Ted backed in a trailer, brandished a sledgehammer, had his way with the room, and hauled it all to the dump within two hours. Dad grabbed a broom before Ted's truck was out of sight, and I crawled around, examining the floor. We were both laughing silly cackles of relief.

Dad sat down to rest and regale. "Can you believe it's all done and gone? How long did you think it would take? I didn't even get to help."

"I know!" I said. "I pictured he would take two days chopping up drywall, prying out nails, and pulling out studs, and then we would cut it all up to fit in the trunk and haul it to the dump for another few days."

"Your brother did a good job building that room. It was a shame we had to tear it down. Chip was a good foreman. He knew exactly what he needed every time we went to Home Depot. He designed the ceiling and walls really strong but easy to take apart. We worked side by side right through the final finish. It only took us a week."

I realized my brother's experience was a lot like mine: He had delegated to Dad specific parts of the job that he could complete successfully. It had clearly worked and had built lasting memories, along with the temporary walls. I hoped I would do as well.

We tidied up the garage, evaluated for repairs needed, and went in for lunch. I was rinsing off dishes after we ate, blankly staring out the kitchen window, when a rumbling erupted, like a helicopter circling near. A dust cloud engulfed my view, and then a hulking lawn tractor swooped across the backyard. I threw Mom a puzzled look.

"Close all the windows!" she shouted over the ruckus. After I scrambled through each room, slamming them shut, she explained, "That's Jeff. He has a lawn-mowing business. If your dad can't mow or Carroll doesn't get to it, Jeff cuts it on his way home. It magically gets mowed whenever it needs it."

When Jeff was finished, Dad walked out to thank him while I eavesdropped at the window. "Thanks so much," my father said, as they shook hands. "Great job. By the way, I want to sell this shed, if you know anyone who needs one." They walked toward it, discussing its features and price, and Dad told Jeff to open the doors and look inside if he wanted.

Jeff checked the interior, opened and closed the windows, circled the outside, and said, "I could really use it, but I can't afford it. I'll ask around to see if anyone wants it. It's big. What is it, ten feet by fifteen?"

Dad nodded and instructed him, "Just take it. Pay when you can. But can you move it?"

Jeff offered to make monthly payments on it and thought he knew a friend who could haul it. Too many ifs for me, but I cleared all the stuff out of it anyhow.

Early the next morning, a long flatbed trailer attached to a big-rig truck plodded by the house in reverse, then *beep-beep-beep*ed backward into the backyard. Dad and I scurried out to watch the procedure; Mom sat by the window. Several men were milling around, so I considered it well orchestrated and stayed at a distance. Dad couldn't see much from our vantage point, but I had a broader perspective than the guys nearer the truck.

"Stop!" I shrieked, running to the driver. "You're going to clip the corner of the house!"

He pulled out and angled differently, high-centering the trailer, when the wheels sank into the drainage ditch. Carroll and a few other neighbors were watching now, too. I was supervising the wheel drama at ground level when Carroll bellowed, "*Wait!*"

The electric lines overhead had tangled on the back of the cab and were stretching like bungee cords. A burly guy in a tight muscle shirt, shorts, and work boots vaulted to the top of the cab and held the lines out of the way as the trailer inched in. I speculated to myself whether Mom and Dad's homeowner's insurance provided coverage for any of these categories of potential disaster.

After a lot of havoc, the shed finally sailed away, leaving a broad, gaping hole in the grass. Carroll saw my face drain white and said, "How are you going to cover that?"

"I don't have a clue," I answered despondently.

"I'll go get some grass and be back in an hour," he said, as he raced out of the yard.

The next time I looked out, Carroll was unloading large crates of grass plants and bags of soil amendments. He explained, "This is the good type of grass your dad planted when he redid the entire lawn a few years ago. It'll grow fast." As I knelt down to help, I marveled that my dad had replanted the huge lawn this way.

I sat back on my heels and said, "Carroll, how can I ever thank you for all you've done?"

He didn't stop working or ponder his words. With his Southern grace, and from his generous heart, he vouched, "I don't need any thanks. Your parents have been our friends for fourteen years. We love them. We're grateful that you can take care of them. That's all we need."

When we finished, I went in and reviewed the shed-moving fiasco with Mom. "What would have happened if those wires had snapped?" she asked frantically.

"I have no idea. It could have been bad. Dad didn't know what was really happening, so don't tell him." From my father's perspective, all he saw was people helping him, and he was filled with gratitude. I saw that, too, and it was amazing. But could I hold on to that and quit picturing the electric lines snapping and burning down the house? Could I hold on to this part of myself that was emerging, at least in appearances, as competent?

"Are we all going to make it through this?" Mom asked, trying unsuccessfully for a joking tone.

"God willin' and the creek don't rise," I chanted, from our Appalachian years in Maryland.

Chapter 13

....

Mom huffed and hefted her failing joints into the car to tackle shopping for clothes. She was silent, so I left her to her thoughts for the ride; I knew she was nervous. I helped her spill out of the car at the curb of the strip-mall store she had selected, pulled up a cart for her to use as a walker, then parked. She waited outside until I returned, and as we entered the store, her eyes swiped the battleground from side to side, sizing up opponents.

"What do you want to look at first?" I asked her with enthusiasm, to make it seem like fun.

"I just want a couple jumpers and some slacks, but nothing here will fit me. Let's just go." She tried to turn around, but I was in the way in the narrow aisle.

I pointed out the cryptically worded sign for big-lady clothes just as an XXL-size woman wheeled by, her cart overflowing with dresses. I suggested, "Let's go over there, and you can show me styles you like so we'll know what to look for." Encouraged by the oversized comrade in arms, Mom followed me.

We found a wide array of fashions and colors in her estimated size. She grabbed and flung garments into the cart like she was in a contest called "All You Can Get in Fifteen Minutes

Is Yours, Free!" "I'll try these on at home," she said, as she piled slacks, shirts, jumpers, shoes, and underwear into the cart. Fashions for large bodies were much more stylish since Mom had last braved the territory, and she left the store excited and relieved.

Relieved enough to let the next worry rise to the surface and bubble out on the way home: "Our finances are a mess. I don't even know how much we owe on the house. We just don't make enough money."

I hated that she framed it that way, but I had to let that go. Where did she think the money should have come from? Dad had worked six days a week for forty years. He had been a cash register repairman when she'd married him. How far up that career ladder was there to climb?

"I just don't want to have to sit on newspapers," she sighed to the window.

I made a clumsy scroll through the card file of my brain but couldn't attach any meaning to *sitting on newspapers*.

"Sit on newspapers?" I questioned reluctantly, still aware there was history I wasn't allowed to know.

"What?" she said. "Oh. When I was in ninth grade, one of the apartments we moved to in South Buffalo was so dirty, my mother covered all the furniture with newspapers so we wouldn't get bedbugs."

"Good grief! Gramma must have hated that. She was so . . . so—"

"Prissy," she interrupted me. "She hated that place, but she loved my dad to the ends of the earth, so she made the best of it. It was a huge old house divided into tiny apartments. We shared a bathroom down the hall on the third floor with two other families. My mother might have had only bread and gravy to serve, but she set the table every day with linens and china. You'll never guess what the refrigerator was: the dumbwaiter! It was cooler inside the walls, so we all stored our food on it and hoped no one stole it."

I knew Mom had finished high school in 1945, so I back-tracked to envision our country's economy when she was in ninth grade, 1942, shortly after the United States entered World War II. *Bye Bye, Buy Bonds*; *Save Chicken Fat;* and *Join the WAC* floated through my brain. Why couldn't I remember the important things?

"Was that when you had to go live with your grand-mother?" I asked, one of the few details I remembered of her childhood.

"No. I was in sixth grade when my parents sent me back to Ohio to live with Gramma Cheeseman; my sister went to live at the Darrows'."

"The Darrows?" I asked. I didn't remember any relatives by that name; I pictured a group of nuns running a home for impoverished children.

"They were my mom's friends," she clarified, "and their daughter was your aunt Kay's best friend. My parents couldn't afford to feed us. Judy was only a baby, and she was very sick, so they kept her with them. I loved living at my grandmother's, though. She ran a tourist home, and there was always enough food. We had cucumber-and-watercress sandwiches for lunch. She bought me a brand-new dress for a singing contest, my first new, store-bought dress—peach-colored shantung. And my first heels—just an inch high, but I felt like a million bucks. She wouldn't let me wear silk stockings, though. I had to wear anklets."

"Didya win?" I asked.

"I did. I represented my school in a city concert. But then I missed my parents too much. I went back home to Buffalo for seventh grade. Aunt Kay still stayed with the Darrows most of the time, though."

"What kind of place did you live in then?" I asked.

"We moved around a lot to different apartments in Buffalo, sometimes in the middle of the night with just our suitcases, linens, the china and the silver. My dad had been selling cars for a few years, but then, after the war started, new-car sales were banned; they were reserved for the military. Car factories made war equipment, like tanks."

Spellbound by her stories, I wondered if riding in the car flipped her talk switch, the opposite of driving a baby around until it fell asleep. I drove slowly, and she continued.

"Everything was rationed. We even had to register the serial numbers on our car tires and were allowed only five tires. We got awards at school for collecting scrap metal. I still have my certificate for twenty-five pounds. Aunt Kay registered for a liquor-rationing card as soon as she was of age, even though she didn't drink. It meant our dad could have more.

"Anyhow, we ended up in that filthy apartment. We stayed there only two weeks; then we all moved in with the Darrows in East Aurora, where Aunt Kay stayed."

"You don't talk about your childhood much," I said. "I didn't know you were that poor." My mother was two years old in 1929 when the stock market crashed, so I knew her childhood collided with the ten-year span of the Great Depression, but she never talked about it.

"We were always poor," she said, without rancor. "In eighth grade, we lived behind a deli, and the owner, Mrs. Schuster, hired me to work after school until she closed at eight o'clock, and all day Saturdays. I made ten dollars a week and gave my mother eight. I waited on customers and broke down the big sacks of sugar into one-pound bags for rationing. I always checked them on the scale, but I could measure exactly right without weighing. I made a game out of it. On Saturdays, I added the week's tabs for customers to pay their bills. That's why I can still add in my head so well. I was only fourteen. Social Security cards had been out only a few years, and I was so proud of mine."

She quizzed me on family trivia: "You know why we moved to Buffalo, don't you?"

"Well, you went there from Ohio after the stock market crashed, so I guess Grampa had hope for a job there."

"He had a job, all right, but not just selling cars. It was during Prohibition, and Buffalo was on the Canadian border. He was in a bootlegging ring with some of his army buddies. We drove cases of booze to Ohio. I was only three, so if we got stopped, I was supposed to pretend to be asleep on a blanket that covered the crates stacked in the footwell of the backseat."

"Were you scared?"

She laughed. "Never. You knew Grampa. Everything was fun with him. We adored him—everyone did. My dad was a nut. He'd come in at two in the morning with a bunch of friends, maybe car salesmen, probably gamblers or gangsters. One time he brought home gallons of oysters and my mother got out of bed and made oyster stew for them in the middle of the night. We were absolutely forbidden to leave our bedroom whenever his friends were there, but Kay and I always peeked. They smoked big cigars, drank whiskey, and played cards. We learned words we could never repeat."

I laughed, too. "Now you probably hear those words every day on TV."

When she didn't answer, I looked over and realized these memories had transformed her face from worried to crinkled with joy, and I knew it originated in the words *everything was fun with him*. She was soothing herself with my grandfather's stories, likely reliving hearing him tell one. She had found the pearl in the memory and used it, just like my father had used his Crossing the Line ceremony story to banish his Navy nightmare. I thought I should start a list of geriatric remedies, like a medicine cabinet for sadness or grief.

She wasn't ready to return to the present and went on, "When Judy was little, she was really sick from malnourishment, and, miraculously, we had expensive medicine, pork chops and steak and butter—things we'd never had before. We were told Grampa's friends had given us those things. We didn't find out until later who his friends were. He didn't tell us until years after we moved back to Ohio."

She paused for dramatic effect, then said, "Al Capone."

"Are you serious?"

"Well, your grandfather liked a good story, but he was pretty convincing about that one. He admitted he smuggled for Capone every time we visited a friend of my mother's at an orphanage in a monastery by the Niagara River. I remember he always went downstairs with a bunch of men and played cards. Then we drove home with the car loaded with crates. Shortly thereafter, we'd take a trip to Ohio to visit relatives. We always traveled at night.

"He said he met Al Capone originally when he sold him a car. Capone invited him to a casino in the basement of a place on Main Street in Buffalo. A speakeasy, you know, with lots of tunnels and escape routes. Al Capone went to jail, but the Mob kept going, and I guess my dad was in with the gang. Maybe they just thought he was fun, too. He sure wasn't dangerous, even though he had certificates and awards for riflery and sharpshooting in World War I."

She wandered in silent memories, then said, "But we didn't get rich from his escapades. Lunch at school was ten cents for soup, but I didn't have enough money. I ate a jar of beans and a piece of bread from home. That soup smelled so good."

As we neared home, she left the past behind. "Can we afford this apartment you picked out?" she asked nervously.

"You can easily afford the apartment. By the way, you probably need to start submitting address changes and closing bank accounts, so maybe you can get a feel for what you owe then."

"I tried to call the bank, but they lost me right after they told me to press something for English. I can't deal with those lists of 'push this for that.'"

"Do you want me to do it?" I knew I needed to take over, but I wanted her to pass the torch.

"Could you? I hate to add one more thing to your list."

"Yes. I'd be happy to do it." Would I ever. The suspense was killing me.

She turned back to the window and murmured to ghosts of her past, "I wonder what would have happened if I hadn't quit singing, if I had signed that contract in Germany."

I knew that by age twenty-three my mother had established a professional singing career, married a CIA agent, given birth to Linda, moved to Greece, divorced, and moved back home. But that was the extent of my knowledge. Those files were sealed before I was born.

How could I empathize with something I knew so little about? I tried, "It was not an easy time to be a divorcée with a child—not a proper thing in the 1950s. I think you made good choices."

She nodded and agreed, "Moving home with a two-year-old and working at Sears was a far cry from my life in Athens as the wife of a big shot. But then, right there in Sears' hardware department, your dad swept me off my feet, and he loved Linda." My mother assessed her almost sixty years of marriage: "I guess it turned out all right."

"It did, Mom. You had beautiful homes, a healthy family, good friends, and plenty of everything. No one of your generation could have predicted how the economy would change or how much the costs of health care would rob your retirement. You thought Social Security and Medicare would take care of you." She sat back and let the system take the blame for her monetary woes.

I offered a silent prayer for my future as their fiduciary agent, then practiced my lying. "It's all gonna be great," I reassured her, "just great."

Chapter 14

....

Before dawn the next morning, I began painting the high garage ceiling, and my hair, while teetering on a tall stepladder straddling the 150 boxes already packed, inventoried, sealed, labeled, and cross-referenced to a master list. If Mom threw another hissy fit about a missing utensil, I could retrieve it and fast-pitch it to her before she slammed her second cupboard door.

My parents' hobbies complicated the packing process. They never pursued purely recreational activities but derived great joy and satisfaction from homemaking. When I was young, no matter what internal demons my mother may have been fighting, or maybe because of them, she baked, sewed, crafted, decorated and redecorated, and reigned as the neighborhood hostess. Our homes resonated with her magnificent soprano as she played songs on the piano from stacks of sheet music ranging from "Ave Maria" to "Yesterday." From hundreds of precious recipes, she filled the table with home-cooked meals from scratch every night and rarely fixed the same dinner twice in one year. Without question, we set a place at the table for any of our friends, neighbors, or relatives who happened to be there at suppertime.

All those homemaking supplies she'd accumulated over the course of a lifetime were being carted to Washington, whether she had used them in the last fifty years or not. Dad had amassed a lifetime of tools, repair parts, and odds and ends, all well organized and clean. He passed along a few things to Chip, but most of it was destined for the cross-country trek. I didn't quibble. I inventoried, packed, and shook my head. Their new apartment was half the square footage of their house, but I would tackle that puzzle later. For now, whatever helped them leap this hurdle was okay with me. I was sure that somewhere in their dark moments they heard a conductor calling, "All aboard. Last stop before nursing home. Tickets, please."

I had just repositioned the ladder in the garage and was stretching to angle my steamed-up bifocals to see the ceiling, dripping sweat in the clammy hundred degrees, when Dad trudged into the garage. With a stiff jaw, he mumbled tearfully, "I just don't feel safe to ride the mower anymore."

Mom and I were both struggling about the probable future of Dad's riding mower. He hadn't used it recently because of his vision loss, but it had been his trusted steed, a work companion, his independence. We suspected that, at over twenty years old, she wasn't going to graze in any grass in Washington, but we hadn't pronounced her dead.

"That's okay, Dad," I tried to console him. "I appreciate it that you don't take risks." I knew I couldn't erase his sadness, but I also knew by this time how courageously and stoically he shouldered and soothed his own emotions. I had a feeling he'd attempted to mow and suffered a scare skidding into a gully or bucking up a hill but was sparing me the details.

"Does the grass need to be cut?" I asked. I knew I could call Jeff or ask Carroll to mow.

"Yeah, before the realtor comes. I can't ask you to do one more thing. But . . . I . . . just . . . don't . . . think . . . I can . . ."

From his tone of voice, I realized this problem felt urgent

to him, not one that could wait for Carroll or Jeff. "I'll do it for you now. I love to mow my lawn." Liar, liar, pants on fire.

I closed the paint can, wrapped up the roller, and switched gears for my day, knowing activity would dissipate his sorrow. I followed him out to his temple, the Barn. Every garden essential stood in its assigned spot, handy, clean, and in good repair. Dad was a perfect fit for the Navy because he was a master of neatness and discipline. When he lost his sight, it was useful to have a place for everything and everything in its place, a common refrain in our childhood. He could locate any tool by memory if it was in its designated location, and it usually was.

He uncovered the mower and pulled out the ol' girl, urging me, "Go ahead and get on." Images of training wheels on a two-wheeler and my first pony ride flashed in my memory.

I saddled up. He turned the key for me and tried to tell me how the gears worked, but the explosive engine noise prevented me from hearing his directions. My father tinkered with the engine, changed the oil, and sharpened the blade regularly, but the mower had never been professionally serviced and didn't have a muffler. I turned it off so he could show me how to engage the blade and use the clutch.

When I started it again, he could tell by the sound that the blade wasn't spinning and signaled me with a hand across his throat to cut the engine.

"This happens a lot. It's easy to fix," he said confidently. "Come over here. Kneel down. Put your hand in there and grab the belt." He patiently began instructing me how to put the belt back on: "Twist it just a little clockwise and slightly rotate it onto that pin in the middle."

I was pretending to listen but was rehearsing a call to have the mower picked up for service. What would I tell the repairman—just fix it enough to mow four more times? My riding mower at home went to the repair shop once or twice a year, when it needed anything more than gas.

I stood up, wiping my greasy hands on my jeans, and said, "I can't get it, Dad. It takes two hands, and my shoulder isn't strong enough." He looked at me like a teacher who knew you could do better if you just tried.

By then, our activity had attracted Carroll. He had owned a car repair shop before he'd retired and was a skilled mechanic.

"Belt off again?" he asked, then knelt down in the right spot, put his hands in the right places, and pulled and twisted for a few minutes. "I can't get it either," he admitted with surprise.

Dad eased his creaky knees down on the ground next to the mower, then said to me, "Put my hand on the belt." I tucked his hand into the tiny access hole and put his fingers on the belt. He spent a moment orienting himself to the pins and gears and then, lickety-split, slid the belt back on.

Carroll clapped Dad on the back. "Tom, you amaze me. I wish I could have had you at my service station. You can fix anything."

Jubilant over Dad's victory in his diminishing world of accomplishments, I hopped back on. *Giddyap! Ride 'em, cowgirl!* I mowed, giggling and giddy at life's little twists and turns.

When he was wiping her down and checking her hooves after my ride, Dad quietly asked, "What should we do with the mower?"

I didn't want this conversation now. I was painting, packing, planning, panicking. I said, "You get to decide, Dad. You could take it and drive it back and forth to my house."

"Let's hitch it to the back of the van and put your mother in her chair on top. Real *Beverly Hillbillies*–style," he laughed.

Finally, clenching his teeth to ward off trembling lips, he quavered, "How about putting her out in the front yard with a FOR SALE sign?" I realized he'd reached a point where he'd rather have resolution than vacillate in the decision-making process. Although he was exhilarated by the price I suggested, he didn't trust that anyone would pay that much for it. We decided if it didn't sell for our price, we wouldn't sell it.

Over dinner, I updated Mom to test the idea out loud again for Dad, reaffirming, "If she doesn't sell for that, we'll take her with us." Mom's watchful antennae went up, and she observed my father all that night and the next morning to see if the choice seemed too hard for him. His antianxiety pills were working, but she always monitored him discreetly every day. Her powers of observation were well honed after decades of his heart disease.

The next morning, we hooked a looker within an hour of staging the mower in the front yard with her FOR SALE sign. Dad was in the bathroom, so I went charging out, knowing I shouldn't appear too eager but not able to contain myself.

A rugged, suntanned man about my age greeted me. "This is a good mower. How come you're selling it?" I noticed his trailer was loaded with grass clippings, and the sign on his pickup said MOWING AND LANDSCAPING.

"My dad can't safely ride it anymore, and I'm moving him and my mom to Washington State so I can take care of them. Do you want to start it up?" I didn't want any illusions about the quality of what he deemed a good mower.

"No. I want to get it for my son; I'm helping him set up his own lawn-mowing business. I'll go tell him and come back later."

"Do you want me to hold it for you?"

"No, that wouldn't be fair if someone comes along with cash in hand."

I had fibbed those same words at garage sales to wangle my polite and permanent exit, so I wrote him off and didn't even bother to report the encounter to Mom or Dad.

The landscaper returned in thirty minutes with his son, a gregarious eighteen-year-old. With just a slight hint from me, they both immediately tuned in to the significance of the occasion, chatting with Dad and confirming what a great mower she was and how excited they were to buy her. They never quibbled about the price, handing Dad a wad of cash with heartfelt handshakes. By the time she was loaded in their trailer, Dad's sadness had turned to relief. He was happy about helping out a kid and darn pleased about the green in his pocket. That didn't last too long, though—as he walked past the car, he said, "Now I guess we have to give up Precious."

My neck muscles cinched.

Chapter 15

....

My parents loved their vehicles and always named and anthropomorphized them. When I was growing up, we accepted selling each of our family cars as a sad but necessary ordeal. It happened rarely because my parents took good care of each one and bonded with them as family members. As a child, I felt honored to be allowed to scrub the whitewalls on the '57 Ford, despite cold hands, wet cuffs, soaked Keds, and gravel indentations on my knees.

Now I needed to coordinate selling their Saturn, named Precious, with precise timing because I didn't want to pay for a rental car any longer than was necessary. She was a good little car, and I used her every day. I also wanted my parents to be prepared to part with her, so I let the decision to sell her just ride, waiting for a sign that they were ready.

Coffee was brewing and Mom was presiding at her post bright and early the next morning, surrounded by scraps of paper fluttering in the fan breeze. "How do you like this?" she asked, then read:

> She's Precious to us in more than name,
> We know that you will feel the same.

Low miles, great shape, good gas mileage, too.
She'd be just the perfect car for you.

I heard the starting gun for *sell the car.* I suspected a protracted, poetic ad was out of our price range, but at least the emotional process had kicked in.

"Cute," I said. "I'll go to the newspaper today to check out prices for ads and figure out the Blue Book value."

I hauled Dad around town to the newspaper, the bank, and the Saturn dealership so he could begin the process of letting go of Precious. After we returned home, I overheard him verifying her fate to Mom, saying, "Can you believe she held her value like that? Selling her will pay for the moving van."

"I know. But I'll miss her. She's been such a good little girl. She never needed a single repair."

I entered the room, and Mom turned to me. "Doesn't Precious just purr? Don't you just love driving her?"

Dad didn't know I was there and thought Mom was still talking to him. He said, "I do. Maybe I'll drive to the hardware store tomorrow."

Mom and I shot each other shocked looks, wondering if we had a battle on our hands.

"Hi, Dad. You want to drive?" I asked.

"Nah. It's okay. You're a good driver. I was just teasing your mother. But I'd like to drive my '38 Lincoln Zephyr. Now, *that* was a car. It purred and roared. I have dreams about driving it all over Youngstown with Johnny and Nelson. I finally impressed them when I got that car."

Mom and I instantly went on silent alert to see where those memories might take him. We knew he had shared his love of cars with his brother, Nelson, who had died in World War II, and with Johnny, his brother-in-law, who had also died tragically and young. Dad was smiling to himself, probably remembering some secret trouble they'd gotten into.

I anxiously ran the ad for Precious with only a few weeks left before our departure. Her price significantly eased the parental pain of separation from their beloved vehicle, but they still talked every day about missing her when she was gone. It sounded like they equated it with sending a child to foster care, but I thought it was more related to losing their last vestige of free mobility.

A week went by, and no one responded to the ad.

"Maybe I should park her out front with a sign," I suggested, needing parental consent to proceed.

"She should get a lot of exposure out there with all this new traffic speeding by," Mom groused.

The county had recently converted the long country road past my parents' home into a calamity of roaring trucks and screeching brakes, a permanent detour intended to ease traffic through the middle of town. It was entirely possible that this bypass plan had been in the works before my parents selected their house, but they weren't ones to conduct consumer research. They spent their money emotionally, not rationally.

They bought this house when they spontaneously decided to move to Florida one winter morning after my dad slipped on the ice in their driveway in Maryland. They stuck a FOR SALE sign in the yard, drove to a Florida town a friend suggested, stopped at a realty office they spotted from the highway, and purchased the first house the realtor showed them. They liked the salesman and bought his product. They were an advertiser's dream—no Consumer Reports for them.

After a week with a sign in her window, Precious still sat. Mom snidely suggested I should have used her poem in the paper, even though it would have cost $125, instead of $25. Precious was a good car in good condition at a good price. I increased the size of the newspaper ad. Nothing. I pulled her closer to the road with eye-catching signs. Nothing.

It was time to turn the Precious predicament over to the angel consortium. I studied the lineup in the clouds of my bed-

room ceiling to choose the best one for the job. Who liked cars?
Who would know what to do? The one who stepped forward was
Johnny, my aunt's husband, who had been killed in a car accident
in 1954, soon after they were married. He was a decorated World
War II Air Force pilot who had been my dad's friend. My parents'
faces turned to unmasked grief whenever they remembered the
day Johnny's car crashed into the back of a semi at the bottom
of an icy hill. He left his young wife, my dad's oldest sister, Jeannette, widowed with a toddler. I never knew Uncle Johnny, but
it was a chapter of family history that, uncharacteristically, was
never rewritten with any happy overtones. I assigned the job to
Johnny and turned to other feelings in my sleepless night.

Before sunrise the next morning, when I was taking out
the garbage, a neighbor I had met once or twice was circling
the car. He looked Precious over and said, "This is a good car.
I might buy it for my wife. Why aren't you taking it with you?"

I stumbled for words as my brain tried to catch up with the
idea. It had never occurred to me that we could take her with
us. "How would we do that?" I asked, as if it were the secret to
a magic trick.

He looked at me as if I were speaking a foreign language,
probably similar to the look I was giving him. With exasperation, he instructed, "You call a hauler; they pick it up, put it on a
trailer, and take it wherever you want. Shouldn't cost much more
than a thousand dollars. I'll call you and give you the number."

Since she wasn't selling, I figured I would need to lower
the price by at least a thousand dollars. Why not just take her
with us?

I went to the dining room to convey this news, aware of
the weight of an unnatural cloak of responsibility and control
over my parents' lives. First I was abandoning their baby; now I
was shipping her cross-country.

"That guy with all those dogs just came by. He was looking at the car for his wife."

"She already has a nice car," Mom protested, as she started gathering up their breakfast dishes to try to end the conversation.

"He said it's a good car and we should take it with us."

Their heads swiveled toward me, and they inhaled in unison. "What?"

"He said we could just call an auto hauler, and the cost seems reasonable."

Again they asked, "What?" They were as befuddled as I had been.

"I think we should take Precious with us."

They both stood up and were suddenly busy at the kitchen counter, with their backs to me. Their wavery voices exposed their emotions. Mom wiped her eyes with her apron. "Precious can go to Washington?"

Dad coughed. "I'd love for you to have that car. It's one way we can repay you for all your work. Put her in your name right away."

Precious was moving to Washington! The family was intact. In my mind, the sad family story of Johnny acquired a redeeming chapter.

Taking advantage of their temporary relief, I presented the next roadblock on my list. "Are you sure you want to take Chip's cat to Washington?" I tried to ask without inflection.

I had witnessed only brief flashes of this cat in all her eleven years, as she hightailed it out of any room I entered, but I knew she was twice the size of an average cat, and fully clawed. Labeling her skittish would have put a positive spin on her personality.

Mom loaded her voice with half persuasion and half *don't question this*. "Tillie doesn't get along with Chip's other cats, and she sleeps with me every night. We're taking her."

The cat was affectionate only with my mother and my brother; all other animate or inanimate objects that moved or made noise were monsters to her. I resented being forced to assume responsibility for it. Who did they think would buy cat food, haul kitty litter, and take it to the doctor?

I sighed in acquiescence. "Then I have to take her to the vet for a health certificate so she can fly."

Mom handed me the phone book and phone, cautioning, "You might have to find a new vet. I don't think ours will take her back after the last time. Somebody got hurt pretty badly."

I called Tillie's doctor, and the receptionist warily scheduled an appointment for the next day, adding a caveat that they might sedate her for the exam. I thanked her and extended my apologies in advance.

"How in the world will we get her in a cage?" I asked Mom irritably, realizing as I said it that my lack of enthusiasm for this whole project was seeping out through the seams of my uniform. I knew they thought I had the authority to say, "No cat in Washington" if any piece of this feline portage went haywire. And I probably did have that power, but my goal, though failed at the moment, was not to foster their vulnerability.

Mom started, "We can get her in her cage."

Dad chimed in, "We can get her in a cage."

They nodded their heads and chanted together, like the Little Train That Could, "Yes, we can get her in a cage. We'll get her in her cage."

I couldn't imagine that feat, between Dad's obvious hunting and trapping limitations and Mom's lack of strength and inability to bend or kneel. However, it was our only option, short of having my brother drive an hour to the house to capture her—a highly likely backup plan, I strategized, as I went to bed.

The next morning, I peeked from the edge of the living room and watched Mom and Dad work together in perfect synchronicity to snare their tiger. Dad sneaked behind the rocking chair where Tillie was sleeping, then stood perfectly still while holding the open cat crate. If he made one rattle, the cat would bolt. Mom walked over to Tillie nonchalantly, cooing her name, then gently picked her up as catnip leaves wafted off her fur like snowflakes. Mom moved very slowly, acting like she was going to give Tillie a little hug, then swiftly dumped the drunk cat into the crate and slammed the door. They were proud trappers as I congratulated them and chortled in relief.

Dad and I dropped the cat off at the vet and headed for "his" grocery store. He bumped the grocery cart along on my heels while I selected lunch fixings for his sister's upcoming visit. One of her grandsons had a small plane and was flying her in the next day from Key West. We trundled through the store where Dad had bagged groceries for ten years, and in each department employees gravitated to him for handshakes and hugs. As he said good-bye to his former coworkers, he handled the departure more like a graduation than an ending. His best old bagger friend, now ninety, loaded our groceries into the trunk. As the parting threatened to well up in their rheumy eyes, I smoothed it over: "We'll be back here to shop a dozen more times before we leave."

Driving away, I quickly changed the subject. "When was the last time you saw Aunt Shookie?" His sister was named Amanda, but Dad still called her by her childhood nickname.

"She came up for a weekend a couple years ago. We went down to Key West to visit her, too. What a beautiful place." He drifted off into his memories, or a nap, a frequent occurrence in the car.

I stopped to pick up the cat from the vet, who had granted her a clean bill of health; whether or not they had ever opened her cage, I didn't ask. Tillie had her ticket to ride, and I had a big scratch off the major column on the list.

The next day, Dad and I arrived at the airport in time to admire an attractive and chic elderly woman deplane. When they hugged, there was no question of their sibling relationship in build, coloring, and carriage.

She chatted on the way home about all her grandchildren. I tried to keep them straight, but there seemed to be a lot of them. I filled her in on my life, my sister's life, and Chip's success with photography. Dad mostly listened, used to my mother carrying on the conversation.

After Shookie and Mom had their hugs and greetings, they settled in at the table with Dad. I prepped the food while Mom asked specific questions about the lives and livelihoods of each of Aunt Shookie's grandchildren. They compared notes on Dad and Shookie's older sister, Jeannette, whose son was now caring for her. My mother's memory and conversational skills always impressed me. After lunch, my aunt said she usually went for a walk at that time of day, and asked if I wanted to join her.

"I want to know how they *really* are," she demanded, as soon as we were out of earshot.

I quickly summed up their medical and financial status, assuring her all would improve once they moved.

"Thank you for taking care of them," she said. "I guess we've all entered that phase; my kids take care of me, too. I'm glad Jeannette is okay, but I've been worried sick about your parents. Your dad has always been special to me; he was my best pal when we were growing up. Of course, your dad and Nelson were inseparable. Losing Nelson was so awful. Our family never recovered. My mother had already been through so much, I didn't think she'd survive. But she was tough. Hard."

"Did you get along with her?" I asked.

"Not really. When I was a child, my great-aunt Amanda—my mother's aunt and my namesake—gave my parents enough money to put away for me to go to college. A lot of money. I didn't find out until I was eighteen that my mother had spent every penny of it. All she said was that she had to buy groceries. No apology."

"Dad told me about that. He said your mother could be a little stern and strict."

"That's putting it mildly. It was lucky everyone in town knew it, because they protected us from her. Like when Nelson almost drowned at the pool. Did your dad tell you about that? Or when he and Nelson got lost at Uncle John's in Struthers? My mother never knew half of what my brothers did, but they still spent a lot of time confined to their room as punishment."

"Dad said he got Nelson in a lot of trouble. He even blames himself for Nelson joining the Marines after he enlisted in the Navy."

"No, it was the other way around," she said with certainty. "Nelson wasn't afraid of anything and lived for adventure. My mother just wanted someone to blame. She was harsh and inflexible. That stiff posture was part of her personality. Did you know she had a fight with her parents and her brother when we were teenagers and didn't ever speak to them again?"

"No, what did they fight about?" I asked.

"Money."

We had circled the block, and before we went in, she said, "Thank you again so much for taking care of your parents."

After we resumed our seats in the dining room, I teased, "Hey, Dad, what's this about you and Nelson getting lost at Uncle John's?"

He looked around guiltily, as if his mother might be ready to send him to his room, then told a long story about being lost for hours while his dad and uncles searched for them. "My dad swore everyone to secrecy and said never to tell our mother. They had been looking for us for a long time, and they were more scared than we were, I think. Even the bloomin' bloody bastard came to help look for us." He spoke the words *bloomin' bloody bastard* in an imitation Cockney.

Aunt Shookie got the British joke, but Mom and I didn't.

Aunt Shookie explained, "Our dad was the youngest of ten kids. The older ones were born in England and talked with a British accent. One time Uncle Charlie, the oldest brother, called someone a bloomin' bloody bastard, and my dad yelled, 'Don't you ever say that in front of my kids again.' Uncle Charlie never said it again, but we sure did. That's what we called him when my dad wasn't around."

"I didn't know you had so many relatives," I said. I realized my father never talked about his family, probably because every story linked back to his brother.

"Between my mother's aunts and uncles and my dad's brothers and sisters, there were a lot," my aunt said. "Not much in the way of grandparents, though. My mother had that rift with her parents, and our dad's father left for the Alaska gold rush when Dad was nine and never came back."

"I just read something about that," I said. "A hundred thousand men went to Alaska and the Yukon seeking their fortunes; only thirty thousand actually made it."

My mother piped up, "My dad's father left for the gold rush, too, when Dad was a toddler; he was never heard from again, either."

Mom continued, "When I was little, my dad told us to look for his father on a mountaintop when we went to a Charlie Chaplin silent movie about the gold rush. We looked and looked."

"Your dad was so much fun; everybody loved him," Aunt Shookie said to my mother. "But no one in my family found any humor in the gold rush subject. My dad's father took off with their life savings and left Dad's mother with all those children to feed."

I mulled over the fact that I had two great-grandfathers who disappeared in the Alaska gold rush. What were the chances of that? Why hadn't I known that?

Dad seemed bored and left the table, returning a few minutes later with a musty, dilapidated box. He set it by Shookie, saying, "Remember this?"

She studied it, then said, "Oh, your kit for making toy soldiers. How did Mother ever let you boys play with something so dangerous?"

"She thought we made them only when Dad was with us. We made them in the basement with a gas burner, so she never knew. It saved my butt one time, though. Do you remember when I broke my sled?"

"Vaguely. Remind me." She winked at me, knowing Dad wanted to relive this story.

He started, but I interrupted, "First, what is all that in the box, Dad? How does it work?"

"You heat lead in this ladle over a flame, then pour it in these molds." He handled the small pieces proficiently, memory overcoming blindness.

I was developing sympathy for his mother. Little boys liquefying lead over an open fire didn't sound safe to me.

"Okay. So tell us about your sled."

"Well," he started, "you know that big hill in front of my mother's house? In the winter when it snowed, cars would have to zigzag back and forth from one side of the street to the other to climb up the hill. When we were sure our mother wasn't watching, Nelson and I flopped on our sleds, flat on our stomachs, and grabbed onto the back bumpers of cars and rode up the hill, then sledded back down. But one time, the car I was hanging onto flew out of control, fishtailed, and threw me off. I crashed into the curb and broke my sled runner. My mother would have grounded me until spring if she had found out how I broke it. I sneaked it down to the basement and welded it together with hot lead. I thought I was home free, until lead splashed and burned a hole in my pants. I guess I made up some story about that to keep me out of trouble."

For hours they laughed and told stories I'd never heard. Until recently, most of the anecdotes my parents had shared with me related to my childhood. As the evening faded, I watched this sojourn into their own childhoods fill them with a new vitality and brightness. Later, I jotted down notes about their stories so I could use them to boost their spirits when needed, making the geriatric antigrief list a reality.

Dad and I drove Aunt Shookie back to the airport, and they chatted about this and that like the old friends they were, with never a maudlin word or tone. We all knew they'd never see each other again, but that was never a piece of the visit. They said their good-byes as if they'd see each other next week. I could hardly bear watching through my tears.

My father basked in the glow of the visit, then fell asleep as I drove us home. I realized that aging gracefully was less about grace and more about strength. I had to toughen up.

Chapter 16

....

At last it was time to list the house for sale. We were painted, washed, primped, and primed as the realtor sat casually at the Command Post with a closed folder, gossiping with Mom about various neighbors. The two nonchatters at the table were silently screaming, *How much is it worth? How much? How much?*

Finally she opened the folder and handed papers to us, saying, "Here are five comps from the neighborhood, and a rough appraisal of your house."

I read the figures to Dad, and he argued, "But our house isn't worth nearly that much."

She jolted up from the papers and questioned, "Is there something about the house I don't know?" She probably wondered if we'd had a gruesome murder, toxic fumes from the soil, or bats in the attic, generating guano.

"No, we just didn't have any idea what houses were selling for," I reassured her.

She said, "That really is ballpark for your house. Your barn, beautiful landscaping, mature trees, and irrigation system all add to the value. You've kept the house in perfect condition."

I couldn't have scripted a better testimony to restore Mom and Dad's pride. The price would pay off their two mortgages, their bills, and the mover. We had never expected that. I wrote down all the numbers and asked her to verify them because I knew we were so slap-happy that later we would wonder if we'd misunderstood.

The house enticed a few prospects but no serious takers. We questioned the price, but the realtor stayed firm in her appraisal, while I envisioned catastrophic scenarios in which the house never sold and I had to manage it as a long-distance rental. Or possibly a hurricane would destroy it before it sold and we'd pay a mortgage on an empty lot because of an unknown insurance glitch. To my parents, I repeated upbeat inanities like "It will sell once it's empty" and "Houses don't sell in the spring; they sell in the fall." Whatever plausible explanation I could invent on the spur of the moment streamed out of my mouth.

As the day of our departure drew closer, I watched my parents weave strands of strength into invisible armors to bear their good-byes with grace. They soothed their last days with light-hearted anecdotes about past moves and discovering new towns together. They laughed and flooded any lurking dark space with humor. Shedding just a few tears, they focused fiercely on the future.

I saw Chip's car in the driveway and knew he'd arrived for his final good-byes. I expected to see him when I went into the dining room, and Mom quickly answered my puzzled look: "He's in the bedroom with Tillie. I don't know if it's harder for him to say good-bye to us or to the cat." I nodded in agreement. I knew she felt sad, not slighted, by that; pets ranked high in our family. Out of the corner of my eye, I saw Chip try to slink out the door unnoticed. I watched him go around to the backyard, then followed him to see what he was doing.

He was kneeling by a flowerbed, and I noticed for the first time the little cross with the name of his beloved cat that had died years earlier. Heaving with tears, he said, "I can't stand it. It's too hard. Maybe I won't see any of them again."

I was determined to stay strong. "Oh, honey. I'm so sorry. It seemed like the only option."

"It is. I know it is. I'm so relieved you are doing it. I'm just sad, and I don't want them to see me this way."

We stood looking at the grave for a long time with our arms around each other. I silently begged every guardian angel we had to bolster him. My reserves were winnowing. After a bit, he said I could go back in and he'd be there in a few minutes.

He came in with a grin pasted on and told funny stories about trying to combine his messy electronics with Jonquil's elegant style in their new apartment. Mom busied herself loading up containers of food for him, and Dad sorted through a collection of antique pocketknives to give to Chip. After a final piece of Mom's chocolate cake, my brother pulled out of the driveway, blowing his horn until he was out of sight. My parents and I headed off in separate directions to spare each other our grief. We all were traversing this rite of passage with tears, laughter, fortitude, and hope.

Suddenly yet finally, moving day dawned. Having extensively rehearsed the day's procedures instead of sleeping, I arranged my mental cue cards in sequential order and acted them out one by one. At the appointed time, Mom and Dad ambushed their pet tiger again and I dropped her at the vet for boarding until we left for the airport, thereby preventing any chance of the scaredy-cat disappearing in the decamping chaos.

The mover rolled in right on schedule, and he and his son worked like they were paid by the minute while maintaining playful banter with my parents. They packed and loaded all day but left our beds so we could stay at home that night, although my bed was useless, as usual. Late the next afternoon, when all my parents' possessions were compressed into the van, its doors were latched and locked under our observation, exactly as the mover had promised. I signed paperwork, wrote a check for half the total cost, and watched the truck rumble away with a wave and a honk, as I wondered, *Did I get the right moving insurance? Did I hire a reputable mover? Will we ever see their belongings again?* Just a few days earlier, the network news had highlighted stories on moving-company scams, as if I weren't worried enough.

Relieved but frazzled by the packing process, I followed my list like a sleepwalker: Take the oldsters to the motel. Go get takeout for dinner and rolls for breakfast. Set up Dad's apnea equipment, the coffeemaker, and alarm clocks for early rising. Try to sleep. Call them at six o'clock to make sure they were awake. They were up, dressed, and sipping coffee in high spirits. I had never expected that.

We retrieved the cat from the vet, drove to the house for a final walk through, and left the keys to Precious with Carroll to hand over to the auto hauler. I started praying for the airport transportation to show up, frantically realizing I had no expedient backup plan. It appeared, twenty minutes late, the driver assuring me we had plenty of time. I swallowed a migraine pill.

Both my parents smiled and waved good-bye to their beloved home as we were whisked away. We were each holding tight to a brave face for one another's sake. After a grueling hour in morning traffic and some anxious confusion delivering the cat to airport cargo, we found our gate with just minutes to spare. Whew! We did it. At nine o'clock, we boarded the plane, with the dominoes in a neat, flat line. Hooray. Next stop: home sweet home.

Chapter 17

....

Katy greeted us at the airport, looking as bedraggled as I felt. It had been a long three months for all of us. As we rolled into the driveway of our serene property, with its soaring cloister of Doug fir trees and native undergrowth, our home cast its calming spell on me.

I had lived on this piece of land for almost thirty years, Katy with me for twenty of them, originally in a ramshackle old place I dubbed Make-Do Manor. A few years before, we'd had it demolished and I had designed a new house, built in the same spot. Whenever I tried to think of a name for the new house, Solace always came to mind.

The manicured lawn, mulched garden beds, and gleaming windows surprised me; I was the homemaker of the two of us. I started to ask Katy how she'd managed it, but the dogs began their welcoming symphony through the front windows.

I said, "Let's get the dogs on leashes before Mom and Dad get out of the car." I asked my parents if they could wait in the car a few minutes.

"We can wait here forever. It is so beautiful," Mom answered.

Tony the Tiger agreed and purred, "Terrrific."

Walking into the house, I admired its clean, orderly calm and told Katy, "It looks great."

She flashed a guilty grin, acknowledging, "I had a little help."

The dogs engulfed me, and I buried my head in them. They were each clean and groomed—another one of my jobs. Our longhaired mixed breed was brushed to a black glimmer, and our standard poodle sported a swanky haircut.

Katy confessed, "For the last three days, a dozen of our friends and my brother have worked here. They washed, weeded, mowed, mulched, or vacuumed every surface. I took the dogs to a groomer."

My parents disobediently cracked open the door and peeked in. I ordered Katy, "Grab Dakota before she knocks them over. I'll take Mica." Dakota was a giant black Lab–golden retriever mix who was prone to seizures from excitement, had a fragile pinned hip, and wielded a tail wag that could topple Dad; Mica twirled and bounced on standard poodle pogo-stick legs, aiming for eye-to-eye contact.

My parents were as eager to see the dogs as the beasts were to see Gramma and Grampa, and none of them were weighing the risks. My parents had spent enough time visiting us to spoil the only grandchildren I offered, and they were all eager for more.

"Let's go sit down before someone gets hurt," I commanded, always the old schoolmarm. Where had I put that dose of serenity and solace that had just soothed me moments earlier? Oh, there it was—on my parents' faces. Good enough.

Early the next morning, I sneaked over to inspect the apartment. My heart stopped. Was I looking in the wrong window? No carpet, no blinds, and emanating from it an odor that could have been bottled for biological warfare. I called the rental agent in a panic, trying not to screech. "When I talked to you five days ago, you promised it would be ready. The mover will be here in four days."

She acted surprised about all of that and rang me off with a noncommittal "okay."

I was prepared for my parents and the cat to stay with us for as long as necessary, but we needed a place to stow what I now estimated to be much more than twice the amount of furniture the apartment would hold. I called the landlord and rented an adjacent garage space we could shove everything into if it came to that.

I professed lame excuses to my parents to postpone their initial viewing of the apartment. I wanted their first impressions to be encouraging and inviting, but the apartment was still rancid and bleak and the bare cement floor was downright depressing. The handyman applied an odor sealer on the concrete that would require two more days to conquer the putrid stench. I ordered a large electronic air purifier just in case the reek persisted. The rental agent assured me the carpets would be down before the mover arrived.

Precisely on schedule, five days after our landing, the movers phoned to announce their anticipated arrival in two hours. I couldn't forestall showing Mom and Dad the apartment any longer and led them over. The apartment complex's owner was scouring the bathtub, her daughter-in-law was washing windows, a workman was hanging new blinds, and the carpet installers were packing up their tools. All the windows were wide open, and my worries blew away in the gentle breeze off the water.

Mom raved, "I can't believe this! It's a vacation home. Look at this! This whole wall of windows overlooks the lake. I'm going to put the table and my chair right here. What a view! Tom, come here! There's a train coming!"

Dad walked over to the patio doors and heard the whistle but couldn't see the train, even though it wasn't far away. Mom painted the scene for him. "There's a trestle over the lake for the trains. There's a red rowboat right under the trestle, going through to the other side of the lake."

As we stood there watching, the clouds covering up Mount Rainier were dissipating, and the mountain slowly appeared above the horizon like a mirage.

"Oh, look!" Mom exclaimed. "Mount Rainier is coming out to greet us! It's just to the left of the trestle, Tom. Can you see it? It's like a painted backdrop. This is unbelievable. What kind of trees are those? Are there animals out here?"

"That's a madrone tree," I said. "You'll see eagles, ducks, otters, deer, and lots of raccoons. Maybe a coyote once in a while." Mom stared with wonderment down the cliff to the rustic shoreline that sheltered large cedars and firs and abundant native vegetation in a protected wildlife habitat.

Dad stepped onto the patio, eager to see the train and the trees. I went with him because, twenty feet from the door, the land fell off in a steep slope to the lake. I cautioned, "Dad, I'll show you where the edge is, right here where the grass stops. Then it drops off."

He stopped in his tracks to get the lay of the land and a hold on his emotions. I hadn't realized tears were running down his face. "This is the best thing that's ever happened to us. Thank you so much," he sobbed, as he wrangled his vision all around to scope out the scene.

"You are so welcome, Dad. Thank you for having the courage to come here and for trusting me. I already love having you here." He was still staring, trying to take everything in, so I rambled, "This is only half the lake. After boats go through the narrow spot under the trestle, there's a whole other part of the lake that's just as big. All of it is a designated fishing lake with a five-mile-an-hour speed limit, so you won't have any roaring motors or Jet Skis."

We slowly circled the building to establish his territory, then went back inside for more of Mom's rapture. "I never dreamed we'd have new carpet, fresh paint, and new blinds. This is almost as big as our house. Doesn't it remind you of

Catawba Island? Tom, we're on vacation for the rest of our lives. I want to die here and have my ashes scattered over the lake."

I was flooded with childhood memories of arriving at the rental cabin for our summer vacations at Catawba Island on Lake Erie. Now, just as then, worries and responsibilities were left behind and stress floated away on the waves. Voices had more lilt, bodies were more languid, laughter rippled.

The apartment was completely ready minutes before the movers pulled up. They unloaded even more quickly than they had loaded and willingly arranged things wherever we needed them at my house, the garage, and the apartment. I predicted a full week's work before the apartment would be organized well enough to be habitable, so I was surprised when, as soon as the movers left, at seven o'clock, Dad proclaimed, "We're going to stay here tonight," in a voice that implied, *Final decision; don't question this.*

Mom said, "I can't leave this view, even though clouds hid Mount Rainier on and off all day. I keep remembering Katy driving us all the way around that mountain. Nine of the most beautiful hours of my life."

I took a moment to consider the logistics, then said, "I'm sorry, I just don't have the energy to set up your beds, relocate Dad's apnea equipment, and move the cat over tonight. We'd have to find sheets, blankets, and pillows, too."

"You can go home," Dad said. "Your mother and I can do it all. We don't want to leave here."

Fortunately, Mom began to visualize the actual process and said, "Maybe we should stay with you one more night. We just thought you'd want to be rid of us. You know, the fish-and-company-start-to-stink-after-three-days thing."

The next day, we assembled their beds, situated the cat and her paraphernalia, organized the kitchen picnic-style, arranged furniture, and stocked some groceries. They were finally tired after a Subway sandwich takeout dinner, so I allowed myself to be shooed home. I left them gazing at the lake, joking about sleeping in their own beds at a vacation resort for the rest of their lives.

The phone harangued me out of a deep slumber at dawn. My irritability dissolved in Mom's poetic joy: "The moonrise shimmered like glittering fairies dancing over the water last night. You should come over right now and see the sun silhouetting the Mountain in every shade of pink God created."

I laughed to myself about the fact that she was already using the vernacular for our beloved snowcapped peak. I had hoped that my parents would be comfortable, but I had never presumed they might be this happy.

Chapter 18

....

I arrived at the apartment for my regular caretaker shift, albeit on a new coast, around ten in the morning, and asked Mom what she wanted to unpack first.

"How about the kitchen?" she quickly responded. "It'll just take a couple hours; then you can be done and we'll do the rest." I suspected that wasn't likely for a month or so but tagged along with her optimism.

I set up Dad to unload canned goods and baking supplies into the pantry. I knew Mom would reorganize it, but at least he wouldn't accidently crack something valuable or cherished.

After unburying five of the fifteen boxes labeled *Dishes*, I hoisted them onto chairs so Mom wouldn't have to bend over. She dug in as if it were long-lost treasure, rather than her blue-and-white Currier & Ives dinnerware, packed just a week ago. She coddled a soup bowl, swooning, "I love these dishes. You remember how I collected them?" she asked me.

"I thought you bought them at the grocery store."

"Nope, I didn't spend a single penny for them. Every week at the A&P, a different piece was free when you bought groceries. My sisters saved theirs for me, and neighbors left pieces on the porch. I collected my whole service for twelve in a year.

That was a great neighborhood. We were all in the same boat in the early 1950s: new marriages, our first homes, new jobs, and relieved the war was over. We were grateful to buy brand-new houses on the GI Bill, even if they were only matchbook size and you could read the neighbor's newspaper from your own kitchen window. We were all friends; a lot of us had gone to high school together."

"You did have good friends there," I agreed. "Eunice right next door, Helen and Carol a few doors down." I was trying to encourage her. I liked her stories to fill in my spotty memory.

"When I was ready for a morning coffee break, I set our venetian-blind code to signal that the coast was clear, and then Eunice came over. If she couldn't come, she closed her blind. Helen and Carol and I gabbed and gossiped almost every afternoon before you kids came home from school. Carol's gone, but Helen writes often. She doesn't do e-mail, though."

Mom's coffee-klatch friends in our first neighborhood had children my age and my sister's age, and eventually some Johnnies-come-lately my brother's age. We roamed the neighborhood freely from the time we were let out in the morning until we were called in for lunch, supper, and bed. I had six or seven friends within a few doors, and many more on adjacent blocks.

The neighborhood husbands and fathers fished together, worked on each other's cars, and shared a few beers after work. It was the land of working-class do-it-yourselfers, and gangs of neighbors converted attics to bedrooms, walled off basements into laundry rooms and workshops, and constructed tool sheds and garages, the men building, the children gofering and cleaning up, and the women feeding, like an Amish barn raising.

As my parents unpacked their boxes, they retold stories about the neighborhood picnics in the summers and all of us ice skating every chance we could, all winter, on ponds and city rinks, as well as at home when the guys flooded three adjacent backyards.

Eventually families grew, incomes rose, and people moved from those starter homes. We upsized a few blocks away, but my parents remained in close contact with all their former neighbors. Mom and Dad made friends with our new neighbors, too, and organized block parties and picnics for the whole neighborhood. Mom accumulated coffee mothers, and Dad gathered guys for projects and a beer. They still exchanged e-mails, Christmas cards, and phone calls with many of those people.

I barely had time to e-mail a friend or two now. How had my parents managed it all? My mother had also participated in church activities, PTA, and a singing group called Mother Singers. Dad made good friends at work for coffee breaks and lunch and sometimes saw them socially on weekends.

Our clean-and-tidy home had been wide open to guests, including our pool table, well-stocked refrigerator, and large aboveground pool that Dad connected to a water heater for three-season swimming. Any of our friends could sleep over anytime and stay as long as they wanted. People of all ages filled our house.

One of my biggest hopes for my parents now was that this apartment complex would provide a ready social life for them, preventing the loneliness and isolation they had experienced the last few years in Florida. While I fervently wanted more social stimulation for them, believing it to be the key to their happiness, I was at a loss about creating it. Was it up to me?

I hoped they would become involved in a church and the senior center, but I knew their immediate neighbors were the best source of friendship for them. I didn't know anyone in the complex well, but I had spread the word that my parents were moving in and were nice people whom everyone would want to know.

We continued emptying boxes and filling cupboards. Dad noticed someone in the backyard and wandered out of the apartment to find out who it was while Mom and I unwrapped and stacked dozens of plates and bowls. She blissfully told me that this kitchen's floor plan replicated her first kitchen's, so she knew right where she wanted each item. I didn't mention the ten additional boxes labeled *Dishes*.

Mom exclaimed, "Oh, here's Sarge and Tin. They made the trip safely." She gently set down the ceramic bank, which depicted an old lady, and hugged the foot-tall Army sergeant bank. These chipped and cracked banks had been purchased from Sears in the 1960s as a gag gift. Now they were treasured mementos of her parents, and all the neighbors and friends in the world couldn't fill the searing hollow left in each of us after they died.

Dad came in with a neighbor in tow. He introduced Ron, who said to me, "You live across the street, right?" I nodded, and we chatted about neighbors a bit.

Mom was still clutching her figurine father, and Ron pointed to it. "That looks like a story waiting to be told," he said, as he pulled out a chair and made himself at home.

She set down Sarge and picked up the gray-haired lady figurine, introducing her: "This is my mother, Matilda, whom my father called Tin. She was a blond-haired beauty, petite and proper, well-educated and intelligent. I didn't take after her, needless to say."

"And the other one?" Ron asked.

"That's my dad, Harland, always called Red." She choked up a little and sat down. Ron just waited with rapt attention, providing a good audience.

She continued, "They started going together in eighth grade and were completely devoted to each other until his death, three days after their fiftieth wedding anniversary."

Mom looked at Sarge's scowling face and said, "He was never grumpy, though. He was an Irish scallywag who liked a cold beer and a good joke. Everyone adored him."

"He was in the Army?" Ron coaxed.

"He passed up a football scholarship from Ohio State University to join the National Guard. He was a private in

the Mexican-American conflict and a sergeant in World War
I in France. Those were the only times he was away from my
mother. He said he brought home medals and nightmares as
souvenirs."

It seemed as if my mother had just welcomed my grandparents in the door and sat them down for a chat. I realized she
was retrofitting her new surroundings with her own foundation, plate by plate, and with each knickknack and story.

I enjoyed Ron's flair for encouraging her to keep sharing
these tales, but I excused myself for lunch. I wanted this relationship between my parents and Ron to develop without my
being an intermediary.

My childhood kept me company as I walked slowly across
the street to my house. My mother's parents had lived nearby
and stopped by our house every Monday, Tuesday, and Wednesday afternoon for happy hour, greeting us when we walked in
the door after school. Mom sliced and diced her dinner prepa-
rations, Grampa enjoyed a beer and a tall tale, and Gramma
twirled an inch of his beer in a glass of her own. On Thursdays
they visited their oldest daughter, Kay, who resided in a Nor-
man Rockwell–rural scene a few miles away. My mother and I
went with them as often as possible, every week when I wasn't
in school.

After Chip was born, he went, too, but my sister suffered
from carsickness and found excuses to stay home. Our beagle,
Dewey, happily rode along with his ears flapping out the Stude-
baker's window. After a lunch of my aunt Kay's homemade soup
and fresh-baked bread, Grampa always said to me, "Patrick,
let's take the dogs hunting."

He never called me Patty or Trish or any other derivative
of Patricia. I was his first grandson, tomboy that I was, and his
willing companion. We'd leash Dewey and my aunt's beagle for
a walk along the river behind her house, setting them free once
they started baying. There were no guns, of course, but plenty of

rabbits and squirrels for the dogs to chase. Grampa and I tramped the dense deciduous forest in sun, rain, or snow, lured by the spell of the unspoiled landscape. We rested on a log jutting over the river and soaked up the season and the spray of the rushing water. Never in a hurry, Grampa headed us back when the dogs were ready, all of us tired and happy with images for sweet dreams that night—images that have lasted a lifetime for me.

I realized now with surprise that it was quite possible that my brother or cousins went along on those walks, but I remembered them as having been just me with Grampa. The other kids probably remembered going alone with Grampa, too. He had a way of making each of us feel like his one and only favorite.

Every Friday through my childhood, as though we were Catholic, Gramma and Grampa arrived at five o'clock, bearing a fish fry of Lake Erie perch, french fries, and coleslaw from Grampa's favorite tavern. On many Saturday nights, my brother, my sister, and I stayed overnight at our grandparents' house, and we all had Sunday dinner there with my mother's sisters and their families.

Because of my new role in caring for them now, and seeing them through my middle-aged eyes, I suddenly and painfully felt the sorrow my parents must have stifled leaving their families behind when NCR transferred my father from Ohio to Maryland in 1968. I knew my parents were proud of my father's promotion to manager of a branch office and were relieved to leave the racial violence of Cleveland after the assassination of Martin Luther King Jr., but at sixteen I was too wrapped up in my own grief at being ripped away from Joey, my boyfriend since age eleven, to consider my parents' sadness. After we moved, we traveled the five hours to see my grandparents (and Joey) at least once a month, but now I realized my mother must have missed her family desperately. Between trips, more and more wine bottles filled her hours of loneliness. Her father died a year after we moved, and my grandmother joined him shortly thereafter. My mother dove deep into her tried-and-true grief remedy and didn't surface for a decade.

I didn't want any more bad decades for any of us. I vowed to myself to do everything possible to help my parents be happy, and I prayed they would work at it, too. I knew I wanted to provide them with every bit of support I could without taking away their own legs to stand on. We were three strong-willed people, so far trying our best to point our wills in the same direction.

Walking through my door, I abandoned my reverie, fixed a sandwich, and contemplated mowing my lawn, until the phone jarred me. Mom whispered tensely, "Could you come back over for just a second? Your dad is getting ready to lift more boxes, and I don't think he should. He's panting."

Chapter 19

....

So ensued my maiden voyage of scrambling across the street, fueled by a rapid heart rate, imagining a red cross on my chest and a rotating emergency light blinking on my head. I raced as far as their door, then, like Wile E. Coyote, slammed on my foot brakes and ambled in with a casual "Hi, Dad. How's it going?"

"Terrrific," he sputtered. His face was red, and he was out of breath, but his smile radiated two hundred watts. "Ron just left. What a great guy! He said he'd bring his wife over tomorrow. She's a nurse."

I distractedly blathered some response because I noticed Dad bracing himself against the fragile antique card table, ready to set it up to hold more boxes.

Dad started unfolding a card-table leg, so I said, "Hey, Dad, how about if I line up boxes on the couch and love seat? That card table might not be strong enough." He agreed and let me lift and locate.

Mom, officially enthroned now at her heirloom dining table, overseeing her new realm, stared wistfully at the card table and narrated my memory: "You kids all ate at that table every

Sunday at Gramma's, and the grown-ups ate at this one." She rapped on the dining table, as if I didn't know what she meant.

"I still see my dad sitting right here with a glass of beer, teasing my mother with some new joke he heard at the bar. This table could tell my life story, good and bad."

Mom continued, "After we moved to the bigger house, Gramma gave me this table and all her linen, crystal, china, and silver so I could have the Sunday dinners and holidays in that beautiful dining room. I've missed that dining room ever since the day we left Ohio. And that giant commercial stove and those double ovens. Why didn't you put double ovens in your new house?"

I didn't answer because I was picturing our extended family with heads bowed at Mom's dining room table, extended with all its leaves, decorated for Christmas, Easter, Thanksgiving, birthdays, and any other reason she could cook up to gather us there. Now that I had a dining room and all the family linen, silver, and china, was I looking forward to holiday meals or dreading them? I certainly had never planned on cooking enough to require double ovens.

Mom said, "Sitting there with all that food, a fancy centerpiece lit with candles, and classical music playing in the background was unreal to me. I felt so out of place, I could barely say grace."

"Grampa never let it get too serious. Or too formal." I laughed, although I was trying to synchronize my memories of those moments with hers. That faraway look on her face that I remembered from my childhood remained a puzzle to me, even now that I had this new piece.

"You're right about that," she agreed. "He'd catch me beginning to choke up and start rolling his napkin into a ball under the table. A freshly ironed, monogrammed, antique linen napkin. I'd see the gleam in his eye, and then the napkin would sail into a water goblet at the other end of the table. He was a good shot. Luckily, even my mother laughed after she gave him her prim 'Harland!'"

Dad joined Mom's meander down memory lane and chuckled. "You kids liked that a lot better than going to my mother's for holidays. For dinner at her house, you had to dress up, sit still, be quiet, and finish everything on your plate before you could ask to please be excused."

"I was worried sick the whole time we were in that fancy dining room," my mother complained, in a voice that meant she still deserved sympathy for having endured it. "You kids in your best clothes, propped up on telephone books on those giant velvet chairs, were a recipe for disaster."

Her change in tone stunned us, and neither Dad nor I could find any words to emit from our gaping mouths.

"She promised me her Limoges china, and I never got it," Mom snarled, still mad at her dead mother-in-law.

"That was all the china she had left. She had to sell her best crystal and china during the Depression to feed us," Dad said, trying to smooth things over and gain some empathy for his mother. To me, the idea of selling her glassware added another tragedy to the elegant but somber house. My father's family had all lived farther away from us and hadn't been as entwined in our lives as my maternal relatives. Traveling in the Midwest in the winter was dicey, so we saw Dad's relatives mostly in the summer. Once in a while, weather permitting, we visited them for Easter, which changed the event from our usual raucous egg hunt, overseen by my mother's comical father, to a solemn event involving frilly pastel dresses, white gloves and lacy hats, cemeteries, manners, and photos. My father's family enforced a strict code governing children's behavior and appearance. My mother had always summed it up before she let us out of the car, warning us, "Remember, children are to be seen and not heard." Even so, I enjoyed visiting the big, old house and I loved my grandmother, my aunts, and my cousins.

While my father continued reminiscing about his family, my eye caught sparks flying from the Command Post as my mother fumed in a noxious, malevolent haze, the result of her accumulated decades of in-law indignation. She was evidently hoping to infuse her own family memories, but not Dad's, into their new apartment.

My mother had loathed the required trips to her mother-in-law's house. I remembered spending the two-hour drive to my father's childhood home monitoring her mood by the depth of her carefully manicured fingernails digging into the back of the car seat as her arm hung "casually" over. Those half-moon indentations were probably the only damage any of our well-maintained cars ever withstood.

I didn't know the truth behind my mother's relationship with her mother-in-law and could barely speculate. My mother was so sensitive to disapproval that she frequently exaggerated and twisted any slightly negative comment. On the other hand, there was never any doubt about her mother-in-law's opinion on every topic. My mother, a former nightclub singer and a divorcée with a child, likely epitomized an unsuitable match for her son, the sole surviving male in the family. I was too young at the time to interpret or understand this subject. Witnessing my mother's humiliation resurfacing now, fifty years later, I saw her underlying pain, not just her anger. I wanted to be sympathetic but couldn't find a quick way to break through our well-practiced family dynamic. Staring was all I had.

Chapter 20

....

I abruptly decided to clear out until Mom blew through her mood, an escape that felt hauntingly familiar from my teens. "Hey, Dad, you want to go up to the garage and put together some of those shelves?"

He understood my intentions, and we scurried out the door before Mom could protest. I watched him hunt and peck his way up the three shallow steps. When I'd signed the lease from Florida, I hadn't realized that while the available apartment was on the ground floor, it had outdoor steps. I pulled out my notebook and wrote *railing*. Dad struggled with the key to the garage door while I pretended to check out the Dumpster. I had to let him learn the feel of the lock.

"The shelves are stacked back there somewhere," he said, as he pointed to a general area. He sat on a stool to catch his breath and said, "Your mother still complains about the way my mother treated her, even after all these years. Did you think your grandmother was mean?"

"No, I never thought she was mean." I didn't know what else to say to my father about it, so I dealt with the task at hand. "How about if we stack the loose shelves here and make a pile of all the hardware on top of this box?" I tried to arrange him in a shaft of daylight.

"My mother was just strict," he offered as an explanation.

"She was," I agreed. "We never dared to find out what would happen if we broke a rule." I listed them like a warden: "Never sit on a bedspread; no food anywhere except the breakfast nook or dining room; no children in the kitchen; back door only; don't question anything."

He laughed, and I continued, "But really, I was more fascinated than intimidated. She was always dressed up, she had that Pennsylvania Dutch way of talking, and she was so skilled in all kinds of needlework. She taught me to embroider, crochet, and knit."

"She loved to sew," he said. "Do you remember the clothes and draperies she made for the rich people in town? The wedding dresses with the beads and jewels sewn into them went for a lot of money. Some of the headdresses alone brought in a bundle."

As we talked, I inserted bolts through the braces and shelves, positioning the nuts lightly, and he followed me, tightening them up by hand—the reverse of our dismantling process in Florida.

After a few minutes, he said, "No matter how bad things were, my mother always worked hard and took care of herself. She fixed her hair, dressed nicely, and cooked healthy meals. Her sewing got us through the Depression and supported her after my dad died. She was too young for his railroad benefits."

"She was beautiful," I said. "Tall, slender, and strong. Statuesque." I knew I was soothing the wounds of fifty-some years of my mother's wrath, but I didn't mind. He needed to move his memories to the new apartment, too, even if they lived in the garage.

"Just like my sisters," he added.

"Your sisters were gorgeous, still are; always dressed up in outfits coordinated with jewelry, heels, purses, and hats. All four of you had movie star smiles, deep dimples, and beautiful wavy jet-black hair in your high school graduation pictures." When I was a young teen, the women in my dad's family dazzled me with a natural grace and glamour I hoped to imitate or acquire genetically, although destiny led me to remain a rough tomboy.

Dad continued, "People always said how much we all looked alike as kids. But then, you cousins all looked alike, too. You could all have been brothers and sisters, instead of cousins."

I uprighted a completed set of shelves and asked, "Do you want to do one more?" He reached toward the pile, so I took that as a yes.

"My mother went through so much," he said. "She raised us four kids during the Depression, and my dad was sick a lot and out of work for months at a time. Your mother didn't know her before Nelson died. That really changed her. Then my father died and left her with no income. It was good that Jeannette and Nelson moved back home after Johnny died."

I instantly sorted out my childhood confusion about my dad's family. Both Dad's brother and his nephew, my beloved cousin, were named Nelson, and there was never any differentiation conversationally about which one was being discussed. There was no Big Nelson/Little Nelson or Old Nelson/Young Nelson. There wasn't any distinction between who was still alive and who wasn't, because no one could choke out the words. No one sat me down and explained, "Your cousin Nelson's uncle Nelson is dead. And so are his father and your grandfather." Everyone just talked about them as if they were out of town.

Dad and I finished the shelves and ventured back into the storm zone, where all appeared calm. A knock, a wave, and a smile at the patio door interrupted our planning session for the next day. Ron and his wife, carrying a plate of cookies, strolled in and made themselves comfortable at the table like old friends. I conjured up a believable excuse and exited, pleased that my hopes for an accessible social life seemed plausible. Mom phoned later, recounting a visit from their upstairs neighbor and Dad's having met a couple guys outside. Success.

My mother grumbled through a brief period of adjustment to the noise of other people's doors slamming and tenants brazenly transgressing through the backyards to go fishing, but the irritation quickly converted to a communication network of knowing who was going where and when. Within a few days, neighbors didn't pass through the yard without dropping by to chat. In the usual pattern, Dad gabbed with the guys outside while he watered the lawn or fed the birds, and women neighbors clustered at the dining room table with Mom.

My phone was ringing the next day as I arrived home from errands and appointments. I rushed in and grabbed it, and Mom said excitedly, "Did you hear all the commotion?"

"No. I just got home from the doctor."

"You didn't hear all the shouting and *beep-beep-beep*ing?"

She wanted me in her game, but my interest was wavering in the wrong direction. "No," I responded in a flat voice—not the best I could do, but better than outright irritation. I was cranky and needed a nap, as she would have informed me when I was five, and still might.

"Precious is home! She beeped her horn all the way down the street."

Mom was so happy, I had to play along. "What was she saying?"

Without a moment's hesitation, my mother hammered a little-girl squeal: "Dad! Mom! I'm here! I wode on a twuck!"

My first thought was, *Thank you, Johnny*. The last few weeks without Precious had proved to me how desperately I needed her. I had hoped to arrange some kind of senior transportation for my parents, but it became clear very quickly that my mother would go nowhere if she had to ride public transportation. She was comfortable with going nowhere, but I wasn't; I wanted her to be active and social. As their sole transport, I needed my own car, not one to coordinate with Katy.

By this time, I was fully exhausted. On the other end of the spectrum, the move revitalized my parents, turning their clocks back twenty years. They were wound up by their new surroundings and just couldn't wait to have pictures hung, shelves installed, furniture arranged and rearranged, and flowers planted. After their recent, barren years in Florida, they were eager to make up for lost time.

Everything they wanted or needed involved me in some way. They wanted to be respectful of my time and energy, but it was impossible. My only hope was to prioritize what they thought they needed and do what I could. Since they both had boundless energy at my age, and plenty now, they couldn't understand my limits. They had spent decades missing their own parents and couldn't comprehend why I couldn't spend all day every day with them. I couldn't either, really. They never overtly pressured me, but the hunger in their eyes for the joy of homemaking was undeniable, and I was the only tool in their toolbox.

For six weeks I unpacked and organized; hung shelves, cabinets, curtains, and aids for the handicapped; ran to the home store and the grocery store more than all the previous accumulated trips of my life; and generally felt happy that they were happy. They were up, groomed, and dressed by eight in the morning and stayed active and cheerful all day long. What more could I hope for? I banished the shadows of Mom's bedridden days in faded muumuus to my list of bad memories. Dad went off his antianxiety pills the first week they were here. They had been a striking couple when they were young, and their smiling faces now regained some of their youthful vibrancy and attractiveness; no one thought they were as old as they were.

I felt chunks of my life reorganizing and rubbing raw spots but hoped I would settle in with more joy than irritation. I was fully aware that at this stage of the game of life, a single health crisis could turn this picture upside down. I needed to savor every moment.

Chapter 21

....

Mom and I were arranging pictures and filling every available inch of wall with photos, paintings, cross-stitched samplers, and framed clippings. I was leveling her two large paint-by-number ship and lighthouse scenes over her bed, when she asked, "Do you know why I painted those?"

"I thought it gave you something to do while you were pregnant with Chip," I answered, fairly sure of my facts.

"That's the when, not the why," she corrected me. "After you were born, I'd had two miscarriages, and then Paul was born with terrible problems. Those eight days that he lived were like eight years—that poor little baby. I don't know how we survived that. Anyhow, I painted to calm myself down while I was terrified about being pregnant again."

She walked out of the room to escape the memories and said, "Let's go hang Gramma Weber," laughing at her pun.

We hung a half dozen large pictures, each with a sentimental story. There was not a single store-bought artwork in her collection. Every frame held a photo or painting of a loved one, or something created by a loved one. As we walked back toward the living room through the short hallway, Mom pointed at the blank walls and asked, "What shall we put here?"

I knew we still had twenty or more mementos to hang, so I suggested a family gallery on both walls, one side for Dad, one for her.

"What a great idea," Mom said, as she dropped into her chair for a rest. She waved toward the cedar chest, saying, "There's family that's been buried in that trunk since we left Ohio in 1968. Go ahead and dig them up if you want."

I pulled a frame out of the trunk, peeling off the wrapping of brittle layers of yellowed newspaper, frayed twine, and crackled cellophane tape. Dad walked in from the backyard, took it out of my hands and held it close to his eye, then ordered, "Shake my hand."

After we shook, he announced, "You just shook the hand that shook the hand of someone who shook hands with President Lincoln."

He was quite proud of his skit, but I was baffled—not the reaction he wanted. He stuck his hand out to try again. Sometimes he confused things, but Mom was snickering, rather than correcting him, so I figured there must be something to it.

After we repeated the scene a third time, I gave in. "What do you mean, Dad?"

"Well, read this about Abe Lincoln and Nelson." He was frustrated and waved the frame at me.

"Nelson?" I asked.

"Yes, Nelson," he answered emphatically.

I gave Mom a puzzled look. I knew my knowledge of history was bad, but I thought I had my Nelson confusion resolved. One Nelson was born in the 1920s, the other in the 1940s; neither had anything to do with Abraham Lincoln's era, as far as I could tell.

Mom clarified, "Another Nelson. That is a newspaper clipping about your dad's great-uncle Nelson, on his mother's side. He died long before you were born."

Dad waited impatiently, not caring about the genealogy, then said, "He was a great guy. Lived into his nineties. He had a big farm, a hardware store, and two houses and went to Florida for vacations every year. All those conch shells I have came from him."

He pointed to the three big shells on the hearth. "Can you still hear the ocean in them?" His smirk twinkled up to his eyes. We'd listened to these shells routinely when we were kids because he'd convinced us the roar of the sea was about to fade any moment. We didn't want to miss our last chance to hear it.

I picked one up and held it to my ear, teasing, "I'd better check. Maybe we should have refilled them before we left Florida. Can they be refilled with Pacific Ocean or only the Atlantic?"

He laughed and continued, "Uncle Nelson was rich; he *gave* my mother that house we lived in. During the Depression, my dad would drive out to Uncle Nelson's farm to work, and Nelson and I would play all day in the barns and the fields. Bert and Ione, the farmhands, said we could eat as much as we wanted." Both of my parents remembered food, and lack of food, from their childhoods—lasting hunger pangs from the Depression.

I realized he was still holding the old picture frame that had started this conversation. I asked him, "But what was all the hand shaking about?"

"Oh, right. Read the article. I haven't read it for years. Read it out loud."

I fixed us each a cup of coffee, and we sat at the table with Mom.

Dad handed me the framed, yellowed clipping. There was no date or newspaper name on the article, and a few letters of each line of the right-hand column were cut off on this copy. I turned it over to see if the date was on the back and saw an obituary. I scanned it and read out loud, "November 17, 1934, Hugh Nelson Walker, ninety-two, last of the Civil War veterans in West Middlesex, died at his home—"

Dad interrupted, "No, read the other side. A reporter interviewed him right before he died."

I turned it back over and began with the title and subtitle: "West Middlesex Veteran Recalls Honest Abe's Warm Greeting. Nelson Walker, Union Soldier, Met President Lincoln in Washington on April 1, 1865; Was Guard at His Funeral Two Weeks Later. By Peter R. Smaltz, Jr."

I was slowly comprehending that as a young Civil War soldier, my father's great-uncle had met President Lincoln on the streets of Washington, DC, and had shaken hands with him. I was reading the long article out loud, when Dad said, "Here comes the good part."

> *"Look," said Private Walker, pointing to an approaching tall, black figure in a great long coat and stovepipe hat, swinging up the avenue with powerful, long strides. "Look, sure as I'm born, here comes our chief-Abrah'm! Stand back."*
>
> *The tall, bent man with the sunken cheeks and the chin whiskers spread out both arms and came nearer. With one hand, as tough as oak, he grasped the hand of Walker, with the other, a companion's.*
>
> *"Hello, my boys, how do you do!" a coarse, deep voice with the soul of the nation in it spoke right out.*
>
> *The three companions, too thrilled to speak, stood rooted.*
>
> *"Don't know how long we'll be at it—maybe not so much longer. But do your best. God bless you!"*
>
> *With the electricity of the contact still tingling in their hands, the men mumbled a thanks and "And same to you too!" And then Abraham Lincoln had passed on. But young Nelson Walker would never forget that fleeting moment as long as he lived.*

"Isn't that amazing? He met President Lincoln and shook his hand!" Dad said. I agreed wholeheartedly and continued reading some more of the interview with his uncle and his aunt about the politics of the day; then Dad said, "Okay, here's the sad part. Slow down."

"I was in Washington the night Lincoln was shot. Let's see, I think it was on a Good Friday, April 14, 1865. On the Sunday before, Lee and Grant made peace. Lee headed south, Grant headed north, and we were all glad. Lincoln went to the theater to forget.

"The next day, April 15, Lincoln died. The whole country stopped breathin'. Bells tolled, flags were at half-mast, newspapers had black borders all around 'em, stores closed up.

"Then on Wednesday they held the funeral. I was a guard. I couldn't see Mr. Lincoln. I hung onto a post to keep the crowds back. The funeral came up Pennsylvania Avenue, where Mr. Lincoln had just spoke to us a few days before. Now I felt sad. The people were crying. First came the twenty pallbearers; then came six white horses with the hearse and Mr. Lincoln. As it passed, people took off their hats and knelt down."

I read through the last few paragraphs, until the reporter said good-bye and "shook the hand that shook Lincoln's."

Dad held out his hand to shake and said, "Now do you get it?"

"Very clever," I said, shaking his hand. "A good conversation starter. I always gave book reports on Lincoln from that little red book of yours. The book was part of the report because it was so old."

"Me too." Dad laughed. "But I took the little book *and* Uncle Nelson. I didn't have to write anything; he said it all. He was in his eighties by then, but he was spry and quick-witted. Always got me a good grade. Teachers loved him."

Mom pointed to a pile. "The book on Lincoln should be in that stack."

I riffled through a dozen musty books until I found it. The binding had disintegrated, and the pages were loose. The faded cloth cover with its picture of Lincoln no longer seemed like ancient history. My father had known someone who'd met Abraham Lincoln!

We hung more pictures as I desperately tried to pay attention to their collection of stories, newly aware that it was a limited, nonrenewable resource.

Chapter 22

....

My parents basked in a storybook first summer of friends, family, farmers' markets, picnics, and parties. My heart was full, even if the rest of me was running on empty. As autumn approached, they reluctantly agreed it was time to begin their medical appointments. I scheduled eye exams, dental appointments, a general doctor for Mom, and the VA for Dad. They both dreaded going to doctors, and I felt like I was dragging two kids for their vaccinations before school started. We'd had plenty of practice going to doctors in Florida, and I slipped into my role of acting as if I enjoyed it, when in fact the responsibility for their health care scared the heck out of me. What if I missed something important?

First up on the schedule was a doctor for Mom. When I drove over to pick her up, she was ready and waiting, and neatly dressed; her purse matched her shoes, she wore makeup and jewelry, and her hair was nicely curled. Once in the car, she crossed her arms over her chest and clamped her jaw firmly shut, with her masseter muscles grinding and flexing in her petulant cheeks. If she'd been in the back, I think she would have been kicking my seat and making faces.

She sat rigidly silent the entire ride and spat a few stilted words in the waiting room. When they called her in, I said, "Have someone come get me if you need me." She hesitated, not knowing which was worse: dealing with the doctor by herself or letting me choreograph her care. She slowly followed the nurse, stiff-legged and solo, but returned thirty minutes later chatty, smiling, and thanking staff members by name.

Success. One safety net in place. How many were required?

Dad's medical care could be provided privately through his National Cash Register Company insurance, but we needed the VA to cover his prescriptions. Our first visit to the VA campus awed us with towering trees, acres of groomed and natural landscapes, Spanish architecture, a soothing lake, and friendly, helpful employees. On entering the grounds, Dad clucked his tongue, shook his head, and said, "Beautiful. Just so beautiful."

After he gave Dad a complete physical and a blood test, Dad's new physician at the VA surprised us with his recommendation for visual therapy and these words: "The program is in Building Five." It was right here at our very own VA, not in San Francisco or Denver, as I had envisioned.

Dad and I walked over to the reception desk for visual programs and asked how we could find out what they offered. A voice from the hallway behind us said, "You schedule an appointment with me, but I'm available right now, so come on back to my office."

He reviewed Dad's VA records and briefly explained how the six-week, inpatient program worked. Veterans from all over the West Coast and Alaska applied to this program, so there could be a year's wait; sometimes they had last-minute cancellations.

Dad got a bewildered look on his face. I explained, "Dad, this is a program for blind veterans. You know, like what Olivia did in Florida."

He nodded tentatively.

When asked if Dad could come on short notice if someone canceled, I answered, "Sure!" even though I doubted he'd agree to go at all.

We toured the facility, with its bright, clean dorm rooms and a big workroom, which was a hive of activity with blind and sight-impaired men learning to use drills, saws, hand tools, computers, and the closed-circuit TV system for reading. In another room, one man was frying eggs while another folded laundry, both under therapists' watchful eyes. A raucous group came in the door after an excursion teaching them to use canes, crosswalks, and curbs. We met the on-site ophthalmologist, a specialist in low-vision patients, who scheduled an exam for Dad. I mentally marked *eye doctor* off my list.

Throughout the tour, Dad was blank. What was he thinking? I couldn't figure out his problem. I realized we were acting like Dad was going to do this, but I still wasn't sure he comprehended any of it. Did he even know what *inpatient* meant?

On the way home, I reviewed the highlights slowly for Dad. I explained that they taught woodworking, cooking, crafts, and computers; went on field trips; and provided individual training tailored to each student's specific needs. He might have to wait up to a year to get in but might be able to go on short notice if they had a last-minute cancellation.

"I don't want to live there for a year," he implored. "I like the apartment."

"I'm sorry I didn't make that clearer, Dad. It was a lot of information all at once. You'd go for six weeks, but you'd come home every weekend."

Dad thought about that, then muttered, "Save it for someone who needs it more."

Beyond reminding him that he had earned and deserved all his VA benefits, I didn't push him. I never expected him to leave the security of his home. I let go of the idea of his attending the program and talked about my amazement with it. I said,

"They teach you how to use the equipment, and then they give it to you, even the CCTV."

He shook out of his fog. "What?"

I repeated the concept.

"Even the TV for reading, like the one Olivia showed me?" he asked incredulously.

"Yep. Those are called closed-circuit TVs. People abbreviate it as CCTV."

"I could get that for free? Do you think I should go?" An irresistible bargain tempted him.

I instantly became worried about his being on his own and tried to dissuade him. Between Mom and me, we watched him and assisted him all day long. Maybe that was his secret reason for wanting to go.

"I think I'll go. Maybe I can get a new computer, too."

The VA called on a Friday night two weeks later, offering admission the following Monday if he was willing. Monday morning at seven o'clock, Dad was spiffed up, as he would have been for any first day of school, with packed suitcases by the door. After his "beautiful—just beautiful" upon entering the VA grounds, we parked, hauled and unpacked his belongings, and set up his sleep apnea equipment.

I felt much more nervous than he appeared to be when his assigned social worker came into his room. Dad smiled and shook hands, but I began a barrage of questions about medications, medical emergencies, and help with his apnea equipment. She said, "We'll take care of everything" and dismissed me.

I wanted to say, *Don't forget, he's* blind! *And* old! *And hasn't been away from my mother since cash register refresher school in 1980.* Then I realized that was like a parent telling the kindergarten teacher the child was only five, and bravely left him there.

Dad phoned home the first night announcing that everything was terrrific, especially the cafeteria. When I picked him up on Friday night, he was more alert and self-assured than he had been since he'd lost his vision. He had accomplishments, friends, and stories to tell.

He loved goofing off with the guys and gaining new skills. He was shyly proud of frying an egg, tooling leather for a belt, and learning to negotiate city streets with a cane. He memorized telephone keypads so he could use the phone if Mom ever let him.

Mom missed him but relaxed into a respite from overseeing him, fixing his meals, and keeping him entertained. She enjoyed being on her own, knowing she had help a few steps away. Her previous alone time had been when Dad was hospitalized and had been cloaked in overtones of what would she do without him; this time alone, she was blithely trying to decide whether she should bake, sew, or stare at the lake.

I spent my time alone studying a long list of household and personal tasks I used to complete on a regular basis to decide which ones were urgent, noticing that my idea of urgency was shifting dramatically. The idea of work I needed to accomplish by myself changed, too. I settled on the things I had to do personally, such as finances, my own medical exams, and the dogs' regular checkups; I hired people to wash windows, clean and treat the roof for moss, and rake leaves. The puzzle pieces of my altered life were wriggling into place.

Dad mastered the CCTV and was rewarded with one. That system in particular reinstated his connection with the world, allowing him to read mail, e-mail, and newspapers. On the weekends at home, he sorted through all his papers and files, reuniting with written words as if they were long-lost photo albums. He was a full-fledged adult again.

Chapter 23

....

When I delivered Dad home from his last VA session in early November, Mom asked, "Do you think we should put up a tree this year?" I knew this question maneuvered *Christmas tree* onto my list in a way only a mother could accomplish. I reminded myself that I intended for this first holiday season together in Washington to make up for the deficiency of their last few Christmases in one fell swoop, particularly in case it became their only swoop.

"Sure, let's do that right after Thanksgiving," I said, regretting the mention of that premier food-related holiday the moment the words fed her hungry ears.

Her knife and fork apparently were poised, and she dug in: "Where do you want to have Thanksgiving, here or at your house? Will Linda, Jack, and Michelle come? Don't you usually have Katy's parents at your house? What about Chris, Dianna, and Carolyn? Katy's brother and his girlfriend? What shall I fix? Do you want me to bake the pies?"

"I don't know" was all I could muster as I staggered out the door under the weight of her expectations. Since she'd moved to Washington a few years before, my sister had spent holidays with her new husband's family. Would that change now? Katy's divorced parents hadn't been in the same room together for decades; could she ask them to attend one big event so I didn't have to cook separate dinners?

Would our customary, long-established gathering of friends be willing to celebrate with our families? Chris and Dianna, our closest friends, lived on our street, and we'd spent every holiday together for decades. Our other close friend, Carolyn, roamed the country in an RV but was usually home for holidays. A tight little group, we were almost always all for one and one for all, but this seemed like a lot to ask of them.

How many people would that be? Over the next few days, I tried to present the idea of one combined event to each person as fun, without a desperate, pleading look in my eyes, and all agreed.

Compiling a to-do list pulled me back in time. During Mom's better years, she cooked, crafted, and exhibited her holiday talents from Valentine's Day through Halloween, but the weeks before Thanksgiving and through Christmas converted our home into a studio and gallery for her annual one-woman shows. For Thanksgiving, she set high standards for blue-ribbon success for her principal passion: food. I felt tired just thinking about it.

The dogs and I went over a few days later to drop off Dad's pills, still a couple weeks before Thanksgiving. Mom acknowledged my task: "Thanks for taking over his pills. I know I could do it if I had to, but it's so complicated now." And it was. Seventeen different medications and supplements from a variety of suppliers, broken down into four separate dispensers for breakfast, lunch, supper, bedtime. I appreciated Mom's gratitude, but taking over the job was much easier than overseeing it.

After giving the dogs their treats, Mom hunkered down at her Command Post, layered under cookbooks and clippings of recipes.

"I can't find my recipe for corn pudding. I know it's here somewhere. The dried corn I ordered from the Amish store just

came. What about cranberry relish? Do you want me to make
that from scratch?"

Evidently, we were planning the Thanksgiving menu
today. I sat down, nixing my plan to slip in and out before cutting the poodle's hair.

"I was hoping you'd make the pies." I tried not to sound
snippy.

"Oh, of course. I thought I'd make two pumpkins and an
apple. How's that sound?"

"That's a lot of work. Don't you think just pumpkin would
be okay?"

"Well, no. Maybe someone doesn't like pumpkin," she
answered, like I had asked a stupid question.

I thought, *It's Thanksgiving; they can eat pumpkin pie, like
all the rest of America.* I said, "Great."

"I'll make those good dinner rolls, too. Everybody likes them."

"Do you think we need rolls when we're having dressing?"
I asked. They both just equaled bread to me.

I could see a tug-of-war beginning in her eyes. She wanted
the meal of her memories but knew she should relinquish some
control to me. Did this same exchange happen the first time her
mother handed off the task to her? Gramma probably backed
into a quiet retreat, just as I was about to do.

She waved a thin, crackled piece of paper toward me. "Do
you want to make Aunt Kay's tomato pudding? You always
liked it."

"I think I'll stick to the traditional dishes: stuffing, yams,
green beans, mashed potatoes, gravy, cranberry sauce. Just that
will be a lot to fix."

"Oh, all right, I'll make it. And succotash." She har-
rumphed, probably wondering why I was so lazy.

"I don't know how you and Dad did it all."

She answered as if she were teaching me how to do it. "I
planned out every day right after Halloween. I put on music and

attacked one room a day, cleaning every cobweb, dust bunny, window, closet, and drawer. You kids helped on the weekends. Remember 'many hands make light'?"

"Oh, yeah. You and your sayings." I laughed. Of course, the word *work* goes on the end of that phrase, but she omitted it so the refrain would sound silly, rather than directive. She preferred willing helpers with no moping to sour the spirit.

My sister, never inclined toward domestic affairs, completed perfunctory assignments and retreated to her room. Of a dreamy nature, she nurtured a burning desire to perform onstage and had inherited the voice to consider it a realistic pursuit. She wanted to learn to sing and act, not cook and clean. I completed my tasks without too much complaint; my Virgo nature generally tilted toward clean and orderly.

"You always helped me get ready. I wish I could help you clean now," she said, with sympathy and lament in her voice. I knew she really did wish she could help.

"Me too. You always had more energy than I ever did."

She continued her holiday planning lesson. "Dad would get up early and start the turkey at five in the electric roaster, but I started making the dressing an hour before that. Gramma always made the pies."

In my memory, Thanksgiving was an overflowing cornucopia of food and family. By the time I woke up, the turkey wafted sage through the house, pans of sweet potatoes were poised for brown sugar, and serving dishes were selected. Linda peeled potatoes for her contribution and dismissal. I fluttered and flattened the antique linens and arranged the good silver, china, and crystal. My enthusiastic parents toiled from the wee hours of morning, preparing the feast, then entertained and fed two dozen relatives and cleaned it all up before they went to bed.

I didn't have a thimble of their energy now, but I hoped if I planned well, I could pull off a manageable meal. By the Sunday before the feast, I felt in pretty good shape with the cleaning and shopping. I stopped in to change Mom's kitchen lightbulb and drop off Dad's week of pills.

Mom presided at the table, rustling cookbook pages with agitation. "This casserole looks good. I'll need lima beans, though. Do you have any?"

"I don't, Mom. And I really don't want to go to the store again. I have to take Dad to the VA tomorrow. Then Tuesday and Wednesday I'll prep and cook." For days she'd been offering me recipes for more side dishes, which I'd declined, reminding her of the eight or ten we'd already planned.

"Ron will get lima beans for me," she declared defiantly. "He's getting marshmallows, too. And a few other things I need." This was her way of warning me that her marshmallow fruit cocktail salad, a sweet and fat-filled dish I wasn't thrilled about serving, would grace my table, as well as other unknown and unauthorized offerings. So much for wholesome, low-fat, and organic. I filed it all in the Not Worth Fussing About category, an overflowing new folder in my brain.

The day arrived, staged with a frosted lawn, a crisp blue sky, and no ominous weather predictions. By late afternoon, the house emanated a holiday aura, the dogs were tired enough to behave, and the food was in the correct stage of warm, hot, or cold. I taxied Precious across the street to retrieve Mom and Dad so they could settle in before anyone else arrived. I had already transferred Mom's Command Post chair, the only chair she was comfortable in, and positioned a chair for Dad where he could see and hear the best.

Katy took over ushering Dad into the house as I followed Mom, pushing her walker toward the double French doors into the dining room, drawn by the long table fully donned in its antique linen gowns and crystal and silver jewels.

"You ironed Gramma's banquet cloth and napkins. I always did, too." She caressed her mother's antique damask tablecloth, then embraced a monogrammed napkin. Mom greeted her crystal goblets, her antique candelabra, and my grandmother's sil-verware like long-lost relatives until the dogs and arriving guests interrupted her reunion.

Everyone showed up safely, high-spirited, and in good health—always precarious goals at this time of year of flu and foul weather. The house burbled with keepsake smells and laughter. Mom presented three prize-winning pies, four dozen lightly browned dinner rolls, and side dishes that drew compliments. I paused to savor the moment and store some in a memory bank, knowing how fleeting the confluence of this many contented heartstrings could be.

Then I felt my gears subtly shifting, careening into the next holiday with a mixture of excitement and exhaustion. Thanksgiving was just the appetizer for the main course in our family holiday schedule.

Mom's last words when I drove them home were, "What time are you bringing the tree over tomorrow?"

Chapter 24

....

I pulled my Santa spirit out of a pocket of my well-worn, invisible caregiver's uniform, loaded my arms with boxes, and burst in with a jovial "ho ho ho." Mom, ensconced on her throne, was surrounded by throngs of loyal subjects, her cookie recipes. "What cookies do you want me to bake for you?" she asked excitedly.

To her, she was offering me a choice of either gold or silver jewelry. To me, she was asking one more question, making one more demand, probably requiring a shopping trip, packaging cookies for mailing to my brother, and a long wait in line at the post office.

I answered, "I always liked those round nut balls, without the powdered sugar." Why spoil her enthusiasm?

"I'll make those for sure. Maybe I can set up a table here like I used to, with all the cookie tins, plates, and napkins, so visitors could help themselves. Do you remember that?"

I did. She baked and we baked. She prepped cookie-baking sessions with crocks of dough, shoeboxes of cookie cutters, soup bowls of white icing with bottles of dye to tint our own unique colors, and a variety of sparkling sprinkles. We munched on snacks and sang along to sleigh bells ringing on the record player. Our friends were welcome, with one caveat: They must be clean—surgical-suite clean. Wash your hands with soap, sit down, and don't touch anything, especially your hair, or you'll be right back at the sink. Most of us rescrubbed at least once. Cough or sneeze, and she excused you from the table.

"That was fun," I said. "You heaped every horizontal surface of the dining room with cookies; then neighbors walked in, loaded a plate, and sat down. Did you ever figure out who sneaked cookies and left a note from Santa all those times when we weren't home?" We never locked our doors, and no one even knocked before coming into our house.

"No, but it wasn't Grampa. He always turned a chair upside down on the table if he stopped by and we weren't home. It was probably Joey."

My teenage sweetheart took the blame for all unexplained pranks and mischief. Most of it he actually committed, along with a variety of genuine crimes that eventually landed him in jail, prison, and an early grave. Stealing cookies was the least of it. Somehow my family remembered him with unfaltering love, even though he broke all our hearts after he took up drugs and crime.

Dad giggled and said, "That Joey was a nut. Remember when he convinced your brother that red stuffed caterpillar was alive? Chip still laughs about how long he believed that."

Then Dad spotted the boxes I was setting on the couch. He hung up his cane and headed for his coat, saying he'd get the containers from the garage. He was peeved when I reported that I'd already stacked them on the porch, because hauling was a Man's Job, but I had to preempt him from teetering with boxes without using his cane. He opened the door and grabbed a box from the entryway. The door hit him in the butt and joggled him as he tottered in. Realizing I was waiting to retrieve another box, he sidled out of my way. I geared into high speed, grabbed two boxes, threw them on the couch, zipped around him, and snagged two more. My conscience screamed, *No one is having fun here. It's not the accomplishment that counts; it's the attitude—remember?*

I ratcheted down my pace and my tenor. "Hey, Dad, could you hold the door for me?"

He held the door while I raced in and out and wedged containers on chairs and end tables; with minimal floor space, I didn't want him to trip over an unexpected obstacle. Mom rattled off a steady stream of fond cookie reminiscences, necessitating only a nod or an "um, those were good" from me.

I started assembling the artificial tree I was loaning them, which suddenly seemed big enough for Rockefeller Center. I interrupted Mom's revels, suggesting, "Maybe a smaller tree would fit better."

"Why?" she snapped. "There's plenty of space. Did you change your mind and want that one at home? We can get our own tree. We want a big tree. We can get one tomorrow. Ron will get us one. He already offered." She underlined and boldfaced her voice: *"We're having a big tree."*

Criminy. I hadn't canceled Christmas. I calmly said, "Okay. You're welcome to this one. I was just worried you'd feel crowded."

Dad suggested moving a chair and table into his bedroom, which I whipped out of the room before he could pick up either one. After thirty minutes, I was already sweaty and claustrophobic and my caregiver's costume was noticeably drooping.

Mom tried to revive my sagging spirit, saying, "Right after Thanksgiving every year, your dad would say, 'We'd better go get the trees before they're all picked over; we can leave them outside in water.' I'd bundle you all up and pack you in the station wagon, and we'd scour the tree lots. The trees never stayed outside in water very long, though."

I knew she said *trees* in plural because we also chose and delivered her parents' tree every year. My dad dragged it down to their basement, where the cousins gussied it up while the adults mused in sentiment and spiked eggnog. Every ornament stored a memory, preserving a family anecdote my grandmother recounted as we gingerly hung the musty, tattered baubles.

Dad began rummaging through the boxes, looking for the lights. As I snapped on the top third of the tree, he stood in front of me and handed me the end of a string of lights, saying, "I'll hold them for you."

"Greeeaaat," I said. Although I was puzzled about the logistics, I knew that stringing the lights was his job, and one more Man's Job that he couldn't do.

I plugged in the string, then methodically unwound it inch by inch as Dad awkwardly spun the twisted mess.

I looped the strand around the tree, weaving around him with every swirl. There was no position he could occupy that wasn't in my trajectory as we slowly draped five strings of lights. I could have finished them by myself in a fraction of the time, but the guilt would have festered long after I packed away the decorations in January.

I tempered my impatience by thinking of my beloved big old bear-dog, Dakota. As with Dad, her shiny black hair was graying, her senses dulling, and her hips wobbling. She plopped right in the middle of every project, but we always maneuvered around her with a kiss and a cookie.

I don't mean to diminish Dad's skills at helping or at inventing improbable, improvisational repairs. He was a genius at it. Much of the time, he was insightfully helpful. There were just occasions when his blindness or aging body—or, more likely, my haste—limited his ability to contribute. Those were the times when he became perplexed, parked himself in the project, and peered at it with his head cocked to one side. I just learned to enjoy it by envisioning the silly pairing with the dog who held my heart.

Under Mom's sovereign supervision, and with Dad's continuous assistance, I bedecked their apartment long after I considered it replete. I overembellished just to their liking with the tree too big for the room, artificial greens swagged from stem to stern, and holiday keepsakes vying for attention no matter where I glanced. I laced outdoor lights over shrubs and suspended them in symmetrical swaths from the patio eaves, framing Mom's perpetual view toward the lake with an embroidered glow, all set on automatic timers. After festooning the mantel and doorway with colored lights, I plugged all the inside lights into easy on-off switches, since Mom couldn't bend to reach the electric outlets and Dad couldn't see the holes to plug into them.

Mom slid a big sheet of vinyl window stickers out from under her recipes, like pulling a rabbit out of a hat. How many other hidden projects did she have for me? "How do you think these would look?" We all knew she meant, "Would you arrange these on the windows?"

I said, "Those will look great. Last year I had the neighborhood kids in to decorate the windows with stencils and Glass Wax, like we used to do." We had daubed every window and mirror in the house, composing frosted masterpieces of angels, reindeer, bells, and snowflakes, with snowdrifts in the corners.

She went back to her recipes, humming "Frosty the Snowman," while I arranged and rearranged cherished Santas and snowmen and cloaked windows and doors with withered wreaths that Mom had made decades earlier. Nary an ornament or surface was overlooked.

Dad pulled their large ceramic Santa out of a box and held it up for directions. "Put Santa on the buffet, where everyone can see him," Mom said. "His poor broken nose. Joey did that." It didn't matter that Joey didn't do it and that every other body part of the sixty-year-old Santa was glued together now, too. It was different for me to have Joey memories to share, so I just enjoyed it. He was every breath of my adolescent and teenage years, but none of my friends here had known him. I smiled to myself, thinking Mom had just moved Joey out West to sit at her table, too.

"I wish we still had the train," Mom said with regret.

"How many cars were there?" I asked. "Three or four?" My mother's artistic sister and woodworking brother-in-law had made our most cherished Christmas decoration, a huge Santa train for the front yard.

"Four," they answered in unison; then Mom continued, "Don't you remember? Aunt Kay painted the big engine with Santa waving out the window, the coal car filled with Christmas trees, a boxcar decorated like a present, and the caboose with *Merry Christmas* on it. Your dad set it up after Thanksgiving, before he slathered cranberry on the first leftover turkey sandwich."

He defended his timing: "Someone was always around to help that weekend."

"Oh, I was happy you did it early," she said. "It kicked off the holiday for the whole street. Everyone came to see it. I served hot chocolate to the kids and hot toddies to the grown-ups."

I left them to their memories and ferried the empty boxes back to the garage, surprised that dusk was falling and I had chalked up a whole day to this endeavor. We sat at the table for a few minutes, reviewing schedules for appointments, haircuts, and other outings. By the time we looked around, it had grown dark enough for the holiday lights to twinkle inside and out. The result was as unexpected and magical as the sliding open of the back doors of the stage in the final scene of *White Christmas*. My parents were speechless and spellbound in their Christmas fairyland. The neighbors all around the lake had filigreed the view with lights that diamond-studded the rippling water. On my way home, I could have sworn I heard Bing Crosby crooning down on the dock.

My phone screeched just as I sank down on my couch with the dogs and my dinner. I was beat but relieved to check *decorate apartment* off my list. I picked up the bleating contraption, and Mom burst forth a rapturous flow before I finished hello. "How can we ever thank you? This is the prettiest tree we've ever had.

Ron came by to say the outside lights looked good and that he would do his the same way. This reminds me of arriving at the park downtown when we took you kids to see Santa. We'd wait for an evening when it was snowing a little, stuff you into snowsuits, and surprise you. But the surprise was for us, too. It was a wonderland of lights."

Dad was on the extension and broke in, "Remember Santa's cottage? And all the stores downtown were lit up and there were carolers strolling. It was magical. Just like this apartment."

Mom added in a wistful voice, "I sang there with the Mother Singers one night a week and Saturday afternoons. That was some cold singing, but I loved every minute of it."

I stifled a yawn and wondered how my parents had found the time and energy to shape all those sweet memories for us. Beyond all the childhood nostalgia, now I had today to fill my heart. It was so unexpected. They were still parenting this child.

Chapter 25

....

I was completing my final Christmas Day pre-party checklist, enjoying the music, cinnamon, and cedar, when my sister pulled into the driveway. I went out to help her carry in packages.

We filled our arms with her loot and started up the walk. She stopped and stared. "Your house is spectacular. It looks like a New England Christmas card. All you need is the train in your front yard."

"Funny you say that—Mom wants me to call the neighbor she gave it to in 1968 and get it back. Chip thinks he might build one from a photo we have of it. He decorates every square inch of his house inside and out, too."

"Me too." She laughed. "I plan my tree while we're passing the turkey and sweet potatoes at Thanksgiving.

"Oh my God," she exclaimed as we went in, "look at your tree. It's exactly like Mom and Dad used to do. Dad's Lionel train, the village, even the bubble lights. You just need to string tinsel, one . . . single . . . strand . . . at . . . a . . . time. That drove me crazy. Just throw it, for cryin' out loud."

I said, "That's why I skip tinsel altogether. And do you remember that Mom also removed each piece of tinsel when she took down the tree, restrung it all back in the container, and saved it for the next year?"

She laughed and said, "A habit left over from Depression-era decorating, I suppose. I recognize all the ornaments you've made. I have every one you ever gave me. You and Mom are so crafty. Remember that year Mom decorated a hundred cookie tins with raw pasta and spray-painted them gold? The pasta actually ended up looking like flowers."

I completed the memory, saying, "Then she baked dozens of cookies to fill the tins and gave them away as presents. They were beautiful, weird as it sounds. Where did Mom find the time to do all that?"

Linda didn't pay attention to me because she was bending down, looking at the village.

"You didn't leave a spot to crawl under the tree with your quilt, a pillow, and a dog. I never understood why you slept there when you were little. So did Chip. It couldn't have been comfortable."

"I was mesmerized by the view of the tree looking up through the branches. I still am. Try it sometime."

She gave me a skeptical grunt, then asked, "Did Mom and Dad go to church last night?"

"No, I offered, but they wanted to stay home and talk to Chip and Jennifer on the phone."

"Hard to imagine them not at church on Christmas Eve," she said, "although that always was one of the most tense car rides of the year. The only sounds were the tires crunching in the snow and Mom fiddling with her purse clasp. I don't know why she was that anxious about a church solo."

In my memory, our childhood Christmas Eve crescendo came too soon and departed too fast, combining two main events: the candlelight midnight church service and Santa. My mother's holiday solo was as anticipated and appreciated as any diva's, and she practiced as if she were the star attraction at Carnegie Hall.

Although a polished performer, she was nervous to sing for this intimately entwined congregation of neighbors, relatives, and lifelong friends. The little church would be standing room only after the extra folding chairs in the aisles filled with once-a-year parishioners, and Mom knew every one of them. She knew the next day her neighbors could be whispering about a missed note or congratulating her on her success. Still, to my knowledge, she never missed a note.

My sister made a trip to the bathroom while I lingered in the memory of the church. I saw us flocking up the dark sidewalk, greeting our friends outside but shushing each other the moment we entered the nave. No one ever spoke unnecessarily or above a whisper, although the plush red carpet and deep velvet seat cushions subdued the sharp edges of any errant baby yelp.

The Christmas service joyously celebrated the holiday in ritual and song. Everyone in our pew sat riveted during Mom's solo, collectively motionless throughout "O Holy Night," until she trilled that very last "deee-*viiine*" in her perfect soprano pitch. We reluctantly held our applause and reverently left the church in candlelit procession into the iridescent snowy hush, the only sound our soft humming of "Silent Night." By the time we arrived at home, Santa had delivered our presents and my grandparents were casually waiting for us, as if they just happened to be passing by.

As Linda wandered through my displays of family knick-knacks and nostalgia, I finished my food prep. I had worked hard through planning, shopping, and cooking to present a crowd-pleasing meal that wouldn't wear me out in the process. Too bad my parents couldn't shop for me. They had been pros in their heyday.

Mom had approached grocery shopping like a purchasing agent for a large corporation. She drafted a list for herself and a list for Dad, each outlined to flow with the floor plan of the targeted store. Dad repaired the cash registers in all the local businesses, so they were his turf and he knew all the clerks. He undertook it as a social event, Mom attacked it as a mission, and kids didn't go.

When they returned home from the store hours later with the chassis scraping the driveway, we all unloaded the loot. That is, my parents and I unloaded; my sister was probably practicing elocution, my brother impishly unwinding a spool of thread around a room. The next step never changed for my parents' whole lives when they returned from the grocery store: Mom took off her rings, watch, and shoes, then constructed a big, dripping mess of a ham-and-Swiss sandwich with mayonnaise, mustard, lettuce, tomato, and pickles. Once she bit into it, she had to truss it together with two hands until the last bite. Dad slapped a slice of bologna and a slab of cheese between two pieces of plain white bread and deemed it terrrific.

It was time to retrieve Mom and Dad, so I told my sister I'd be right back. I hesitated in the car in front of their apartment and gathered my holiday spirit, amused by the illuminated deer statues waving their heads in the garden. Every day my parents were sharing stories of their delight with the decorations, neighbors visiting, and "Merry Christmas" long-distance phone calls. My parents each thanked me profusely for everything I did. I imagined their gratitude as fuel and soaked it in to replenish my waning energy.

Since Thanksgiving, Mom's Christmas spirit had been on a roll and I was its designated driver. She studied the Sunday newspaper ads and recited her lists to me as if she were sitting on Santa's lap. I shopped, helped my parents wrap, and prepared everything for shipping in time to arrive cross-country. Weather and achy joints permitting, they had ventured out with me to absorb the spice of the season, singing along with Christmas carols ringing on the stores' PA systems and smiling at the bustling crowds. I drove them around to ogle Christmas lights at night.

I couldn't deny them their joy, and they weren't really demanding things, just suggesting, but to me it was the same thing. I didn't want my last conversation before a heart attack or stroke to be "Do you really need electric deer in the yard?" I firmly believed in guilt prevention.

I found them waiting at the dining room table with coats folded on their laps. "We're ready," Mom said. "We left the lights on for you to see. Aren't they beautiful?"

My crinkled parents were as sparkly as any Christmas decoration with their holiday sweaters, ear-to-ear smiles, and twinkling eyes. To see them so happy rekindled my holiday cheer. I snapped dress-up photos by their tree, then packed pies, presents, and their old bones into the car for the one-minute drive. They oohed and aahed all the way up my driveway and were awestruck when they entered the house, immersed in holiday fragrances, Christmas carols, and shimmering lights. The dogs demanded their attention first, but then Mom admired each decoration while I helped Dad inch down onto his hands and knees to see the train and village. I figured if he couldn't get up again, I'd get him a quilt, a pillow, and a dog.

Other guests were arriving, pretty much the same crowd as we had for Thanksgiving, unloading presents and greeting Mom and Dad. I detoured to the kitchen, overhearing snips of conversations with the hors d'oeuvres.

Dianna said to Mom, "I loved your Christmas letter."

"Thanks. I made some notes; then my Christmas elf composed the letter, added the photos, and printed seventy-five copies for me." Mailing a computerized Christmas letter symbolized a full, contemporary life to her, and she was proud of it. I was glad I'd made the time.

"That's good news about the house selling."

"It was a blessing," Mom said. "I kept worrying a hurricane would blow it away and we'd pay a mortgage on an empty lot the rest of our lives, or the kids would have to manage it as a rental." I hadn't realized we'd shared the same secret disaster scenarios.

Dinner drew more praise than I'd hoped for, and everyone resettled in the living room for the pre-dessert entertainment. This was Mom and Dad's first time to cast their lines into our traditional game, the Fish Pond. Each guest contributed two wrapped gifts valued around ten dollars. The pond was above flood stage this year because several of us overstocked it, making sure there were presents geared toward my parents.

We piled all the gifts in the middle of the living room floor and one by one hooked packages with a modified fishing pole. We fished and poached and laughed until we each weighed in quite a catch and had stories about the ones that got away.

When there were only two minnows left, Katy suggested that Mom and Dad, as the newest anglers at the pond, should fish again. Mom happily declined, saying, "No, I have enough. Let someone else have an extra turn." I had rarely heard my mother utter the words "I have enough." It was a measure of success I had never expected to achieve.

For entertainment during dessert, the dogs ripped open their gifts—big stuffed animals from the Goodwill—while we found places in our bellies to tuck in my elaborate Yule log cake. The evening settled over me as a satisfying blend of festivity and fulfillment. I basked in the spirit and soaked in every memorable moment. If this were the only late-life Christmas I was to have with my parents, it would serve as a perfect recollection.

Precious taxied home two tired but sated oldsters. The next day they were still reflecting their holiday glow and called to compliment me on the meal, presents, dessert, and atmosphere. I said I'd had good teachers.

After I hung up, I suddenly and sadly remembered that every year of my childhood, minutes after one of us tore open the first present, my mother's post-Christmas depression started dripping over her like India ink. Mom didn't even pretend to enjoy her presents or anything else from that point on, and all her glitter gradually dimmed and lost its sparkle by the end of Christmas Day. We each persistently attempted to astonish her with as much joy on Christmas as she created for us, to no avail. Her depression resurfaced tenaciously each year as part of her tradition and held her hostage until the first bright, clear-blue, snowmelt day. Inspired by the rich, invigorating air, she opened the windows, hung sheets on the line, and dove into a project. Painting, upholstering, planning a party: It didn't matter what—she was back. Maybe she suffered from seasonal affective disorder, or maybe from something much more complex. It was never open for discussion.

This first year in Washington, my mother's cheer held on tight through the dark days of winter. I skeptically searched for a black scourge seeping over her smile but found only gratitude and grace. Maybe she had abandoned her traditional postholiday depression in Florida, leaving it behind with the bottle. I was not going to drop a bad memory on her mood by asking about it now. It would remain another mystery from my childhood, sealed safely in the corners of her heart, where "don't ask, don't tell" stalwartly guarded her secret.

Chapter 26

Our lives settled into an erratic pattern of shopping, doctors' appointments, homemaking, and holidays. As I turned the calendar page at the end of each exhausting month and year, I reminded myself I was lucky to have my parents at this ripe age. I *was* genuinely glad they were thriving, although when I had packed up their ailing bodies in Florida I had anticipated about six months of managing everything from lightbulbs to surgery before I began evaluating nursing homes and funeral parlors.

After several years of their dependence, I believed I had a handle on my role as caregiver. I heard what they weren't saying, embedded flexibility in all my plans, practiced Pilates to relax my body, and minimized extracurricular activities to conserve my energy. We never argued or fought. Our saddest challenge so far was the death of our beloved old dog, Dakota, and we all survived that, as we had the losses of so many other adored pets.

My parents had been holding their own physically, mentally, and financially, and so had I. Until three days ago.

At daybreak I bundled into down and wool and cautiously picked my way through the knee-deep knotted branches burying every square inch of our neighborhood. A ferocious storm had ushered in our fourth Christmas season and crushed my fledgling caregiver's confidence. Hurling itself off the ocean, it slashed apart our serenity, shuddering through western Washington all night with more savage intensity than predicted. It decimated wind gauges, so many areas had no record of peak gusts. Our power had blown out with an ominous convulsion and a jolting, distant explosion around midnight three nights ago. Line workers were flocking in from other states, but trees were down and power was knocked out all across this half of the state; our little neighborhood of a few dozen would be a low priority.

Dad was at the table, buttering a bagel with shaking hands. "Oh, hi," he said glumly. "I just fell into the piano trying to see if it was daylight. I forgot you moved it. It's so dark all the time, I don't know if it's day or night."

"Did you get hurt?" I asked, while searching for blood in the dim light. His skin was so fragile that he bled with the slightest provocation.

"No, it was just stupid. I should have turned on the lantern first."

I had moved the piano and Christmas tree away from the fireplace when I had convinced them to allow me to build a tiny pressed-log fire. They had considered the fireplace only decorative, since they were both afraid of fire. They were too cold to wonder why I had two boxes of pressed logs available when the roads were impassable. I had thought I was prepared for an emergency like this by storing the boxes three years earlier.

I commiserated about the darkness: "Even on a good day in the winter, sometimes it's so dark the daylight-sensing lights in my yard never turn off."

I was pouring him some hot coffee I'd made on my grill, when Ron came in with his empty cup and a gallon of muddy water. I poured his coffee while Dad pushed the bagels over to him. Ron thanked us for the daily treats.

"Thanks for the toilet water," I joked. We both laughed, but Dad just grumbled. Ron hauled gallons of water up from the lake so residents could flush their toilets.

Even in this bleakness, we had fallen into a pattern.

I took a good look at Dad and noticed he was blue and shivering. I put a blanket around him and added a pressed log to the dying fire. I rubbed my purple hands by the open hearth and persuaded myself that it was warmer, but it was still damn cold. It was cheerier, though, and the illusion toasted our hearts for a few minutes, until the chill took precedence again. The thermometer read fifty-one degrees inside and twenty-eight outside.

"Are you sure you don't want some firewood?" Ron asked me. "We got your friend Dianna's tree all cut and split."

"No!" Dad shouted. "The house across the street caught fire that way."

"But we had a housekeeper and a gardener for a month," I teased. Usually this turned the story away from lingering in the frightening moments when we didn't know if the kids had all safely gotten out of the burning house across the street from us in the 1960s. The family was fine and stayed with us while their house was restored, bringing their housekeeper and gardener.

"No firewood, just Presto logs. They don't spark," Dad rasped, now short of breath from the stress.

"Okay, Dad. No problem. What's the daily update, Ron? I thought I heard a power truck beeping down the street." I tried to move on, while watching Dad's breathing.

"It was just a scout checking out the problem," he said. "The trees blocking the road have to be cleared before they can fix the lines, and the tree guys are backed up for two or three days. At least we can get out now through the dirt road. It's cleared."

After Ron left, I swathed Dad in blankets in his recliner by the fireplace and went home, saying I'd be back in three hours, the life span of a pressed log.

My coping skills were running out. Dad had described towing Mom to the bathroom in a crippled midnight stagger, and I realized even if I could find a motel with electricity, I probably couldn't propel her frozen joints up those troublesome outside steps.

With no predictions about power restoration, I trudged over every three hours to stoke the fire and rekindle my parents' spirits. Chain saws and generators rumbled from every direction.

"Hi, Dad," I said quietly from across the room, trying not to startle him.

"Oh, hi," he said. "You poor thing; is it time already?" He threw off layers of blankets and uprighted his recliner. "I put on long underwear and then closed my bedroom door to keep more heat out here. I'll sleep out here; your mother went to bed with her live heat pad, Tillie."

"Hey, I've got an idea," I said, as if proposing something really fun to do on a winter's night, like toast marshmallows or tell ghost stories. "How about if we set up your oxygen tank, since you can't use your apnea equipment when the electricity is off?"

"No," he answered adamantly, shaking his head. I didn't force the issue, understanding his inability to contend with one more glitch in his shadowy confines.

He turned on the portable radio while I rekindled the fire. "Did you hear that?" he asked. "Most of western Washington is still without electricity. Trees fell on houses everywhere. I guess we should consider ourselves lucky. What's it like at your house?"

"Our propane fireplace keeps us about as warm as a candle, so we cordoned off the area around it by thumbtacking blankets up like curtains. We put sleeping bags and the dog's bed in front of the fireplace and stayed pretty warm. It's cold once we step outside those curtains, though. I had to put a jacket on Mica, but poodles don't seem to mind wearing clothes."

Mom and Dad perked up for a lunchtime visit from Dianna, bearing a big pot of piping-hot homemade stew. She lived on the other side of the uprooted trees that had severed our power line, and her electricity was back. Thankful for the food and for the reminder that they had people to take care of them, my parents dug deep into their resource bag and pulled out gratitude.

Dianna also offered her electrified house to Mom and Dad, but I couldn't persuade Mom to emerge from her cocoon. She wouldn't leave Tillie.

When I dragged myself over for the next log run, I spied a serpentine extension cord swirling across the parking lot, ultimately swooping into my parents' apartment. I had no clue what it meant and couldn't organize a logical explanation in my burned-out brain.

I walked in as the microwave beeped, utterly baffling me. My mother's teeth chattered while she said, "Jim ran an extension cord from the generator on his RV into our apartment. We had coffee, and I reheated some stew in the microwave."

My father's complexion had plummeted to an odd shade of purple, so I suggested they plug in a space heater. Mom declined, grumbling, "We don't want to waste Jim's power."

I knew they were too distraught to fight with me, so I said, "Let's just see if it works," while I grabbed the heater and aimed it at them.

She thawed enough to prattle, "All the guys are taking turns checking on tenants and delivering firewood. They'll rotate the extension cord every few hours so each apartment gets a little time. Take some stew up to Jim when you leave, okay? Maybe we should give him some cash for gas for the generator, too."

"That's a good idea. How did you like the stew, Dad?"

"What?" he mumbled.

"The stew Dianna made—was it good?"

He bumbled over to the patio door as if I were talking about something outside that he should look at. "I don't see anything," he griped.

In the flicker of daylight through the window, I was alarmed to discover that he had paled from purple to a cadaverous gray.

Chapter 27

....

It dawned on me that since he now seemed muddled and sullen, maybe he wasn't just cold; maybe he was low on oxygen. Had I really blown it by not convincing him to use his oxygen tank at night?

I used my "oh boy!" voice again and said, "Hey, Dad, let's try out that oxygen while we're just sitting here at the table and see how it works." I quickly left to retrieve it so any naysaying wouldn't be in my hearing range. I adjusted it to his face, and he pinked and perked up within minutes. He practiced adjusting the tubing to his face and turning the tank on and off. He managed it well by feel alone, so I said, "Great! Since you're sleeping right there in your chair, it will be easy for you to use it."

"No."

This was one of those pivotal points where I wanted him to feel in charge of his own decisions, but he had to change his mind. I looked at Mom with a question on my face, and she shrugged her shoulders.

"Dad, this is why we have the oxygen—so you can use it when the power's out."

"I'm fine. I don't need it," he huffed.

I really didn't want to tell him he had been rummy and the wrong color. "Why don't you want to use it?"

"It's too close to the fireplace. It's dangerous."

I should have realized that was the problem. My parents had tried to return the tank after its initial delivery because they were afraid it would spontaneously ignite as soon as they read the warnings. "I'll call the company and find out if it's safe," I said.

I placed the call within Dad's earshot so he wouldn't think I was inventing the conversation. I described our setup, including its proximity to the fireplace, and the technician assured me it was okay. When I told Dad it was safe, his ambiguous responses did not convince me that he had resolved to use it. I knew the oxygen presented one more complicated contraption to perturb him in the pitch-black, frozen night.

I ran out of tools to sway him, so I switched to my last resort: the truth. "Dad, you were gray and fuzzy-brained when I got here, but you're already better after just a few minutes on the oxygen. Could you just trust me and put it on every night?"

"Fuzzy-brained?" he asked, while the meaning sank in. "Okay. Every night," he assured me.

That resolved, Mom took her turn at a problem, demanding, "We need supper. Aren't you going out? I'm hungry. Can't you do something about the electricity? This has gone beyond ridiculous."

Supper was not on my priority list, since they had plenty of stew left. I excused myself before the wrong words came out of my mouth. They didn't know we were starting to worry about frozen water lines rupturing or that Katy was in the process of relocating her difficult mother and cat to our house because her mother had no heat at all at her house.

I didn't want my exhaustion to burn through my empathy. How terrifying was this loss of electric power superimposed on the powerlessness of aging and disability? I could not fathom it and tried not to be judgmental about my parents' reactions.

How did it feel not seeing well to begin with and then functioning by flashlight? How did it feel to depend on others for your heat, water, and food? Grateful, with a fringe of bitterness, in Mom's case; grateful and worried about burdening others, in Dad's case.

Even though the storm had worn us all down, Dad and I stuck to our daily routine. As the gloomy days dragged on, Dad focused on maintaining himself and the apartment, but Mom was losing ground physically and emotionally. She stayed in bed a lot and occasionally waddled to her post, grimacing and grumbling. I felt guilty thinking the word *waddled*, but it was sadly descriptive. She shuffled and hobbled each pain-provoking footstep a few inches at a time. She didn't use her walker in the house; she braced on the wall-to-wall furniture for any route she chose.

My friend Carolyn dropped by, bearing lunch and warm wishes for my parents. She still had no electricity at her house, either, but brought Mom and Dad microwavable bed warmers, two more boxes of logs, deli sandwiches, and a roll of plastic to make storm windows. She saw Dad's exercise bike in the living room and asked him about it.

"It's too cold in my bedroom to ride, especially when I get splashed crossing the ford," he explained, trying to keep a straight face.

Carolyn played right along: "Can't you roll your pants up?"

"That's a good idea. Do you want to see it?" he asked.

Always agreeable, she followed him into his bedroom. He showed her the huge poster of the ford that crossed a river in our hometown in Ohio. He always pretended that was where he was riding his exercise bike, so I had taken the photo on my last trip and Katy had enlarged it into the poster. I heard him telling Carolyn about the trees and cliffs and the steep road winding down to the bottom of the river gorge.

When they came back, Mom confirmed the story. "So, did you see that the road goes right through the river?"

"I did. Tom said sometimes it was barricaded if the river was running too fast, but usually he just drove in and took his chances. Was that scary or fun for you?"

Mom said, "I guess it was as much adventure as I could stand. He'd pretend the brakes weren't working at the top of the hill and act like the car was careening down the twisting road. As the car whooshed into the water, he'd always tell the kids to lift up their feet because they were going to get wet. I just sang the part of 'Climb Every Mountain' about fording the stream and prayed we didn't get water in the engine."

"I love that song," Carolyn said.

"It has carried me through many a dark hour. Maybe we should sing a verse or two now," Mom quipped.

We laughed, ate lunch, and gabbed. I contemplated how often during difficult times in my life, my subliminal soundtrack replayed my mother's arias, encouraging and comforting me.

Carolyn helped me tape clear plastic over the big picture windows in an effort to keep out the Nordic wind, then left with my thanks for having brightened the noon hour. Her attention provided a few degrees of warmth, as well as the comfort of more hands on deck. We needed all we could get.

I went home humming "Climb Every Mountain" and hoped I could ford this stream.

Chapter 28

On my late-afternoon log run, I spotted the male apartment residents clumped in the parking lot by the firewood they had neatly stacked in a communal pile. They had come out in force like bears to protect and supply their den of twelve apartments. They had already hauled, cut, and split all seventy-five feet of the Doug fir that had fallen in Dianna's yard and were now delivering it in wheelbarrows to each apartment.

I headed over to chat with them, and they introduced me to the newcomer in the group, a well-known local newspaper reporter. An anonymous caller had tipped off the paper to the post-storm camaraderie in our powerless pocket of paradise. Most people in the area had their electricity back on, so we were still a story. We rambled on about the rotating extension cord to keep tenants' freezers cold, provide heat, or warm up soup, and described the firewood and lake-water brigades. When I mentioned my parents' age and infirmity and how the neighbors and my friends were all pitching in to care for them, the reporter's ears perked up like a German shepherd's on a search. He wanted to meet them. I hesitated, because my parents' emotions had covered the map these last few days, but agreed, thinking this could go really well or really badly. And either way, it could be in print.

I knew both of my parents would get a big kick out of being in the newspaper, so I was willing to chance it.

My folks were huddled at the dining room table, enjoying bowls of hot chili Chris had just delivered. Mom welcomed the reporter, acknowledging and admiring his success, and explained to Dad who he was. Wearing their best personalities, they babbled uplifting storm stories for an hour, without any self-consciousness about their words showing up in black and white for all to read. The reporter praised their strength, saying they were the best example of glass-half-full people he'd ever met.

His visit had warmed the cockles of our hearts but nothing else. It was nigh on suppertime, and I needed to plan dinner for my parents. Their meals so far had been either fast food or homemade soups and stews from friends with electricity, but all organized by me.

I drove to Safeway and bought deli chicken nuggets and macaroni and cheese containing enough sodium for a football team. I would have preferred to offer them tossed salads and fruit but knew it was pointless. I'd been dealing with their grocery shopping for several years and was thankful beer and wine hadn't worked their way back in, but Mom's cart was always chock-full of sodium, cholesterol, and sugar. After my half dozen sermons about the fact that a single serving of SPAM Lite provides one quarter of a day's allotment of sodium, it was still on every list.

The electricity blessed us around noon after almost a week of no power, and life quickly returned to normal, or as normal as a few days before Christmas could be after we'd lost all that prep time. Instead of planning Christmas dinner, I threw out every soggy, smelly remnant from my freezer and refrigerator. It was a significant sacrifice of money and time-consuming, homemade, organic soups and sauces, baked goods, and pet food.

I dreaded the prospect of cleaning out my folks' refrigerator and mammoth freezer, for fear of how they would weather the ruin. They didn't tolerate waste or squandering and felt financial losses like physical wounds. But the three of us pawed through it together, and it went surprisingly well, since my mother held a broader definition of "still okay" for partially thawed foods than I did, and since her jam-packed jumble had retained the cold better than my more sparsely organized shelves.

Christmas number four arrived and followed our established friends, family, food, and fishing pattern, while we regaled one another with storm stories and affirmed gratitude for heat and lights. I read aloud the long, heartwarming newspaper article prominently featuring Mom and Dad in the Christmas Eve edition of the local paper.

My friends had memorized the steps for providing perfect family holidays, and that made the performance easier for me. Mom's pain was sufficient to trap her in her chair, so Chris fished as her proxy and entertained us all in the process with her stand-up comedy. Carolyn described every present to my father so he could decide whether he would fish or steal when it was his turn. Everyone engaged them in conversation. It was support that allowed me to relax and soak in the moment. "Merry Christmas to all, and to all a good night" were Mom's last words after I dropped them off.

When the phone rang and showed their caller ID early the next morning, I expected it was Mom calling to thank me. Instead, she whispered, "You'd better get over here. Gerald Ford died."

Chapter 29

....

I gave Katy a *what the hell?* look, saying I had to go over
because Gerald Ford had died. She just shook her head in
mutual confusion as the dog and I hurried out the door.

My parents were at the table, holding a wake.

Mom eulogized, "A reporter put it well; he said President
Ford represented a better time in America, living by his faith every
day. He never flaunted his religion to promote a political agenda."

My father's head was bent forward so far, I couldn't tell
whether he was praying, crying, sleeping, or listening, until he
piped up, "They were talking about Ford's Navy record on the
news. He was on a ship in the same typhoon I was, in December
of '44. Three ships sank, and eight hundred men died in that
storm. Ford's ship caught fire, and he helped put it out. I wonder
if he had nightmares for the rest of his life, too." He started choking up and left the room.

My mother said, "I hope your dad doesn't have a bad reaction from thinking about that storm. The TV reporter went on
and on about Gerald Ford and that damn typhoon."

"His Dilantin level is fine," I reassured her. "So he
shouldn't have a seizure—probably just nightmares."

"We'll both have those," she said. "We went through lots of scary storms in our lives. Your dad still broods about the clothes tangled in the treetops when we went to Johnstown to help after the flood in 1977."

I went to check on Dad. He was six inches from the TV screen, trying to see a football game. I sat on his bed and watched the game with him for a while. He murmured, "I said a prayer for Gerald Ford's family. I guess sometimes that's all you can do, isn't it?"

"It is a pretty good cushion to lay your worries on," I answered. He nodded and went back to his game.

I left, pondering my parents' spirituality and strength. Their religion was never something they talked about, aside from offering a brief grace at big meals. They simply tried to abide by the Ten Commandments as best they could, with occasional lapses of racism and prejudice and fractured promises of fidelity.

They expressed their spirituality most often in their belief that complaining showed a lack of gratitude to God. I knew they battled sorrow and despair and had secret places where they stored pain, but they each tried to start every day in a good mood, pulling on a smile like a sweater. The sweater might stretch or tear by nightfall, but it was patched by the next morning. They were appreciative of their lot in life and grateful to God for it.

While they weren't particularly strident with rules for us as children, we were forbidden to wallow in melancholy, self-pity, or any other misery. My parents' abiding philosophy was "get over it," and they held fast to that. They stowed "it could be worse" scenarios to pull out of a hat and dispel sudden anguish. During hard times, they reliably produced optimistic topics tangential to any problem—a resource they used like a thesaurus.

I learned this lesson from them, although my life taking care of them was sufficiently complicated that I didn't always have time to conjure up positive alternative situations to help them feel better. I abbreviated the doctrine in my frequent retort "worse things can happen." If the situation wasn't dire and I thought they could handle some levity, I added, "And probably will."

I knew my parents' strength was forged through the decades by tragedies, crises, and storms. They both vividly remembered the Dust Bowl in the 1930s, whirling a black cloud of dirt and poverty through the Great Depression, dropping grit and despair across the country. My mother retold bleak stories of streetlights on all day as the grimy dust fell like rain in New York. Dad remembered distraught, out-of-work farmers showing up at his family's back door, asking for food and nonexistent work, and his mother always feeding them.

My parents' fortitude spun through many hurricanes, most notably Andrew, which had destroyed the town of Homestead shortly after they had moved to Florida. Now, our recent Northwest winter storm, named the Hanukkah Eve storm, left its mark on them.

Mom called later to say Dad seemed okay and was taking a nap. "I'm going to try to keep him from watching any more news today. After the storm we just had, he can't take much more. He started talking about the hurricanes in Florida. The hurricanes were bad, but Pittsfield was the worst," my mother went on. "That whole town was wiped off the face of the earth."

I knew *Pittsfield* was code for the Palm Sunday tornado of 1965. I said, "I remember people claiming it was an omen from God because it was on Palm Sunday."

"It was eerie to have a tragedy like that on a religious holiday," Mom said. "But on that Easter our pastor gave a sermon about an all-loving God who offered challenges, not punishments. I've never forgotten that."

The Easter Sunday following that horrific Midwest tornado that destroyed Pittsfield, Ohio, was burned on my teenage memory because everyone's emotions were charged by the destruction, yet the adults adhered resolutely to our prescribed family rituals of church followed by a big family dinner. Our church, lined with Easter lilies and extra chairs, offered prayers and fund-raisers for the displaced families. Usually a jubilant service, this one was somber, as my mother's solo resonated. Afterward, all the relatives at our dining room table seemed jittery, passing the ham with propped-up smiles.

Mom continued with her memories of the tornado: "Your dad went to Pittsfield after the tornado to help with the cleanup. He was so upset when he came home, he couldn't talk about it without crying. Ten miles away from us, and every single building in that little village was leveled. The only thing left standing was the statue in the middle of town. The whole place was rubble. A lot of people were killed."

"I remember being holed up in the basement all night during that storm," I said.

"I herded you all down there with sleeping bags, popcorn, and Monopoly. I trusted my own warning system, luckily, because there was no official warning."

"What do you mean?" I asked.

"Well, the storm knocked out all the long-distance phone lines when it started, so no one could warn us it was on the way. But I knew a tornado was coming when the temperature suddenly went from bitter cold to balmy and there was no air, just that ominous, dead vacuum before a tornado hits. And my joints hurt terribly; they're still the most reliable weather forecasters. I warned the neighbors, Aunt Kay, and Gramma and took you all downstairs."

That tornado outbreak remained one of the most intense ever recorded in terms of strength, width, length, and total number of reported tornadoes involved. More than 250 people across six states were killed—60 in Ohio alone. It served as a lifelong storm gauge for my parents. My parents rated windstorms as "not as bad as Pittsfield," "just as bad," or "worse than Pittsfield."

Although storms had strengthened them like the tempering of steel, I prayed we didn't have too many storms left to weather in their lifetimes. That old steel was getting brittle, and I was never as strong as they were.

Chapter 30

....

After our storm and the holiday rush, I danced the rhythm of regular life with renewed appreciation. Before daybreak, I sneaked off to the grocery store with just Mica and Mom's list. After a week of inactivity and stress during the storm, my mother's back was too painful to scrunch into the car and Dad wouldn't be awake quite this early. My elation at shopping alone ended when I unfolded Mom's list. Pencil smudges smeared the page, items were scratched off and scribbled over in red ink, a few things were double-underlined and asterisked, obliterating adjacent words. What I couldn't decipher, I guessed at: ice cream or sour cream? As only the *cream* was legible, I bought both. The essentials weren't listed. No milk, bread, lettuce, or cheese? Had she lost her grasp on her area of expertise? What did it mean? Was this a permanent or temporary problem? Should I make a grocery checklist for her, or a doctor's appointment?

I threw in staples and six frozen meals for them to try. My mother never served any prepared foods when we were growing up, and my parents still considered them an unaffordable luxury. I stashed all their food in the trunk of the car to stay cold until I could deliver it later, at a reasonable hour.

My mood for the drive home was the opposite of my brief

joy at having gone shopping alone. Maybe some music would soothe my soul. I rummaged through my CDs at the stoplight. No to Joni Mitchell. No to Elvis. No to John Lennon. Try the radio. No. No. No. Where was my personality? I distinctly remembered, as a teenager, dueling Jimi Hendrix against my mother's Bach and swearing I'd never fizzle into an old fogey. Damn. The bumper sticker on the minivan in front of me read DON'T RUSH ME. I'M SEARCHING FOR WHO I WAS BEFORE I PUT MYSELF LAST. *Maybe I should follow her,* I thought.

When I walked in with their groceries before noon, the apartment was airless and dark and the silence sucked the life out of me. Mom's racked joints after the freezing power outage had confined her to bed; her absence from the Command Post had left a black hole. I opened the blinds and turned on lights to ward off the mental demons taunting me that this foretold my future.

I found Dad in his bedroom, leaning over the computer keyboard with his face an inch from the blank e-mail screen, his eye pressed into a magnifier. I hesitated at his door, not wanting to startle him. I puzzled over a wet pair of underwear draped on his exercise bike's handlebars as I slowly went in. When he noticed me, he grumbled, "I messed this whole thing up again. What does *unauthorized user* mean?"

I was tired and hungry and wanted to bolt, but I knew wrestling with my conscience would prevent me from accomplishing anything worthwhile at home. "I don't know, Dad. I've never understood your system very well. But I brought groceries; let's put the frozen stuff away first and then figure out the e-mail."

After we dealt with the perishables and the e-mail problem, I went home, still managing to lug along my guilty conscience. Dad had nothing interesting to do when Mom stayed in bed, and he wouldn't leave the house, in case she needed something. He'd occupy himself putting away the rest of the groceries, watching TV, tidying up something or other. I'd occupy myself worrying about them.

In my frettings, I remembered that damp underwear slung over the handles of his bike. I knew it would embarrass him if he realized I had noticed it, so I hadn't mentioned it. But now that I thought about it, I recalled that he had recently told his doctor he was having a problem with dribbling. The doctor had downplayed it as normal aging, and I had forgotten about it. I pulled out my pocket notebook and added *male incontinence pads* to my drugstore list. I already bought plenty of geriatric supplies like that for them. The first time I loaded up my cart with pads, stool softeners, and other assorted body-care products, I wanted to hang a NOT FOR ME sign on it. Now I just threw the junk in the cart.

My mother's inability to grocery shop reminded me about a wheelchair. I had been afraid to mention it to Mom because I had no idea how she might react, but recently, on a particularly painful day for her, I had casually said, "Maybe we should research a wheelchair for you so we can have it on hand in case of an emergency. It could take months to get one."

Much to my surprise, she said, "I've seen those scooters on TV. It might be a good idea to have something like that."

I never accurately predicted how she would respond to anything.

In our childhood, her responses were reliable only in their unpredictability. They were definitive and dramatic, in the mode of whichever temperament took charge at the time. She might be effusive and gracious or bitter and snide. We constantly evaluated her prevailing personality because it tinted or tainted our entire universe. I can picture her hanging sheets on the line in our picket-fenced backyard when I was about eight years old. I'd stroll past on a reconnaissance mission to decode her cryptic expressions. Was she smiling in the fresh air or frowning with tight lips while jamming on the clothespins? My next step was to experiment with a harmless question like "What's for supper?" to evaluate her tone of voice; her response determined whether I hung around or skedaddled.

Now I was painfully aware that my mood shaped their dependent world. My responses had to be predictable and non-critical. If I wanted to say, *You what? I can't believe you did that! What were you thinking?* I translated it to my new oldster-speak, which came out as, "Okay. That should be fine. No problem. Thanks for letting me know."

For example, their phone had recently gone dead, so Mom had used her cell phone to call the phone company and had been on hold for almost an hour before she had given up. We shared minutes among five cell phones, and she'd blown an hour. But the heart of the matter was that she had tried to take care of it without bothering me, so I had to approach it that way, not by the cost of minutes. When she had realized her blunder and called to fill me in, I'd recited, "Okay. No problem. Thanks for letting me know."

In addition to fretting about their needs and health, I managed to squeeze in time to worry about myself. New Year's Day of caretaker year five was rousing the reflections-and-resolutions monster for its annual reunion with my mirror. Could I consider my care for my parents an achievement? What was I accomplishing in this life of caretaking? Was that the headline of my life now? Who was I? How did I define myself? Did it matter? Did I need to achieve something?

In the past year, I had managed to study Spanish, exercise regularly, and follow a regimented antifatigue diet. But mostly I took care of everything and everyone near me. I wasn't saving the planet. Did it matter? Time is such a precious commodity. Was I spending it well? Well enough?

My cognitive functions swirled and stirred in an emotional stew, the mediocrity of my activities overwhelming me. When I read the paper, I considered new interests: citizen liaison to the city council, the Master Gardener program, or volunteer work at the free dental clinic. Why did I value those tasks but not what I was doing? I told myself it was not what I did that mattered, it was who I was, but it was rhetoric. I had no forward motion, no goals, no ascent toward achievement.

I stopped myself and decided the only thing I really wanted to accomplish was to get over my bleak mood, but I wallowed in it a little longer, wading in deeper.

I kept searching for a way to change my attitude about the things I did. It used to work. There were many permutations: *Smile and you'll be happy. Laugh and you'll feel better. It could be so much worse; it will be so much worse, guaranteed. Enjoy today.*

I wasn't.

That was as long as my day allotted me for cranky contemplation before the dryer buzzed, the dog scratched at the door, and the phone rang. It was all I could stand of my own thoughts anyhow.

I checked caller ID and answered the phone: "Happy New Year."

My parents responded in unison with the same greeting. Mom continued, "I feel a lot better. It *is* a happy new year. How can we ever thank you for all you've done? I just gaze out over the lake and think how lucky we are."

"You're welcome. That apartment is a little bit of heaven. How was the dance last night?"

"We decided not to go; my feet hurt, and Kay had a cold. Anyhow, Vienna seems so far away; next year I think we'll plan to go to New York. I was just too happy sitting here to think about going anywhere else."

Every year, my mother and her sisters, Kay and Judy, pretended they spent New Year's Eve dining and dancing in Vienna. Over the phone they planned their gowns, accessories, and hairstyles and discussed hors d'oeuvres and music.

My mother continued, adding details to the fantasy about dancing while I was staring at a list that said *wheelchair, ramp, pain medication,* and *cortisone shot.* We gabbed a little longer, and I said I'd be over at ten the next morning for our appointment. I didn't define the appointment, trying not to spoil Mom's mood. The wheelchair representative was coming to evaluate her.

"We'll be ready," she answered flatly.

I'd shot down her good spirits in record time, for a complete caregiver failure.

Chapter 31

....

I walked over to my parents' apartment fifteen minutes before the scheduled wheelchair evaluation appointment and found them scrubbed and polished at the table. Their rosy-cheeked complexions, full heads of wavy, dark hair, and beautiful smiles defied their health histories. After the usual "how are you todays," I launched into my prep.

"Mom, remember that Medicare's criteria for electric wheelchairs are based solely on your ability to get around *inside* the house."

"I get around fine inside the house," she protested.

"I know you do, but you hold on to furniture to walk, and some days you're in so much pain you can't get out of bed. I just want to have it in case we need it." I wanted to convince her that this was not the time to be her perky, glass-half-full self, but I didn't want to depress her with a complete reality check.

The wheelchair salesman arrived and began Mom's health history by reading from the doctor's notes: "Left knee replaced twice because first replacement shattered; right hip replacement redone after being completely loose for ten years; five severely degenerated vertebrae in lower back; breast cancer; kidney cancer. Is that correct?"

"Oh, I guess so," she answered unconvincingly.

"Do you have any trouble getting around in the house?" he asked her, while glancing around at the contiguous embankments of furniture.

In her cheeriest voice, she said, "Oh, no, I don't have any trouble at all in the house."

Had she heard anything I had told her earlier about justifying the need for this wheelchair? I calmly added, "She walks by hanging on to wall-to-wall furniture."

In a tearful, jagged voice, Dad added, "Last week I had to help her get in and out of bed and hold her up while she shuffled to the bathroom, hunched over in pain."

My mother defiantly interrupted him, her fist whacking the table in time with her words: "We aren't leaving here."

Now I understood. I reassured her, "Mom, this is about keeping you *in* your apartment, not taking you out of it." I described to the salesman how convenient it was to have them right across the street from me, and said I wanted them to stay there, knowing the words would carry more truth to Mom's ears if I were telling someone else.

He continued his evaluation, asking if she had ever fallen. She quickly and adamantly responded, "No! Never!"

I said, "Twice," and she agreed in a despondent voice.

The salesman concluded that Mom likely would qualify for a power chair and went outside to unload his sample. He quickly ramped the stairs, hopped into the chair, sped down the ramps, and reeled into the apartment. I questioned him about the ramps, and he assured me they would come with it.

He rolled the snazzy little chair close to Mom, then made lengthy additions to his notes after watching her groan and hoist herself out of her chair, then gimp and grab furniture to cover the two feet from her chair to the wheelchair. She plunged into it and easily steered it around, transforming it into a carnival ride, not another signpost of decline. He left us with the forms for the doctor, saying it might take sixty days or so.

After two redeliveries of the necessary documentation and two dozen phone calls, three months later the wheelchair was scheduled for delivery, with specific assurance from the secretary that ramps were included.

When the salesman arrived, I greeted him in the driveway but had no sense that he recognized me. "I'm Margaret's daughter," I clarified. "We met when you completed her evaluation."

Without acknowledgment, he pointed at the stairs and asked irritably, "How am I supposed to get this thing in the house?"

I looked at his name tag and the name on the original order; they matched. He had ridden down his own ramps over these stairs three months ago. Had he suffered a head injury in the interim?

I couldn't stifle my shock. "You promised me ramps came with it. The secretary confirmed they were being delivered today."

"We don't provide ramps; they are your responsibility."

I pressed, but he offered no responses, apologies, or troubleshooting help. The topic was a complete nonstarter. We had a very expensive wheelchair and no way to use it.

After I rocked and rolled the wheelchair through spongy grass, over gullies and molehills, and in the back door, I lied to Mom about how easy and cheap it would be for me to order ramps online and dragged myself home. Damn it. One more thing.

I wanted to use portable ramps to minimize inconvenience and liability for other tenants. I carefully calculated the slope, and while it was slightly steeper than ADA requirements, it was well within the recommendations for electric wheelchairs. After contacting a dozen businesses about portable ramps, I discovered why the wheelchair salesman had played dumb: No one could legally provide a non-ADA-compliant ramp to an apartment building.

My only immediate plan of action involved lying awake every night and worrying, a tactic I had begun in Florida and had practiced frequently ever since. That finally produced the courage to phone the landlord and ask his permission to build a non-ADA-compliant, semipermanent ramp. I was prepared for "no" and completely shocked by "sure, no problem." Maybe I should have called him sooner, or maybe I just had to send enough distraught energy into the universe for a guardian angel to intercept it.

Which angel? My father's father seemed a likely candidate to have sprinkled a little benevolence powder on the landlord just before his phone rang. My mother described her father-in-law as the most loving man she had ever met. An otherwise reliably harsh critic, she used the words *fun*, *charming*, *loyal*, *kind*, and *easygoing* to portray him. He took Mom to antiques sales, always buying her something she still remembered fondly. She had recently reminisced about him when we were unpacking: "He bought me that colander"—she pointed—"and remember that cute percolator you kids played with in the sandbox? That was from a swap meet he took me to; I wish I still had that, even though the bottom burned out."

He had died a few months after I was born. Both my parents reminded me often how he held me and carried me around wherever he went when we visited, and I'd felt buffered by that embrace my whole life. I still treasured the stuffed animal he had given me at birth; Sugarloaf sopped up many tears and shared many dreams through an inseparable childhood.

Now that my paternal grandfather was onboard, my phone rang the next morning. An old friend needed work right away; he was a skilled plumber and a talented carpenter, waylaid by a sick wife. I hoped this was my answer. A full year had passed since Dad's doctor had said, "Stairs? He shouldn't be using any stairs." And then, of course, we had Mom's thwarted wheels.

My friend constructed a sturdy work of art for us. Dad sailed up the ramp like the young Navy recruit he once was. It was a huge relief not to watch him scrabble his way up and down the stairs. Mom rode the wheelchair up and back, then tried her walker, her legs lumbering the rise of the ramp better than her lungs did. I couldn't fathom why she didn't try to move around more. I didn't even think of it in terms of exercise anymore; just being more mobile around the apartment would help. She went from bed to Command Post to bathroom bracing herself on furniture or using a walker. *Should I look into oxygen for her?* I wondered.

Was I going to let that percolate to the top of the worry list, now that the ramp and wheelchair were checked off? Or would some unknown problem hiding around the corner stick its leg out and trip me with an unforeseen crisis?

Chapter 32

....

Dad creaked his rusting joints into Precious on a sunny March day for our monthly drive to the VA for his blood tests. After clicking on his seat belt, he stated, without preamble, "Today is the anniversary of my brother's death."

The airspace in the car went dead, like when a radio signal unexpectedly fails and there isn't even static. I didn't remember him ever using the words *my brother*; he had always referred to him by name, Nelson. What should I say? I didn't want to summon more emotion than he could bear, but I wanted him to talk if he felt like it.

"What a terrible loss," I knew I'd responded inadequately as soon as it hit the vacuum between us. It didn't matter, though; there was no salve for this.

We merged into the freeway traffic, which always scared Dad as the cars raced in and out of his pinpoint of vision. He usually said, "I didn't even see that car until it was right on us. I'm glad I'm not driving." Today he was silent.

After we settled into the slow lane, he began reminiscing in a flat voice: "I had seen him at Great Lakes in 1943 when he joined the Marines. He was just starting boot camp, but I was finishing my training. They needed guys so bad that boot camp was only a few weeks, but I had been there for a couple months in classes on maintaining equipment and guns."

He had never talked about this, and I wanted to keep him going. I asked, "Great Lakes Naval Training Center? You were pretty close to Youngstown from there; did you get to go home sometimes?"

"Not much; it was too hard on my mother every time we left. She didn't want either of us to go in the service. She was so mad, and she blamed me for Nelson's joining because I was older and enlisted first. She thought he was just following in my footsteps, but there was a lot of pressure to go into the service after Pearl Harbor. One time while I was still in high school, a complete stranger grabbed my arm and shook me and yelled in my face, 'My son's in the Army. Why aren't you in the service?' It was unpatriotic not to sign up."

After a somber mile or so, he continued wistfully, "Nelson and I were both in San Francisco right before I shipped out. The fall of 1944, I guess. We went carousing and drinking with his CO; then, after the bars closed, Nelson and I sat under one of those big signs . . . What are they called?"

"Um, billboards?"

"Right. We sat there and drank beer and laughed. We both loved San Francisco and decided we'd live there when we left the service. I'd been on shore patrol for a few weeks and got to know the town pretty well. Anyhow, Nelson and I stayed out all night because he didn't have to get back to base." He was chuckling. "I got back late, and the gangplank was already pulled up. The guys on the dock threw me in the cargo net, and the crew hauled me on board. I got in a little trouble for that. Thirteen days confined to ship—at sea! Ha! Some punishment. Our captain was a good guy."

He was silent again, and I didn't know where he was going or where to lead him. I turned off at our exit from the freeway, then stopped at the light at the end of the ramp. I appreciated the quiet after the turbulence of the freeway, but it was too quiet. Sullen.

He turned toward the window and wiped his face with his handkerchief. Then, very slowly, in a hollow voice, he sobbed, "That was the last time I ever saw him."

I choked on his sorrow. No one in his family had ever recovered from Nelson's death. It was a deep wound bandaged by a carefully protected piece of gauze, ready to ooze anytime it was bumped. Dad had guarded this heartbreaking gash from me all my life, protecting me. Now I was the adult, the caretaker, the one to hear his troubles. His *brother* was a loss suddenly more exposed, more raw, than any stories of Nelson.

Cars behind us started tapping their horns, and we both flinched at the sounds interrupting our gloom. I turned onto the road to the VA, still unable to talk.

He lamented, with a bitter tone, "Nelson could have stayed in San Francisco because he was a rifle instructor. He was good at everything he did and moved up the ranks fast. But he was a daredevil. He wanted action. He was always tough. But Iwo Jima took him and around seven thousand other Marines."

"Seven thousand guys died on Iwo Jima?" I asked incredulously. Why hadn't I known that?

"Almost—sixty-eight hundred, if you want to be exact. It's called the bloodiest battle in Marine history. Twenty thousand more were wounded. The Japanese were hiding in caves with connecting tunnels five stories deep all over the island. I can't imagine we needed that island that bad. Eight lousy square miles. A sniper shot Nelson in the neck four days before the US declared victory. Four days."

We stewed in the fate of those four days before he went on.

"I was still in the South Pacific, and after they told me about him, I sat on the floor in the ship's boiler room for twenty-four hours without moving. The captain didn't bother me, and the guys left me alone. I was embarrassed afterward, but they knew from my stories that we were as close as twins. I felt dead. You have his Purple Heart, right?"

I reassured him with specifics: "I do. I have his medals, his certificates, his letters home, all the funeral announcements and letters from the government. Your mother saved everything."

"Good. I want you to have it."

I knew he meant: *I want my brother's life and loss to have mattered.*

I asked, "It was a long time after he was killed before his remains came back, wasn't it? A month or more? April?"

He bristled and gave me a puzzled glare. I was usually the fact-checker, but I was evidently way off on this one. He tersely clarified, "It was in April, three *years* later." I couldn't share his sorrow if I didn't know the facts.

"Three years?" I realized I had seen telegrams notifying his parents that Nelson's remains were arriving in April, and assumed it was the April following his death in March.

"Three years," he repeated, with exasperation. Shaking his head in frustration, he added, "Mr. McCauley wouldn't let me open the casket, but I wanted to. I begged him. Even though Nelson and I had worked at McCauley Funeral Home in high school, driving the hearse and picking up bodies, I couldn't get Mr. McCauley to change his mind." He slapped his thigh with his fist. "I didn't get to say good-bye."

His sigh was almost a moan, before he continued, "My mother wrote a lot of letters and pulled a lot of strings to get Nelson back after he was buried on Iwo Jima. Then she devoted her life to his memory. You remember that big flag on the porch? That was from his casket. And she was president of the Gold Star Mothers."

I remembered the melancholy shrouding my grandmother's house, Nelson's medals and photos enshrined on her desk; the pilgrimages to the cemetery each Memorial Day, known then as Decoration Day; and my grandmother wearing her white suit with her Gold Star pin.

"I remember the flag and that Gramma was in the Gold Star Mothers, but I don't know what they did."

"They helped veterans and their families, mostly, and conducted ceremonies on holidays. I think it gave my mother a place where other people understood her. Even at the end, she wanted to be buried in her white Gold Star Mothers suit. She never got over it."

I slowed to fifteen miles an hour over the speed bump as we entered the VA grounds, with its pergola of cherry trees budding chartreuse, framed by evergreens so dense and tall we couldn't see the sky.

"Beautiful. Just beautiful," Dad greeted the trees, as they soothed him. "These trees will be pink soon, then cover the ground in confetti."

I knew he was focusing on the trees to shift his thoughts. He concluded his eulogy by saying, "I love it here. Thank you for bringing me."

I pulled up to the handicapped walkway. A volunteer helped him out of the car and started escorting him toward the building. The VA immersed Dad in tangible appreciation for his service to the country in World War II, briefly mitigating the lingering trauma of the war and the sacrifice of his brother. Dad could tell me about his pain, but here his burden was shared every time his hands and eyes greeted another old man. Many times I had seen a knowing look pass between them, the empathy consoling Dad with every handshake. I thought of his words describing his mother and the Gold Star Mothers and knew the VA gave him a place where people understood him.

As I parked, I resolved that Nelson's death and every military holiday would be acknowledged differently now by this "make love, not war" baby boomer. As I proudly joined my veteran in the waiting room, I thought maybe my mother was right; maybe I should replace my peace-sign flag with one of the three American flags she had gently pressed on me over the years.

Chapter 33

....

It was a gorgeous day in late May, and my friends were joining us for lunch at my parents' apartment to celebrate Mom's birthday. I arrived early and deposited seven Subway sandwiches in her kitchen, along with a "happy birthday" to her. I reflexively read her mood in the scene: hair combed, cheeks rouged, apartment clean and tidy, Mother's Day and birthday cards decorating the shelves, a fresh apple pie tantalizing my senses. It seemed like a party atmosphere, but I wouldn't know for sure until she spoke. While she generally appeared in a good mood, a bitter scourge still erupted now and again without warning.

Turning to me from her dining table throne, as the TV ranted about a miracle cleaning gel, she scowled and snarled, "Did you hear that? He ended every sentence with a preposition. Don't they teach grammar anymore?" I offered no response beyond a blank stare and a bobbing head, obeying my training not to ask what was wrong. She pushed on: "Well, don't they? Doesn't anyone care what's proper? I'm sick of it."

No party hats here. Dad waved me out the back door, and I slid out to plant the Mother's Day petunias my sister had delivered the previous weekend. I had originally planted low-maintenance shrubs in the little garden but replaced them with flowers when Mom had pouted about the lack of color. It was one of those oh-so-familiar, easier-to-do-what-she-wanted situations. Now, every spring, I dreaded buying, hauling, and planting multiple flats of flowers but conceded it was an important seasonal ritual for them and a daily escape for my father when he watered and weeded.

Dad and I hunkered down on our knees in the dirt, and I pulled the petunias out of their pots. "Why is Mom in such a bad mood?"

"She's constipated," he said.

Dad began digging holes with his trowel, and I crept behind him, filling each hole with fertilizer and tamping in the plants. I could have finished it all myself in a fraction of the time, but he needed to feel useful.

"This bad a mood for constipation?" I questioned.

"That's all I can figure out. She's been bossing me around and correcting me all morning. I finally told her if she didn't like the way I opened the blinds or answered the door, she could get up and do it herself. She just sits there and orders me around like a servant. If she moved around more, she probably could shi . . . go."

He stopped himself from saying the word, but he didn't swear very often, so I knew he was in a bad mood, too. We crawled our way through the flowerbed in our inefficient but practiced routine while I tried and failed to think of something comforting to say. We both felt helpless and hopeless about Mom's weight and failing joints and the ramifications of her inactivity.

Unsuccessfully trying to hide the resignation and defeat in my voice, I sighed, "We'd better go in and see how she is. It's about time for the girls to get here."

He began his arduous ascent to his feet, his hands climbing his cane, saying, "At least now the weather's better and I can get out every day to water the flowers. Someone's usually around to gab with. What a great place to live." He still found a rainbow in every storm.

We brushed off our knees and went in exclaiming about how nice the additional flowers looked, acting out our usual roles of pretending everything was fine. By the time everyone arrived for lunch, I wore my customary headache. As planner and host, I hated coordinating these events but valued them and appreciated that Katy, Chris, Dianna, and Carolyn obliged me. The fact that they always claimed to enjoy my parents was some consolation.

As I sorted out the sandwiches, Dianna commented on all the presents and cards, then pointed to Mom's pie. "That's a perfect birthday cake. You have an excuse not to mess around with candles."

"Exactly," Mom replied. "I always have pie for my birthday, and I make pineapple upside-down cake for Tom's. That's his favorite."

I grabbed the party momentum, saying, "For my sister, Mom always baked a five-layer chocolate-mint cake, decorated as fancy as a wedding cake." Like so many of our family memories, it might really have happened only once or twice, but the occasion had blossomed into the whole story.

Mom added, with a touch of irritation, "You never liked sugar, even as a baby, so I made angel food cake with confetti sprinkles inside it for you. No frosting. We put ice cream on ours, but you ate it plain. Your eating habits were always so strange."

As we sat down and started to eat, I tried to prevent the conversation from further derailment. "For Chip's birthdays, Mom decorated big sheet cakes with racetracks for his Matchbox hotrods and arranged the candles like streetlights. We each had big parties, too. Lots of kids for pool parties and slumber parties. Mom churned out food like she ran a diner."

Dad set his sandwich back on his plate and cleared his throat to talk. "The best party was the carnival for your tenth birthday. I made all those booths in the basement for games, like at the fair. You kids threw Ping-Pong balls in fishbowls, rolled bowling balls, or threw darts for prizes. The whole neighborhood played."

"It was great," I told my friends. "My sister's friend Cyndy dressed up as a fortune teller, and Dad put dry ice around a crystal ball to make an eerie fog.

"Here's another tidbit about our birthdays," I continued. "All three of us were given presents on each other's birthdays. We thought that was normal."

Mom laughed. "I couldn't bring myself to give presents to just one of them. It didn't seem fair."

I guess in return I could make a little birthday party for her without all this grousing in my head.

My raging headache abated somewhat amid the horseplay and laughter all around the table. Chris finished a long, hilarious story, and everyone was still tittering when Mom brought the chattering group to a sudden silence: "You used the word *funnest*; is that a word now? Shouldn't it be *most fun* to be correct?"

The veins in my temples bulged as my teeth ground behind my stricken smile. "Oh, Mom," I said, in what I hoped was a lighthearted tone, "just enjoy the story. The grammar doesn't matter."

"No, I want to know," she insisted. "I've heard it on TV, too. Is it correct? It sounds terrible. What are they teaching in schools now?"

Maybe I should have announced she was constipated, so please excuse her impertinence.

Dad shoved back his chair to start clearing the table and the air, and we paraded after him, leaving Mom alone at the table to boil. No one was going to touch this. Conversation resumed at the sink with "Aren't the peonies beautiful this year?"

We stacked all of Mom's presents in front of her, and she shifted gears. By the time the party wrapped up everything was smoothed over by stories and laughter.

My beloved buddies, each a well-educated, accomplished career woman with strong self-esteem and a good sense of humor, had defused the harsh words, minimized the eruption, and moved on. Over the last thirty years, we had all been involved with one another's families and rode out the bad with the good.

It was sad, though, to witness Mom carrying this level of judgment into old age, because I wanted her to reap the limited social stimulation available in her immobile world. I hoped all the people she met would be as gracious as my friends.

My mother held fast to her belief that good grammar was a virtue and signified intelligence, sophistication, social status, and wealth. Class was important to her, and she flaunted language as her ticket to a higher rung on the ladder. She had suffered from this unfortunate barrier as long as I could remember. I say *suffered* because I imagined it threw roadblocks into relationships that she couldn't explain. I knew some of her friendships had ended unexpectedly, and I was sometimes surprised it hadn't caused her to lose her marriage, too.

All through their relationship, she had ridiculed and humiliated my father's spoken words. He sprinkled his sentences with sufficient mispronunciations to fuel my mother's superiority fire whenever she needed to stoke it. Dad grew up in a Scotch-Irish enclave on the edge of Amish country and retained a tiny bit of its melting-pot vernacular. He said *warter* for *water*, a common pronunciation that locals would not have registered as odd without my mother ringing bells and shining spotlights on him every time he said it. *Doll*, used often enough with two daughters who dragged them everywhere, came out of his mouth as a combination of *dowel* and *dawl*. Not being a fighting man, he shrugged off her reprovals. It was entirely possible that my mother used those attacks as punishment for some marital transgression he had committed and he accepted it as his due.

My father's mother had a few language idiosyncrasies, too, mispronouncing dozens of common words that allowed my mother to gloat in her own apparent better breeding. My grandmother called November *Lovember* for the one hundred Lovembers she lived. She had reason to enunciate it often for my mother's ears, since my father's birthday was in Lovember and we saw her in Lovember sometimes for Thanksgiving—unlucky coincidences. My mother corrected her without apology.

A forbidding foe, my paternal grandmother aimed the language artillery right back at my mother. My childhood nickname, Patty, ended with a *y*, but my grandmother spelled it with an *ie*. Not sometimes, not haphazardly, and not because she didn't know how it was spelled— she wrote it that way on every piece of correspondence regarding me because she ordained it correct. I didn't know all the politics behind it, but my mother interpreted that *ie* as a complete denunciation of her intelligence and status.

My mother declared war on my father based on those two vowels with every birthday, Easter, or Christmas card I received. When she started, "Why can't your mother spell your own daughter's name correctly?" my father grinned sheepishly and headed for the basement, correctly called the storm cellar in his family's language. Mom usually continued the tirade on the telephone with one of her sisters, the rest of us in hiding until it blew over.

Granted, my mother possessed a genuine knack for grammar and words, and I valued her knowledge, but its mutation into this persnickety intolerance was distressing. Constipated or not, Mom spat and sputtered daily about words misused in the newspaper and the people who wrote them. She made snap judgments about neighbors based on the way they spoke, and that was often the final pronouncement of their status.

She valiantly tried to convince me not to use the word *got*— not an acceptable term for any use. I decided not to give that any energy, not to spite her by overusing it, and not to succumb to her skewed standards, but just to let her be.

I got over it.

I thought I should put this quality on my watch list, though. My language skills weren't half what hers were, but I still noticed misuse or mispronunciations. I didn't want to hear her judgments coming out of my mouth someday. Maybe what really bothered me was the common notion that one day I would recite her lines and look down and see her hands coming out of my sleeves. There was no getting over that.

Chapter 34

....

Saturday morning I was up at four thirty, staring at two columns of tasks on an eight-by-eleven yellow legal pad, crossing off *mom's birthday party*. The page presented a well-rounded accumulation of stressful reminders, with everything from *check my investments* and *research osteoporosis treatments* to *mow the lawn* and *clean the dog's ears*. I plodded through my chores and was booting up my Quicken financial program, when the phone rang before lunch. Caller ID said MOM & DAD, and I answered, like I always did—part of my "do it now" mentality.

Ostensibly, Mom was calling to tell me the bill for her wheelchair had come. She paused, probably trying to evaluate my mood, then rattled off a honey-do list for me.

I was trying to concoct a polite response while she hemmed and hawed a little more, then she added, "Dad thinks he has something you could use to seal up that mouse hole. He wants you to seal any holes around pipes, too." It wasn't a mouse hole; it was a tiny trough I had whittled in the doorframe the previous winter for the generator's electric cord. Only a mouse named Houdini could squeeze through, after first opening the heavy storm door Katy had installed for them. But critters did get into the apartment somehow, so I knew I had to find and fill gaps.

My overwhelmed side wanted to say, *I have been working for six hours already today while you sat and drank coffee. Leave me alone.* My better side thought, *They're over eighty. Be glad they know there's a hole in the doorframe.*

My voice said, "I'll be over after lunch."

It was this weighing, balancing, and juggling that wore me out. They threw all the balls at me, and I had to decide which ones to catch. My conscience tiptoed back and forth across a fine line between service and servant. Maybe the problem was that I liked to do a job well and to completion. This job didn't provide me with a sense of accomplishment, though, and what did *completion* mean? There was always something more I could be doing. I thought *could*, but my brain interpreted it as *should*—my Virgo downfall.

A few months earlier, I had tried tackling my chronic need for productive time utilization by keeping track of the hours I spent taking care of my parents. After a few weeks, my grand total was many more hours per week than I averaged during my entire career. No wonder I was tired.

I'd seen an ad for a lecture on fatigue but didn't really plan to go, knowing I was always too tired by that time of night—though the irony was not lost on me. The speaker's advertisement contended that fatigue was the number-one reason women went to their doctors. I decided to attend the lecture at the last minute, without showering or changing my clothes. I didn't plan to see anyone I knew, figuring there would be thirty or forty exhausted strangers there.

To my dismay, hundreds of women lined the sidewalk, waiting for the doors to open. I considered leaving, rather than dealing with a crowd, but headed for the ticket booth while debating.

Someone tapped me on the shoulder, saying, "Hi! How are you?"

I didn't remember exactly who she was, but she had the giveaway robust, clean look and perfect teeth of a dental hygienist. She pointed to a group of familiar faces waving at me and offered me an extra ticket.

No shower, and already six people I knew professionally. One had been a student of mine when I'd taught dental hygiene. Darn.

I joined them and sat next to a former classmate I had seen from time to time over the twenty-five years since our training. Our dental hygiene class had been a cohesive group, and the two of us immediately dove into comfortable conversation.

She filled me in about her job and family, then asked, "How are you?"

"I haven't worked for a few years. I'm taking care of my parents."

"I heard about that," she said. "Do you miss it?"

"Yes, I really miss my patients and the camaraderie of the office," I admitted. "It was the only type of work I ever did. Right out of high school, I worked as a dental assistant to pay for college; then I went to dental hygiene school."

The physician speaker began, and it was apparent from the get-go that she proposed a psychological, rather than physiological, cause of our problems. The big screen flashed a long list of items women naturally take care of, then two questions: Who takes care of us? What feeds our self-esteem?

My classmate groaned, wrote a note on the paper, and slid it to me like we had done in school. It said, *I just want to take a vitamin to fight my fatigue. I'm too tired to try to figure it out.*

I wrote back, *Me too. I don't have the energy to reassess my life.*

She scribbled on the paper and passed it back to me. *I wish I could leave now, but it would be too conspicuous. How come you write left-handed? You weren't left-handed in school.*

I answered, *I had to learn how. I can't do any repetitive motion with my right hand. I should have quit working years before I did. I wrecked my arm.*

She splayed her arthritic fingers and wrote, *My hands hurt, but I love it too much to stop. It's the one place where I feel a sense of accomplishment at the end of every day.*

The presenter's premise that women's instincts for taking care of others doesn't feed us shook me up. It described my life, down to the atomic level. She adamantly recommended setting limits and nurturing one's self-esteem.

I was electrified by the confluence of circumstances that presented this information so relevant to my current life in the midst of elements of my former, fulfilling occupation. I felt my magnetic poles attracting and repelling information and emotions. I never would have processed the information the way I did if I hadn't been sitting with the remnants of my career.

Currently, my dental hygiene memories mostly evoked sadness at the continuing pain in my shoulder and limited use of my hand. But I had loved my work and had derived great satisfaction and a good paycheck from it. It had fed me in many ways. The last two years I had worked, however, had been a painful, minute-by-minute push to complete my tasks in the time allotted, and without my patients' awareness of my struggle. It was depressing, terrifying, and exhausting to have achieved a high level of skill and professional respect, to work in a practice I loved and valued, and to become physically unable to accomplish the task.

I didn't know what I was going to do with this shift in thinking about feeding my self-esteem, but I knew I was looking at my struggle through different eyes, whether I wanted to or not.

On my way home, I considered possibilities for new activities. I created a long list, but each item seemed like a Band-Aid, not a cure. I promised myself to sit in my discomfort, not just fill up my time, until the right answer presented itself to invigorate my spirit.

Unbeknownst to me, the foundation for my paradigm shift had begun the Christmas of the big storm, when we were

without electricity for almost a week. To pass the dark hours
of freezing worry, I had taken to journal writing, documenting
the events of the power outage. Until then, I had rarely written
at all because of my right-arm problem, but during the storm
I had felt compelled and scribbled left-handed. I had rambled
on about my parents' bravery and my bewilderment for many
candlelit pages. After that, I occasionally penned some tidbit or
anecdote that I wanted to remember or wished I could forget.

A few months after the fatigue lecture, I read some of my
anecdotes to Katy. They seemed kind of fun and funny to me,
but she loved them. She immediately ordered a laptop for me,
providing a keyboard small enough for one-handed typing. It
arrived three days later, and my life changed within hours.

I'm not sure why seeing my words in print gave value to
my caregiving role, but my stock in myself soared. It wasn't that I
suddenly believed in the importance of what I was doing; it was
that I viewed it from an entirely new angle. The creativity fed me.

The routine tasks of caregiving didn't change, though,
even if my new perspective viewed them through a literary eye.
I sat at my kitchen counter, sorting Dad's pills after typing notes
about Mom's birthday party. How many times would I fill these
boxes with his daily medicines and vitamins? It was so odd to
know that the burden of my obligations would be relieved by
death. Death. I couldn't reconcile the slight annoyance of the
task with the enormity of its conclusion.

The truth was that, in between the annoyance and worry,
I genuinely enjoyed my parents. While I made notes about the
highlights and lowlights, there were days and days amid those
incidents that flowed in a normal pattern of a sturdy familial
relationship filled with contentment. I knew now that I would
miss them more than I would ever have imagined at any point
earlier in my life.

I started making a list of what I could do while grieving:
paint the inside of the house in cheerful colors, visit relatives,

204 | While They're Still Here

go to Ireland. But how does one plan for grief? Why was I even trying to? There was no way to predict what was going to happen or how I would deal with it. I needed to trust myself and my band of guardians.

Suddenly, my mother's voice singing "Que Sera, Sera" came into my head and filled me with calm. *That* was how I'd get through it.

Chapter 35

....

I walked over to their apartment after noon to deliver the week's worth of pills, all labeled, color-coded, and sorted by time of day. Their door was always unlocked, so I walked in and sat at the table while they ate their sandwiches. I had left my wheelbarrow filled with tools, duct tape, caulk, and a large piece of Styrofoam outside.

"Thanks so much for the birthday party," Mom gushed. "Judy and Kay both called and laughed so hard they couldn't talk after I told them Chris's funny story."

I didn't soil her mood by asking if she had used the word *funnest*.

"You're welcome. It was fun." Then I casually added, "I brought a piece of Styrofoam to seal up the fireplace if you want me to. It won't be pretty, though. I'll spray foam around all the water pipes, too."

"I don't care how it looks," she answered quickly. "Just seal it up. The sooner the better."

We didn't know where a bat had gotten in, but I knew we'd feel better making any attempt to thwart another encounter. As I was hermetically sealing the fireplace, I remembered the recent bat episode.

It was the essence of a caring-for-my-parents experience. Precious and I had picked up the oldsters to deliver them to the podiatrist for their routine foot care, and then to the grocery store. Dad folded himself into the backseat, and Mom hefted and grunted herself into the front. We were rolling along, making generic chitchat about the glorious day, while I covertly ran a timer in my head to decide which chores I would be able to accomplish after shopping and schlepping. Sunny, warm days are precious few in our climate, and I tried to spend them wisely. Clean the garage roof? Fertilize the grass? Weed the garden? I noticed my good-weather list didn't include canoeing, roller skating, bike riding, reading, or napping in the sun, but I didn't care—I'd learned to live with myself.

Mom was prattling away when my channel tuned back in to hear her say, "Your father caught a bat this morning."

"*Whaaat?*" I screeched, hoping I had misunderstood her or that she'd done one of her clever plays on words. Besides, what was the likelihood that a man who was blind as a bat and terrified of mice could actually catch a furry, flying animal?

"Tell her, Tom." No response. "*Tom!*" she yelled.

He couldn't hear anything in the backseat. She shouted at him again: "Tell her about the bat." No matter that auditory tests confirmed him deaf in one ear, she discredited his hearing loss as personally selective against her.

"Oh. It was nothing," he said. "I was in the bathroom and thought I spotted something crawling under the door. I didn't want to touch it, so I threw that bucket from under the sink over it, grabbed the whole thing up in the rug, and took it outside. Your mother saw it fly away; that's how we knew it was a bat."

"That's amazing, Dad. I thought you hated mice and bats as much as I do."

"I don't just hate them; I'm downright scared of them. But there was no other choice."

This was quintessentially my father: Just do whatever must be done.

I was still driving as my brain lurched into overdrive. We were on a jovial little jaunt for nail trimming and groceries when he might need a rabies shot? They thought this was a cute story? My mother frequently phoned me to detail the antics of a squirrel in the backyard but couldn't have bothered me with this potential medical emergency? I focused on breathing—*in-two-three-four, out-two-three-four*—with a placid expression plastered on my face. I'd get nowhere if they felt punished; they were proud of this misadventure. In their interpretation, they had resolved a problem without pestering me.

Can an eighty-something-year-old tolerate rabies treatment? Dad was adamant he hadn't been bitten, and I examined his hands thoroughly for marks. I remembered from when I lived in Maryland that the health department had recommended shots even for humans in close proximity to bats, because sometimes you didn't know you'd been bitten. Was that the protocol here?

Are there other bats lurking in my parents' apartment? Where did the bat get in? How long can I keep this stupid look on my face and feign congratulations for their prowess? Will I have to take Dad to the VA today? What about my sunshine jobs?

I deposited them at the podiatrist and muttered that I'd be right back after running an errand. *Breathe. Breathe. Breathe. Try to move your shoulders before they calcify.* I called the health department and, after winding my way through several menus, left a message. Not knowing whether the health department would call back in an hour or a week, I started strategizing about my next call: 911? VA? My own doctor? What was the window of time before this became an emergency? *Was* this an emergency?

My phone bugled, and, to my surprise, the caller ID read HEALTH DEPARTMENT. The nurse asked and answered sufficient questions that I felt confident in her advice. The lucky part was that since my father hadn't wanted to touch the bat, he was certain he hadn't been bitten. She reported there was almost no rabies in our county, so contagion was highly unlikely. Whew! What a difference it made to have someone promptly return my call, answer my questions definitively, and announce that there was no problem. That was a rare pattern in this morass of responsibility for cryptic geriatric predicaments. I laid the seat back in the car, wiggled my shoulders, opened the windows, and tuned in to the bird choir, thanking my true guardian angels.

I sealed up the fireplace opening while searching my peripheral vision for small moving objects. Since my parents were equally afraid of fire and bats, it seemed a safe bet we'd leave it covered permanently, and it looked terrible. Mom must have thought so, too, and suggested I take the artificial-flower wreath off the front door and hang it on the fire screen. I fastened it on, and we all agreed that it looked great, but I knew we were lying; we were just relieved.

After I sealed around the pipes and doorframe, I joined them at the table for a cup of coffee. "How can we ever thank you for all this?" Dad said. "All the work you did on the house in Florida, getting us here, taking care of everything." He was teary-eyed and out of breath. I didn't know what had brought on this sentimentality or where it was leading.

"You are so welcome. I'm just glad to have you here," I responded truthfully.

I hadn't seen them the day before, so I gave them a good going-over for color, speech, and mobility, saying, "How are you? Anything I should know about?"

Dad chewed while Mom reported, "Look at that bruise on his arm. Do you think his Coumadin is off?"

I answered, "He goes for blood tests Wednesday, so we can check then."

"You take such good care of us. Thank you. Thanks again for doing Dad's pills. It was just too much for me."

With a serious look on his face, Dad cleared his throat and said, "You do take good care of us. You always did understand health, even as a kid, when you had to convince us to take you to the hospital. You were only nine."

Mom agreed, "That was so terrible. We drove right by the hospital with you moaning and vomiting in the back of the station wagon, begging us to leave you at the emergency room. We never imagined you had appendicitis. And we'd just gotten you out of the hospital a month before, after your accident."

For my ninth birthday, I'd been thrown from a horse and landed in a coma for a week. It was understandable that they hadn't wanted to take me back to the hospital after that trauma.

"It wasn't just driving right past the hospital that was so bad," Dad said. "We drove her two hours to Columbus, left her at Aunt Judy's, went to a football game, and then drove back home. She cried and threw up the whole time, screaming over every bump in the road. It was unforgivable."

Dad frequently apologized to me for this medical nightmare, and I tried to reduce his guilt. "I was sick a lot, so it wasn't surprising that you thought I had the flu." It wasn't until I was much older that I discovered I couldn't digest fats.

Mom justified the trip differently: "Well, it *was* Ohio State and the homecoming game, it was the only time we ever had tickets to a college football game. It was a great game, but by the time we got back to Judy's, you were even worse. We'd planned to stay overnight, but you were too sick, so we went home. I didn't want everyone else getting sick if you were contagious."

My undiagnosed digestive problems made for a childhood gushing with stories highlighting embarrassing vomiting episodes in prominent locations. Prior to my near-death experience of a ruptured appendix, my parents tried to convince me that throwing up was something I could learn to control, alternately praising me and shaming me. They approached it like toilet training, which, in a pitiful sense, it was: I learned to find out where the bathroom was wherever we were and could get there before I missed the target. After serious lecturing from the ER doctors about their negligence when my appendix ruptured, and a strong possibility that I wouldn't live, they treated my problem more compassionately.

I trusted they always *tried* to do what they thought was right, and that was enough for me not to bear any malice. But I had also sensed very early that I'd better be in charge medically and had donned my little nurse's cap.

"Remember how you took care of Betsey?" my mother asked me, in a teasing voice.

Dad and I both gave her a puzzled look, and she explained, "All those times she was suddenly blind?"

I smiled at the thought, then clarified for Dad, "On our first day of kindergarten, Betsey claimed she couldn't see. I walked her all the way to school, holding her hand, telling her when to step over curbs, then up the stairs to her classroom. I can still feel her pigtails slapping my face as she shook her head *no!* when the teacher told me to go to my own class. By then she was acting blind and mute."

I had turned five just six days earlier, but I knew how to take care of Betsey. She was my bride when we played wedding, my wife when we played house. A dainty, delicate girl, she was my constant playmate and first charge. I had a strong suspicion she could see, or she would have been at a doctor's office, instead of walking a mile to school with another five-year-old, but I never questioned her need to pretend.

When the teacher peeled Betsey's fingers off mine and ordered me to my classroom, I felt relieved of my burden. Miraculously, Betsey's sight and voice returned on our way home, when some boys were fighting and it was too good to miss. She had occasional spontaneous relapses, but I was always at the ready.

Yes, I was always at the ready.

Dad chortled about Betsey, then, returning to the appendicitis topic, said to me, "I'm still sorry I made you bend over and tie your own shoes." He had apologized to me hundreds of times for this. I had screamed and cried that I couldn't bend over because my stomach hurt; he still believed he had caused my appendix to rupture at that moment.

Mom said, "It was just so odd that you were sick on every holiday or whenever we went to restaurants. We thought it was emotional, because you were so shy, and we needed to help you get over it. No one thought then that a child couldn't digest fat, or connected it to having rich food on holidays or milkshakes in restaurants. Everyone else was eating the same things you ate. You were always different."

The conversation was hurtling toward objections about my stringent diet, so I said I needed to go home. I handed Dad his pills and finalized arrangements for the next day's outing. I wanted to gather their stories and fold them into my caregiving chronicle without rancor, but some days were more challenging than others. I hoped the good parts spilled out in ink and the bad floated away.

Chapter 36

....

My parents pulled and packed themselves into Precious for appointments and errands. They were always ready on time, and almost always pleasant.

Mom asked, "Did you see that special on FDR last night? There was good information for your book in it."

Hoping to encourage them to reminisce, I had recently mentioned to my parents that I wanted to write a story based loosely on our family. I didn't want them to feel self-conscious about what I might write, but I wanted to get them talking.

"I saw the beginning. I'll watch the rest tonight." I turned my head and shouted so Dad could hear in the backseat. "I had no idea the polio epidemic was that bad."

He grumbled, "We played in a big drainage pipe at the bottom of the hill. They thought that's how I got it. We weren't allowed to go down there. I should have obeyed my mother." He lowered his head, still ashamed of his misbehavior.

Mom said, "Everyone was afraid of polio, and no one knew for sure how it was spread. It was always worse in the summer, so they kept us out of swimming pools and lakes; that was the only prevention we knew. Anytime one of our friends got a sore throat or a headache, they were quarantined. My friend Alice had the sniffles one morning and a couple days later was paralyzed."

"My mother told us not to go near the creek, and the pool was shut down," Dad said. "We were never allowed to go in the culverts, but we did it all the time. That's fifteen minutes I wish I could've undone, just for the trouble I caused her."

Mom continued, "By the time I was old enough to feel safe from it for myself, I had you kids and started worrying all over again. Doctors were working on a vaccine, but it wasn't ready yet. The year you were born was one of the worst years ever for polio. Every day the news got worse. Lots of kids died or lived in iron lungs, some for weeks, some for years, some forever. They looked like coffins to me."

"How did those work?" I asked.

"They had bellows in them that acted like lungs," Mom said.

Dad said, "The iron lung was invented right about the time I had polio. My mother promised me I wouldn't ever have to go in one or have my legs in casts. There was a nurse from Australia who used hot packs and massage to treat polio, and FDR said it worked, so my mother tried it. She massaged my legs for hours every day for weeks, down to my ankles, then apologized to me for the rest of her life for not including my feet. That's why my feet are . . . the way they are."

His feet were severely deformed, but he never used any words describing them. Thankfully, when he had shoes on he walked almost normally, just a little stiff-legged. I wondered what kind of names bullying boys in the locker room had called him. I said, "I remember your mother telling you she was sorry for not massaging your feet."

"I was just glad she saved my legs. The doctor gave me electric-current treatments every day, with one metal plate at the top of my leg and one at the bottom. I missed six months of school, but then I could finally walk with crutches. That's why I graduated late."

"So those were your crutches in Gramma's garage? I never could understand why Aunt Jeannette wouldn't let us play with them. She snapped at us and said they weren't toys."

He said, "My mother kept them in case somebody needed them, but they were a reminder of an awful time. It was hard on the whole family. Things were already bad, there was no work and no money in 1933, and then, while my mother had appendicitis, I got sick. The neighbor saw me crawling when I was nine and called the doctor."

They were quiet for a while; then Mom asked me, "Do you remember going to the school gymnasium for our vaccines?"

"I do; we took it in little paper cups. We were happy not to have shots."

"For me it was a real leap of faith, though," she said, "an act of sheer desperation. A few of the first vaccines had been contaminated and actually caused polio. But the threat of the disease was worse than the possibility of a bad vaccine, so we all marched in."

We were approaching the store, and my parents turned their chatter to buying birdseed and peanuts and to the antics of their well-fed squirrels. So much sorrow and so much strength.

We dropped Mom at the grocery store, and Dad moved into the front seat for the ride to the lab for his blood test. I hadn't washed the insides of the car windows before I'd picked up my parents, and the sun highlighted traces of the dog's nose prints. He stared at them, then said, "It's a message from Mica!" He read it slowly, as if deciphering canine language. "I love you, Grampa."

We both laughed, and I was glad to move on to a lighter subject, but my head was swimming with my parents' recollections. They had talked about sending dimes directly to the White House for FDR's March of Dimes, and how that had become a charity to fight birth defects. I silently remembered my parents' sadness when we went door-to-door, filling our annual fund-raising cards with dimes. I had always thought the sadness was because of Dad's polio, but now I realized it was for their baby Paul's birth defects and death, which they never discussed when we were children. They had borne that sorrow stoically, trying to protect us from it.

I questioned the wisdom of encouraging them to talk about the past. Were they enjoying their stories, or was I dredging up too many bad memories?

Chapter 37

....

Ushering Mom home from a doctor's appointment a few days later, I held the apartment screen door open while she maneuvered her walker over the threshold. She gasped, "Tom!" and moved aside, waving me to hurry around her. Dad stood hunched over the kitchen sink with fluids streaming from his face.

What the hell is this? I thought, as I scrolled through triage. *Head injury? Stroke? Seizure? Why did we leave him home alone?*

I shifted gears to a calm voice: "Hi, Dad. What's going on? Are you okay?"

He spasmodically nodded his head up and down and then back and forth.

As I got closer, I realized he was crying. *Different triage. Who died? Is one of his sisters sick?*

He couldn't talk through his convulsive crying, confining Mom and me in a terror-filled suspense.

He finally choked out, "Printer."

I reasoned that he'd read bad news in an e-mail. *Is my brother okay? Did someone have a bad accident?*

Then he sobbed, "Ink. Broke it."

I was still medically focused and thought he had broken the arm he was now clutching across his retching chest, maybe by having dropped the printer.

"Just relax a little and try to take some deep breaths, Dad. Everything's going to be okay." I wished I knew *what* was going to be okay. "Let's go sit down." I guided him to his chair. Mom was already in hers, now also gasping.

He flung himself down, grabbed the wad of tissues Mom handed him, and strung together "I broke the printer."

I was so relieved that I wanted to laugh, but clearly this was serious, so I said, "It was a really old printer, Dad. We have an extra one at home you can have."

That helped, but I had definitely not addressed the issue. He was still forlorn, crying, blowing his nose, and unable to converse.

After more consolation, he explained, "I wanted to change the ink cartridge. I studied the directions yesterday so I could surprise you with it today. I broke the holder completely off."

In his mind, he had broken an expensive piece of equipment. The career cash register mechanic couldn't change an ink cartridge—how devastating. I felt so sad for him. I realized he used so much energy being brave every day that this one thing had tipped the balance. I'd never seen him this distraught.

"It's complicated, Dad. I can't do ours at home. Katy has to do it."

He stopped crying.

"Maybe it's not really broken. Let's go check it out," I suggested.

Mom brushed her hand across her forehead and mouthed, *Whew.*

Dad followed me into his bedroom and pulled the printer's manual out from his CCTV. "I followed all the directions exactly," he lamented.

I sat down in front of the open carcass of the printer and read the pamphlet he handed me. While I studied it, I tried

218 | While They're Still Here

to convince him that printers were inexpensive and had to be replaced every few years to keep up with technology, but that just didn't ring true to him. In his generation, you took care of things and fixed them until they deteriorated completely.

"You did everything right, Dad. Here's the problem: The instructions are for all the models made by this company. They picture the color cartridge on the left, but yours is on the right. I would have done the same thing you did. Nowhere in all these instructions do they even mention that the colored ink might be on the right."

He wasn't convinced. I think he imagined I was just trying to make him feel better. I had to repeat how poor the directions were to Mom, in his presence, before he accepted that was the problem.

All the while, I had the knowledge that he had asked me two weeks earlier to change that cartridge. It was on my list, but with no urgency. I was still learning priorities, obviously—a difficult way to learn, laced with plenty of guilt.

I was getting ready to leave, but he still looked dejected. I said, "I was thinking about finalizing the plan for adding more lights to the dollhouse this afternoon. Want to help me?" Truthfully, I was thinking about falling into a coma on my couch, but he needed a diversion worse than I needed a nap.

"Sure. I'll get my jacket. Maybe I'd better change my shirt. It's wet. Can you wait that long?"

On the way to my house, I complimented Dad on the complicated wiring he had installed in the dollhouse that my grandfather had built. It was a beautiful house, displayed prominently in my dining room. I sadly remembered that Dad had wired it the year before he had lost his sight, but didn't mention that. "Oh, right," he said. "I forgot about that. That was our last vacation out here before you moved us, wasn't it?" We were probably both calculating how long he'd been struggling with blindness.

After I let Mica out to greet us, we all crammed into my workshop. I was refurbishing the dollhouse Dad built, the one we had brought from Florida. I planned on upgrading the lighting, wall coverings, trim, flooring, and fixtures from a kid's "play" level to an adult "look at" level.

I pointed to the chalk lines where the grooves needed to be cut to run all the new wires, thinking we would look at the plan and discuss the hookups and then he would go home.

Taking off his coat, he asked, "Where is your Dremel tool?"

When he had it in his hand, he said, "A big round bit works the best."

I fastened one in the collet, and he aimed for the dollhouse. I quickly made the chalk lines heavier and turned on a high intensity light.

"Put the bit on the line," he requested.

I had planned on carving the tiniest, tidiest little grooves in dollhouse history—some sort of dental hygiene quirk about quality work in microscopic locations—but quickly let that idea go. Flooring and wallpaper would ultimately cover the grooves.

"Okay, let's start in the master bedroom," I said, setting the bit on the line, then turning on the Dremel.

He stood there for an hour and a half and cut every groove perfectly. I guided him verbally for every millimeter, but he accomplished all the cutting himself. He was exhausted and content when he was done. I was so glad I hadn't tried to prevent a failure by not letting him attempt it. One day when I needed a memory to fill a hole in my heart, it would be a wonderful reminder, and a precious part of the provenance of that house.

Chapter 38

....

Dad and I were tending their garden when he started telling me that he had just seen on the news that a professional ice-skater had been struck in the face by her partner's skate. He said she was badly injured, and he was visibly shaken by it.

I scoured my sack of segues to find a way to reroute the topic. "Remember that great skating rink at the end of our street?"

He laughed. "I'll never forget the first time I took you and your sister skating. You were only three or four years old, but we bundled you both up and walked down the street, and I laced up your skates while you sat on a log by the fire. I told you both to stay there until I could get my skates on and help you, but you just skated off together like you had been doing it for years."

He continued reminiscing. "A neighbor gave me my first pair of skates for helping him clean out his basement. I loved to ice-skate."

"How old were you?"

"It was after I had polio, so I was probably eleven or twelve. They had wide blades and were good to learn on. Nelson and I skated on the lakes and rivers all over town. We roller-skated everywhere, too. My roller skates were the only reason I didn't run away."

He paused, giving me a Cheshire-cat smile to let me take the bait.

"Why was that?"

"I was mad at my mother and told her I was running away. I sat on the front steps to hook on my skates, and she said, 'You're not taking those skates. Your father bought those.' So I didn't go. I loved my skates."

The freedom of skating must have been powerful after months of crawling, then crutches, then finally walking again.

I asked, "Why were you helping a neighbor clean his basement?"

"I did lots of odd jobs for spending money. I ran errands and lit the furnace on the Sabbath for the Orthodox Jewish family across the street. I worked at Isaly's ice cream shop; they had huge vats of ice cream and a V shaped scoop so the ice cream went all the way to the bottom of the cone. I swept the floor at the dry cleaner's, then started helping with deliveries. I ran the laundry to the customers' doors so the driver could get more done."

Running after polio, I thought.

"What did you do with the money you earned?" I asked, trying to prolong the memory.

"Spent it," he answered, shaking his head in disgrace.

"On what?"

"Well, the first thing I bought with my own money was a beautiful brown leather bomber jacket.

He was quiet for a moment, then admitted, "Mostly pinball machines, though. My mother would have killed us if she'd known."

"You weren't allowed to play pinball machines?"

"She considered it gambling. The machines were all owned by the Mob; the store owner got a cut, but not much. The machines were rigged so you couldn't win, but we figured out a way."

"What did you do?"

He gave me a guilty *don't tell my mother* look, then confessed, "Well, probably ten or twelve of us huddled around the machine so no one could see what we were doing. Then we drilled a hole in the side, slid in a wire, and rolled the score up. We won a big payout, but then we couldn't ever go back, in case they caught on. We kept playing the Bug, though. Everybody played the Bug. Except my mother."

"What was the Bug?"

"Penny bets on the last three digits of the closing number of the stock market that day. The odds were five hundred to one. My friend's mother issued the papers, then collected the bets right before the market closed."

"Did the Mob run that game, too?"

"Probably. Gangsters were powerful in Youngstown, since it was located between Pittsburgh and Cleveland. Did you ever hear of the Jungle Inn? You should write about that place."

"No. What was that?'

"It started as a brothel, but then it turned into a casino. It was pretty famous. When I went into the service, lots of guys from all over knew about it. The door even had a little window they slid open to see who was there before letting people in, just like in the movies. It was during Prohibition, you know, but it was two miles out of town, so the local cops didn't have any authority."

"Did you go there?"

"No!" he shouted. Then he confessed, "Well, we rode our bikes out there and hid in the weeds to watch. There were a lot of fancy cars in that parking lot. You ever hear of a Youngstown tune-up?"

"No. What was that?"

"Assassination in a car by rigging the ignition to a bomb. Really. Look it up on the computer, but don't put it in your book. It makes Youngstown seem worse than it was."

"You were lucky you didn't get caught seeing something you shouldn't have."

"Or, worse than that, if my mother found out we went there," he conceded.

"I was thinking about all my jobs yesterday," he went on. "I always worked, but after I was discharged from the Navy when Nelson died, I went home to nothing—no job, no money, no skills, no car. I lived with Shookie and Bob. Susie was about four; Robbie wasn't born yet. Bob got me a job at Thew Shovel in Lorain. I had to work his shift, three to eleven, so I could ride with him, but I hated those hours."

"So that was when Susie wanted to play wedding all the time. She said you were a good sport about marrying her over and over."

It took him a moment to locate that memory, but then he said, "She dressed up in Shookie's lacey slips with a crocheted doily on her head and played the wedding march on the record player. She was the first baby in the family, and she was a doll."

"Susie told me that during the war, she and Aunt Shookie lived with your parents while her dad was overseas."

"I think they did. Nelson and I were both away in the service by then, too."

"She said she was the only one home with Gramma when the telegram came saying Nelson had been killed. She said Gramma started wailing, and she just hid behind a chair. Gramma couldn't stop crying long enough to tell her what happened. Susie was only three."

"I didn't know that. Poor Susie."

I immediately wished I hadn't told him. He felt it as a fresh tragedy for his beloved first niece, now in her sixties. I needed to redirect.

"Susie said she loved it when you stayed with them, especially the pranks you played on each other."

"We had fun. There was a balcony over the back porch. One really hot day I sneaked up there with ice water and poured a whole bucket on them while they were sunbathing."

He continued, in a wistful tone, "I finally moved out and bought a car for three hundred dollars. She was a beauty—a 1938 white, four-door Lincoln Zephyr. Red interior." He paused with a faraway look, seeing it in his mind's eye. "I had to sell her, though, in exchange for room and board when I went to work at NCR. I was so lucky to get that job. The company was good to me for forty years. I just found some papers that said my job title was district supervisor, not just office manager." He was as proud at that moment as he would have been if he had just been promoted.

"And then, of course, there were the Green Stamp bonuses every year," he said.

"Those were from NCR?" I asked. The Green Stamp Store annual shopping spree was unforgettable. My parents didn't buy frivolous items as a rule, although my mother did manage to spend my dad's entire paycheck on what she loosely defined as necessities. The Green Stamp Store was different, though. We were allowed to pick out whatever we wanted, and the atmosphere was about as madcap as we ever got; this was free money.

"Yes," he said, "in the 1960s, NCR gave repairmen bonuses if we sold fifty-two or more maintenance agreements for cash registers in a year. They gave us the bonus in Green Stamps."

"So every year that we had a Green Stamp bonanza, you met or exceeded that quota?"

"That's right. I sold a lot of machines and contracts."

It was a feather in his cap that we had all enjoyed; I just hadn't known about the feather at the time.

We reminisced about his cronies over the years at the company until I went home. Jotting down the highlights of his stories, I realized he was still filled with emotion about things that had happened in his younger days, yet we had never talked about them. Did he think about these things routinely and keep them inside intentionally? Was I finally a good listener? What if I had never been given this opportunity, or had been offered it but not taken it?

When I originally envisioned caring for my parents, I hadn't an inkling of thought that years of deepening companionship would be a part of the package. I thanked my guardian angels for guiding us in those early days, somehow lighting the path for us to put down our swords and start fresh with each other.

Chapter 39

....

The moment the phone jarred me awake at two in the morning, I flashed through possible emergencies. Caller ID flung me up on my feet, scrambling for the light. Before I finished saying hello, Dad said, "Your mother fell. Can you come over?" I pulled out my jeans from the folded pile I intentionally prepared at my bedside every night like a fireman and nodded yes to Katy's questioning point toward her clothes. We'd raced to emergency rooms in the middle of the night for sick dogs, friends' diabetic comas, and heart attacks. I'd survived windstorms, floods, earthquakes, and a volcanic eruption, but this phone call rendered me weak in the knees.

I was responsible for this one, and my hands were shaking, even though I had rehearsed this scenario a thousand times since my parents had moved here. There was no fairy-tale ending to this chapter of our lives, and I had no idea when the last paragraph was coming or how it read. Was this it? Katy often chided me that the light at the end of the tunnel was a freight train or two.

"Did you call 911?" I asked Dad, knowing he hadn't. I was their emergency number.

"No. She thinks we can help her get up. We don't want to wake everyone up with a siren." I kept him on the phone long enough to get a trace on his condition. He seemed calm; his breathing was regular.

"Okay. I'll be right there. I'll call 911 and see if they'll come without a siren, just in case we need them."

"Thanks. I unlocked the door." I knew the conversation was over when his phone clattered as he searched for the base to hang it up.

He was inexperienced at phone use; my mother, who had aggressively guarded her job as family phone operator their whole life, had hampered him. When we were kids, even teen agers, it didn't matter who was closest to the phone—Mom answered. We didn't question it. She called me once or twice a day now, with tidbits of information, questions, or problems. If Dad called, my heartbeat increased and I started looking for my jacket; something was going to require action.

The first call I remember my father initiating was shortly after my parents moved to Florida in 1989, during one of my mother's darker decades. After a terse "Hi, it's Dad," he spurted, "Yourmotherhadabreastremovedtodayandshe'sfine."

Whoa, I thought. *Back up here. Back way up.* I knew I needed to stay calm, because I didn't want him to have a heart attack on the phone, but I was lost. "Sorry, Dad. I couldn't hear you."

"Your mother had a breast removed today and she's fine." He'd rehearsed the line, and that was all he could deliver.

"Why?" I asked, completely shocked. How could she have cancer and I not know? Even though she was drinking heavily, I called early every Saturday morning before she hit the bottle; if I called after noon or so, bitter ranting lashed across the phone line.

"The doctor found cancer three days ago, but your mother didn't want to worry you."

While there was truth to that, I knew she needed to handle her own emotions without someone hovering, and she needed to drink at her own dosage, unimpeded by a judgmental daughter.

By the time I had arranged to be off work and flew to Florida, my mother had acquired a few doses of radiation, two cemetery niches, and sets of keys to the mausoleum for each of us. We toured the mausoleum, reenacting the cemetery excursions of my childhood. I wanted to stride through, view the spot, and get out. Mom sat, admired the building, sang along with the piped-in melodies, and made light conversation. Dad paced in a slow circle around the perimeter. I settled down, realizing my mother was preparing us by painting living memories, weaving bandages for our future wounds. She missed her own parents every minute of her life.

A fire truck and a medic van, noisy even without sirens, roared me back to the present. Four clean-cut, strapping young men disembarked from the truck, racing toward the steps; I halted them against their will, feeling like I had a hand on their chests while their feet were still spinning.

I hurriedly summarized, "I'm their daughter. My mom's down; she's alert and okay. But my father has a very serious heart condition. Don't upset him."

They sauntered into the apartment as if dropping by an old friend's house for a midnight snack.

One took me aside for records, one occupied Dad, and two went to Mom. The head honcho was a handsome black male, and I wondered how Mom's prejudices would play out. He knelt down beside her and cradled her contorted shoulders where she was pinned against the sharp edge of the bathroom doorframe. His voice was soft and reassuring. "I just want to ask a few questions before we help you get up. Is that okay?"

She rested her head on his chest. "I feel better already." Her prejudices were blanket judgments that often didn't pertain to individuals, so she latched on to him as her savior. He assessed her condition, and they gracefully lifted her up and helped her walk to her bedroom. They left, saying, "Call us if you need us again," which held an ominous tone of prediction to me.

Katy and I stayed and chatted for a few minutes, until I was satisfied with my parents' vital signs, before going home. It was four in the morning, but I was too stressed to go back to bed. I made coffee and worried. Would Dad have a reaction to the stress—a stroke, perhaps? Was Mom's back injured? Should I call her orthopedist? Why had she fallen?

The phone shrilled directly into my nervous system an hour later. Mom said tremulously, "I need to go to the hospital. I can't move my left leg. I think I broke my artificial knee again." I said I would be there in a few minutes and that I'd call 911 after I had a chance to wake up Dad.

"I can't get out of bed to unlock the door," she said, sounding terrified and trapped.

"I'll bring my key. You just try to relax and focus on breathing nice and slow." I hung up, questioning whether we should have gone to the hospital three hours ago; had there been irreparable damage?

I dreaded the hospital, but at least it wasn't her right leg, the one with the brand-new hip re-replacement. Remembering the details of that recent episode made my stomach lurch, and I didn't want either of us to relive them. For a month after her risky surgery to remove a broken hip replacement and install a new one, ambulances had carted her back and forth between the rehab center and the hospital when medication changes caused unexpected, life-threatening electrolyte imbalances.

I unlocked their door, told Mom I was there, and went to Dad's room. How should I wake up a blind, partially deaf person with a noisy oxygen machine on his face without scaring him into an angina attack? I stood in his door and delivered my usual greeting. "Hi, Dad. It's me." He woke up calmly and fully alert. I had my pitch prepared. "Mom thinks her knee should be X-rayed, so we're going to the hospital."

Always pragmatic, he asked, "Are you driving or taking an ambulance?"

"I guess we'll take the ambulance so she doesn't have to get in the car," I answered, pretending the choice had nothing to do with the fact that she couldn't move her leg. He didn't need to know that yet.

The same paramedic crew was still on shift and stormed in this time with a mission: extract an oversize, immobile, frail body racked with pain from a warren of wall-to-wall furniture. Scrambling as if the house were on fire, they left the gurney in the driveway and scuttled by me with a tarp, ignoring my advice to push aside some furniture and wheel the gurney in the back door.

They rocked and rolled Mom back and forth, over her groans and whimpers, sliding a large tarp under her. She shrieked as they hoisted her up and wedged her through doors, curving her into the hallway, then squeezed her screeching body past a bulky cabinet in the hallway and seesawed her up and down as they lugged her up the stairs.

Dad, Katy, and I were dumbstruck by our inability to help, shooting each other questioning appeals from saucer eyes. It was hard to believe what we were witnessing. The medics were determined to move her quickly, yet her pain wrenched by us in slow motion.

Why hadn't I planned for access for a gurney?

I entrusted Dad to Katy and followed the medic van as it crawled along at twenty miles an hour. I knew they were creeping at a snail's pace because Mom was harnessed flat on her crumpled back, moaning, or possibly screaming, over every bump. She squawked in the car at every little chuckhole under the best circumstances, always comparing it to her calamitous foray down the basement steps on her tricycle as a four-year-old. She had recently added the detail that she'd pulled the bike out of someone's trash and it had no tires.

The ER was full tilt at six o'clock. After we'd waited ninety grueling minutes for a doctor, a nurse passed by the room, noticed Mom's level of pain, and returned immediately with morphine. Mom grew quiet and stopped grimacing. When the nurse asked if the meds were working, Mom sang the Alka-Seltzer jingle about what a relief it was.

Hours of X-rays, CT scans, and blood tests later, the doctor reported, "Good news. Your artificial hip is fine, and there is no damage to the artificial knee hardware, just a hairline bone fracture above it. If you can put pressure on it, you can go home." The nurses translated my panic-stricken face as they followed the doctor out the curtain. I heard them verifying that Mom was in excruciating pain and had limited mobility under normal conditions, referring him to her previous hospital records. With agitation, the doctor agreed to admit her for one day.

I set Dad up with food, rearranged the apartment for gurney access, and resumed the "Mom's in the hospital" schedule that we'd established after her hip surgery. I went to the hospital at daybreak, picked up Dad at noon to take him back to the hospital with me, drove him home, then finished my day with a final check-in at the hospital. I knew from previous experience that I needed to be at the hospital as much as possible to supervise and advocate for Mom's care.

After five days, an ambulance transferred Mom to the rehab wing of the nursing home—coincidentally, the same room she'd been in and out of a few times the previous year. I helped her settle in, then left to check on Dad. The apartment was laundered, vacuumed, dusted, and tidy. Everything appeared shipshape, except him. Was he just tired? Had he done something strenuous and was now experiencing the aftermath of nitroglycerin for his angina?

"Whatcha been doin' today?" I casually conversed.

"Nothing. I didn't even get up until ten."

That was very unlike him and took me down a different part of the "What's Going on Here?" flowchart. Breathing normally: check. Walking okay: check. Using both hands equally: check. Coffeepot still on: whoops.

"Do you want the coffeepot off, Dad?" He was surprised he had forgotten to turn it off. That called for more direct questioning: "How do you feel?"

"Fine."

"You seem tired."

"Oh."

My questions weren't eliciting the information I needed. "Did something happen that you don't want to worry me about?" I could ask that because he would not lie under any circumstances. He assured me he was fine, nothing was wrong.

"Do you want to skip seeing Mom today?" He had seemed disoriented the previous day when we had visited Mom, and I'd had to repeat conversations to keep him included. I couldn't figure out why he couldn't focus. Background noise? Too many people coming and going? Bad memories? I didn't know and hoped it was a short-term, situational problem.

He answered, with a heavy sigh, "I have to go. What would she think if I didn't?"

"She'd want you to take care of yourself."

He challenged that and we volleyed a few times before he acknowledged he was tired and could use the rest. I left hoping I wasn't on the verge of a gruesome story where I had to tell my mother in the nursing home that her husband was in the hospital, or worse.

Chapter 40

....

Two weeks later, Mom was still immobile, black and blue from head to toe, and hurting everywhere. Her bruised ribs made breathing and moving difficult. Her arms were completely beaten up from multiple failed attempts at blood draws to monitor her chronic electrolyte problem. She knew that the two criteria for going home from the rehab center were to get in and out of bed without help, and on and off the toilet by herself, yet she opted for a bedpan. How long was this going to go on?

I spent plenty of time with her, but Dad visited only briefly every few days. He couldn't explain his feelings, but I could tell seeing her immobilized unnerved him, so I provided excuses for him not to go.

They finally decided to discharge her after three weeks of very little progress. Precious and I arrived at the nursing home to pick up Mom, not knowing how she would get in or out of the car; it had never been easy for her to begin with and would be much worse now. She had spent the last two days telling me how well she was doing and how much she was walking in the halls, so I tried to hope for the best. My doubts rested on the flaw that she recounted her achievements from her bed, never leaving it in my presence, despite my encouragements.

I'd rasped around my house all morning, anxious and angry. How would I manage all this? I reminded myself to deal with what was in front of me, not fifteen feet into a future that might never appear. Today all I had to do was drive to the nursing home, compress my mother's stiffened limbs into the car, drive home, and extract her. There were people doing truly hard things in their lives, and this wasn't in the running. Nevertheless, I was stressed. I looked up and asked my troupe to rescue me. They wafted me up, swaddled me in a cloud, and reminded me I was never alone. Call it creative visualization or creative craziness—I felt better.

"Hi, Mom. Ready to go home?"

"Am I ever. Yesterday they gave me the worst bath of my life: cold water, a rough washcloth, shoving me this way and that. It was—"

I'd heard enough and interrupted her. "Where's your stuff?"

"It's still in the closet. No one's been in to help me. I need the bedpan."

I noticed she wasn't dressed. "Are they still releasing you today?"

"Yes," she answered, as she buzzed for a nurse.

"Mom, there's no bedpan at home. Maybe you should use the bedside commode."

"Oh, all right. Help me, then."

I was stunned when she could not stand at all without her walker and could not take a step without extreme effort. The facility evidently had a much looser interpretation of her meeting the goals for discharge than I had envisioned. Maybe she should have stayed longer, but I knew she would have more activity at home, if I could get her there. Finally, the nurses packed her belongings and stuffed her into the car, and I listened all the way home to her complaints about the bad bath.

I sidled Precious as close to their back door as possible, over the grass and dangerously close to the edge of the cliff, while neighbors streamed out of their apartments to welcome Mom home. Four men gently raised her out of the car and assisted her into the apartment, giving us all a boost. Dad was swimming in sentiment and gratitude for her arrival and reception. I settled her at the table, said I'd be back after a bit, and turned her over to Dad's care.

An hour later, he called me in a breathless panic. "Your mother can't get out of her bed. It's too high. Can you bring some boards over and we'll take out the box spring?"

I knew that made perfect sense to him, but there wasn't enough room to stand the mattress aside to remove the box spring. Also, I didn't have the energy to measure and cut wood and wasn't strong enough to lift a mattress. None of those reasons would sway him, so I didn't bother explaining.

"I'll be right over. But don't do anything. Maybe she can use the sofa bed." I imagined him trying to lift an extra-thick, full-size mattress by himself to save me the trouble.

We decided Mom would use Dad's hospital bed and he'd sleep in his recliner. Mom remained stuck in her bed and afraid to try to get out. She froze in place and demanded that I roust neighbors to help her move to Dad's room.

All three of us were alarmed at her condition. Mom was wild-eyed, and Dad was frazzled.

"I don't think you can call a neighbor every time you need to get up. Do it like you did at the nursing home. Grab the walker, sit up, swing your legs over."

She angrily relented, and we moved her to Dad's room. I retreated to the dining room to regroup while Dad organized his apnea equipment in the living room, with the TV blaring.

"Tom." "Tom." "*Tom!*" He couldn't hear her.

I went to see what she wanted, handed her the tissues she'd requested, and returned to the dining room. Now I was wild-eyed and frazzled. The phone rang; an upstairs neighbor had heard Mom yelling and offered their baby monitor, a solution that had never occurred to me.

After setting it up and having Mom and Dad practice listening and talking on the monitor, I was ready to say good-bye, but Mom was still a deer in headlights. I said, "Call me when you need to get up, and I'll come over. I don't think you'll need me, because you really did it on your own last time, but I'll come over just in case."

That didn't help—she was trembling and biting her lip—so I pulled out the big guns. "Mom, you have to get past this. You're stuck in that brain-trap thing you do where you remember the pain, instead of focusing on the present and future." We'd been through this after her hip surgery.

"I know. I just keep thinking about falling, and I'm afraid to walk."

"Put all that worry in a little box and throw it away. Think about walking gracefully, going wherever you want, dancing."

As I passed the photo of my father's mother in the hallway, she reached out and stopped me. She stared deep into my eyes, thanking me and assuring me she was with us. Even so, I walked home more depressed than ever. Should Mom go back to the nursing home? Should I stay over there? Both choices deflated me. I'd search for fresh ideas tomorrow.

The phone rang minutes after I was home. Already? It was Mom, saying calmly, "Don't worry, everything is fine. I'm up and in the dining room. I'm going to have something to eat. You cured me. Thank you. I love you."

"Mom, I'm so impressed that you jumped that hurdle. You are remarkable."

"You made it possible."

What more could a daughter/caregiver want? Many people have said to me they wish they could have, or had, cared for their parents. It could be very gratifying when you weren't too worn out to notice.

I rounded up a free hospital bed, including rails and a trapeze; experimented with various prescriptions to treat Mom's blood pressure, pain, and electrolyte imbalance; prepared meals for them; supervised visiting nurses; and tried to maintain some order in my own household. All the time, lurking at the edge of my energy, was the question *What's next?*

Chapter 41

....

Next was a surprise visit to the ER, but I suppose they all are. Three days after the nursing home released Mom, we were hunkered down in a full ER waiting room because of Mom's critically low sodium, the result of a new diuretic.

Mom shivered and turned blue, even though she was bundled in a wheelchair with every jacket, towel, and dog seat cover I had retrieved from the car. I pleaded repeatedly with the clerk to advance her in the queue, to no avail. There were well over a hundred people in the waiting room, pacing, crying, vomiting, wailing: teens with toothaches, babies with rashes, every age with appendages trussed in bandages.

Many hours later, she was finally admitted and tucked into a warm bed. After seeing her bruises, every nurse and doctor found some subtle way to determine whether Mom was an abuse victim. They casually asked questions about her home life, eliciting her knight-in-shining-armor narratives. I could have told them that Dad still apologized to me for the one and only time he ever spanked me when I was a child.

Leaving the hospital, I had flashes of the long-term impact of this piece of our life story, while my mother's voice sang in my head "You'll Never Walk Alone." I knew that at some point, today would be another page in my book. Would it fill a paragraph or a sentence? By then, would it be more intellectual memory than crushing pain? How many times would I walk out these hospital doors, wondering what I needed to do next to assure a good outcome?

Inevitably, the day will come when there will be only me to take care of at the end of a hospital trip. Will I be able to write in the midst of grief? Will Mom's beautiful soprano still be the soundtrack refueling my strength?

When I went over to their apartment on that warm, sunny day with a breeze off the lake and Dad sitting at the table, having his plain bologna sandwich for lunch, I realized how unprepared I was for this part of their lives to end or even change. They had been so happy here.

Days later, Mom was still in the hospital, with her pain, pain meds, fluids, and electrolytes out of control. She had a joke ready for the nurse the next time she came in. "Here's how the IV bag works: As the bag goes down"—Mom sucked in her cheeks—"I go up." She puffed up her cheeks. Though Mom was consistently considerate with the nurses, this one obviously hadn't expected humor from her aged, infirm patient and had a good laugh.

I washed her face, straightened her covers, and found a 1940s channel on the hospital's music network. Mom started singing along right away, then stopped and announced, "This was my theme song."

Her theme song? Is she delirious? Has she had a stroke? Is she hallucinating from a medication error?

"What song is that, Mom?"

"'Laura,'" she answered with élan. "Whenever I entered a nightclub in Washington, DC, or Athens, the band would break into this song."

This was big news to me. I didn't know she had enjoyed that level of renown; the topic was verboten. In my lifetime, she had acknowledged events of her first marriage only one time, when I expressed confusion about marriage and birth dates when I was twelve. Aside from a vague remark about her life in Athens when we were still in Florida, she had never made any reference to it. Ever.

From the serene look on my mother's face, I knew she was enjoying reminiscing, medication error or not. "Did you go up and sing along with the band then?" I asked, hoping to keep the story going.

"Oh, sometimes the audience would clap and I'd do a song or two. Sometimes they'd give us the floor and we'd dance."

Was I in the wrong room? *Dance? We?*

"You were a good dancer," I said. "I remember you dancing around the house, singing."

"I was pretty good, but Fritz danced like Fred Astaire. He was tall and elegant and floated across the floor. We always ended to a big round of applause, and he'd bow with a flourish and twirl me."

My mother had never uttered the name Fritz, my sister's father, out loud in my presence. He had been persona non grata until this moment. Like a newspaper reporter with a juicy tip, I dug for all I could get.

"How did you meet him?" I asked—my way of saying, *Start at the beginning.*

"At a roller-skating rink in Buffalo. He skated like he danced and was so handsome; it was love at first sight, even though I was only fifteen. He was eighteen and leaving for the Air Force, and my family was moving back to Ohio. I dated other boys, but he was the only one for me.

"Then, on my eighteenth birthday, I was sitting on the porch and glanced down the street and there he appeared like a mirage, walking toward me in his dress uniform. It was a complete surprise. He gave me my engagement ring that day."

"When did you get married?"

"September 9, 1945. His mother called my mother and told her not to let me marry him, claiming he was too wild. But they didn't like me much, anyhow. His grandmother said I had a false laugh." She frowned, still hurt by the comment.

"Did you move to DC right away?"

She nodded yes and went on, "The war was over, and he was working for the Diplomatic Corps as a cryptographer. We had a nice apartment on Quinn in Arlington, just across the river from all the monuments."

"Were you happy?"

"Very. I felt like I was in a fairy tale. He worked a lot, especially after he joined the CIA, but I walked everywhere and knew every inch of DC after three years."

"Did you work?"

"I worked at the Federal Housing building, filing. It was boring, but it was right downtown, so that was fun. I made friends, and we explored the monuments and museums together. A couple of them sang, so we formed a trio."

"So you sang in nightclubs in DC?"

"Oh, yes. I modeled, too. Have you seen those photos?"

Photos? Modeling? My fuses were blowing. I said, "No, I don't think so," hoping my voice wasn't tainted with disbelief

"Well, they're in an envelope somewhere. I quit when the photographer wanted me to do nudes. But DC was the best place I ever lived. There was always something to do. I remember sitting on a hillside overlooking the Potomac and listening to music from a floating platform in the Tidal Basin, with Lee's mansion magically suspended in the dark above it."

Mom rambled on, "Fritz was transferred to Greece right after Linda was born, but I stayed behind a few months before making the trip with a newborn. It was a terrible flight, but she was a good baby. We had to stop in Shannon, Ireland, because of bad weather in the Azores. They bunked us in a hostel, and the only thing to eat was mutton soup. It was awful. The thing I

remember the most, though, is the Alps. They were more beautiful than anyone could ever describe."

I knew my mother had a good memory, but this was out-
rageous. What were the Azores, and how had she remembered
that? Mutton soup? The Alps? The Tidal Basin and Lee's mansion? Who was this?

"What was it like in Greece?" I asked, trying to sound casual.

"We lived in northern Athens, in a ritzy neighborhood
called Kifissia. Fritz had rented a beautiful villa made of marble
and stone, with vine-covered verandas upstairs and down. My
maid, Maria, didn't speak English, but I learned Greek fast."

She rattled off a dozen Greek words and their English
counterparts to prove her point.

"Maria showed me all the ruins the first week I was there.
There were signs all over the Parthenon about not touching or
taking anything, under penalty of law. But it was crumbling
right before our eyes, and a piece fell right in my shoe! Can you
believe it? It was a painful walk down the Acropolis with a rock
in my shoe, but I saved that shard of marble. I might still have it
somewhere. I never told Maria."

After a pause, she continued, "There was destruction from
the war everywhere. Even across the street from our house, there
was an abandoned orphanage full of bullet holes, and a bombed-
out monastery. But the World Wars and the Greek Civil War
were over and we didn't think about it much. It was so exciting to
live in an ancient world. You should go there sometime."

"You had a maid?" I knew I should compose an intelligent
question about relics and statues, but the idea of my mother
having had a maid interested me more.

"I had lots of household help. Your sister learned Greek
from her nanny before she learned English. Sanitation was
hard, though. Potable water ran only two hours a day, and the
public pit toilets were sickening.

"I traveled all over with my girlfriends from the American Club. One time we took a boat to Crete and rented a house for the weekend. We went sightseeing to the Cave of Zeus. It was ninety degrees outside and went down to fifteen degrees inside the cave. I passed out; they called it heatstroke. I didn't see much of the cave."

"Did you sing in Greece?" I asked.

"Well, Fritz entertained visiting ambassadors and bigwigs with parties at our house. After I made my entrance down the staircase, Fritz would escort me to our grand piano, and my trio and I would sing for the audience. It was pretty exotic for a poor girl from Buffalo. Too good to last."

"Did you have fancy clothes to perform in?" I expected this to lead down another avenue of pleasant meanderings

"No. Fritz wore beautiful hand-tailored clothes, but I had only what my mother sent me. He wouldn't give me any money. He didn't want me to outshine him."

She hesitated, then continued, "I knew when he packed his white dinner suit for a supposed business trip to Corfu that he was having an affair. I found out it was with the other girl in my trio, my friend. There I was, alone in a foreign country, with a toddler and no money."

She hesitated, and I saw a brief but familiar distant sorrow take over her face. My mother had carried this sadness every day of her life, and it slipped out on rare occasions.

"My family took up a collection and wired money to me, and I sailed home. We stopped in Naples, and I rolled Linda's stroller all over the brick streets, *clankety-clank*, to see everything I could in twenty-four hours. The food was awful in Italy. But then we arrived in Boston and they served us lobster dinners. I ate two! That was the best part of the trip."

She lowered her voice in a conspiratorial way. "Did you know Fritz called from time to time, wanting to talk to Linda? Sometimes he would say how much he missed me and how beautiful I was. Until he died in 1972, I was terrified one of you kids or your dad would answer the phone sometime when he called."

Aha! The answer to her control of the phone all those years.

Her hospital dinner arrived, distracting her from the past to the present. I said my good-byes and left, hoping my memory would hold until I could write down what she had described. I doubted I would remember the details or trust my imagination if it weren't in ink. Theme song. Modeling photos. A nanny and maids. Entertaining ambassadors. Maybe *I* was hallucinating.

I lobbied hard for her release after a week of unsuccessful experiments to balance her electrolytes and pain meds, and finally packaged her up and smushed her into Precious. By the time I drove her home, neighbors extricated her from the car, and we scootched her into the apartment, she was ready for bed. So was I. Unfortunately, tomorrow's list was boxing inside my brain. How much care would she need?

We limped along in a new routine, yet, five weeks after she fell, Mom was still wearing a nightgown all day, wasn't fixing any of her own food or drink, and was shuffling from the bedroom to the bathroom to the dining room with the aid of a walker. She wasn't attempting any of her physical therapy, her oxygen was low, and the home health nurse expressed concern about pneumonia. Mom girded herself with nasty retorts, armed and loaded for anyone who mentioned diet or exercise.

The summer was slipping away, so I focused on the mountains of mundane tasks to complete at my house and their apartment before winter—things I could actually fix, since I was making no progress repairing my mother. She *was* feeling well enough to find things for me to do—a mixed blessing. She ordered me to tighten this, move that, or glue those together. I resumed my normal level of simmering irritability, the specter of losing my parents recessing into the shadows.

By late September, my mother began improving, creating a ripple effect in my mood. On my way to their apartment, the rich, crisp air was interspersed with floating pools of warmth like a spring-fed lake. The only sounds were birds singing, squirrels rustling, and the occasional train aria at the crossing. I knew I would return home with three new things on my list (one that I meant to do but had forgotten, one that I would forget, and one that would enter triage), but I willed myself to bask in the moment. Someday I would wish so hard I could walk across the street and see them.

Their door was open, and soup smells welcomed me through the screen door. Mom was at her Command Post, dressed, combed, and rouged, her face radiating a reminder of her youthful beauty. Ohio State football blared from the TV, and they were both cheering, completing my familial autumn scene. I absorbed the warmth, fragrance, and sentimentality and bottled the essence for my memory bank.

By the first of October, I was beginning to feel caught up but didn't delude myself into thinking this was more than a brief pause in the chaos called my life.

Chapter 42

·······························

Three months after Mom's tumble, things were returning to what we considered normal by then. I sat at my clean kitchen counter, eerily happy, enjoying a fresh cup of coffee and the newspaper, uncannily conscious of being up, dressed, exercised, and fed by six thirty. I had cleaned the house the day before—no longer a routine chore, just something to fit in when the time was available. The dog was groomed and bathed. I was too calm.

Brrrring, demanded the phone, never good this early.

"Did I wake you up?" Mom asked.

"No. I've already had breakfast and walked the dog."

"I've been vomiting all night. My stomach hurts."

She had frequent digestive upsets from what I imagined was overeating, so I wasn't too worried. I told her I'd call the doctor.

The doctor saw us at nine, examined her, and issued the fateful conclusion: ER. Although it brought up bad memories for both of us, we were willing by then, Mom because of the pain, and I because a doctor validated that it was more than a tummy ache. My vision of a little gas pain had been deflating as Mom's grimacing had escalated. She said she'd never been this sick.

Experienced ER users now, we faced it with blankets, a basin, ginger ale for Mom, and food for me.

"Do you know why I brought this blanket?" she asked, as she adjusted the red wool draped over her in the hospital wheelchair.

"No. I know it's always been in the cedar chest, but I don't know where it came from."

"It saved Grampa's legs in the Argonne Forest."

This meant nothing to me, and she could tell. I heard *argon*, like the gas.

"The Battle of the Argonne Forest—you know, the Meuse-Argonne Offensive."

I shook my head apologetically.

She continued, "It was the bloodiest battle of World War I. It began in September, 1918, and they were in the trenches for months, even after the armistice was signed in November. My dad had frostbite; they wrapped him in this blanket, and he said it saved him. That battle helped win the war. More than a hundred thousand soldiers died there. Your grandfather was a war hero, but for the rest of his life his legs hurt and he had nightmares. He was offered a teaching position at West Point after the war, but he'd had enough of the military."

"I remember his medals and his helmet. Was he married to Gramma then?" I asked.

"Not yet. They married when he came home, on her birthday. Have you seen the letter he wrote her from France?"

"No. What letter?" Why hadn't I ever seen it? Was this another secret?

"It's in the cedar chest, too. I couldn't read it after he died. But I knew it by heart, I'd read it so many times. He wrote it from Brest, France, in February, 1919. It begins, *My own sweetheart*, and it's signed, *All the love in the world*. He writes about going over the top at Verdun on September 25 and how scared he was. I'd like to read it again; will you get it out for me sometime? And get his little pocket Bible, too. He said he kept it in his shirt pocket over his heart during the war and that it saved him from many a bullet."

I wondered how much of what she remembered was an impressionable child's memory. Had his Bible literally deflected bullets? Did it matter? He lived and thousands died.

Snug in the red blanket, I realized, she was wrapping herself in her father's protection. His free-flowing, unconditional love had surrounded and soothed us all and was now comforting her through his blanket, Bible, and love letter. Warmth, faith, and love—what more could a person need?

Once an hour, I begged the triage nurse to consider Mom's age and infirmity to advance her in the queue, but vomiting rated low and we kept getting bumped down the list by convoys of ambulances with priority.

Finally, she was examined and transferred to a room, twelve hours after our arrival, with a plan for gallbladder removal in three days, "if she stabilizes." The next morning, I was glumly fascinated by how easily we all slid into our hospital routine. Dad called every morning to tell me he was up. My backpack still held energy bars, an empty bottle for water, and a crossword-puzzle book. The dog went back to bed with a disgusted *umph* as she circled and flopped.

I was set for my morning trek to the hospital, but Dad hadn't checked in yet. I didn't want to call him, because the ringing might jolt him awake into a blind tangle of apnea hoses, phone cords, and electric bed controls. It was abnormal for him not to wake up by seven, and it was now eight thirty. I stopped at the apartment and unlocked the door into the dark, cold kitchen. This was all wrong, and my body lunged into full fight-or-flight chemistry.

Dad came shuffling out of his bedroom and saw me. "I just got up! I just made my bed! I slept through the night! I haven't even made coffee yet." He was happy to have slept so well; I just had to shake my head at my capacity for worst-case scenarios.

I walked into a similar anticrisis with my mother that same morning. When I arrived at the hospital, she was dopey and confused and her eyes were cloudy. I was cataloging the symptoms when I noticed that, little by little, she was growing more alert. When she asked for a cup of coffee, it dawned on me that she was just waking up, not suffering some new syndrome.

I'd asked the nurse what she meant by "if she stabilizes and gets well enough for surgery." She suddenly had to leave, making a remark about the unpredictability of things in older patients.

There was no forecast for my next three days, although I searched for any clues. It was hard to plan for contingencies in the face of so much unknown. I read my horoscope, drew tarot cards, and peered into the shadows, searching for clues to the future. I read the obituaries and tried to practice seeing theirs. Dad had started writing his obituary years ago and had given me the notes. I thought he wanted to know if his life had value. But what would it be like when one of their names waited in black and white in the newspaper to startle me into the next phase? Maybe I should buy a Ouija board.

Mom underwent surgery and recovered well, petting and crediting her red blanket. Christmas was barreling in our direction, but I felt that I knew the routine by now and geared up to perform my duties. The first Saturday in December, I stopped in at the apartment around ten in the morning to drop off some milk, expecting a long, preholiday wish list.

Mom was stationed at her post. She reported on the day's birdfeeder activities and antics of squirrels, cats, raccoons, and deer, before her voice assumed an ominous tone. "Dad's not up yet."

I didn't have to read between the lines or ask for clarification. "I'll look," my voice responded, with no tone at all. I'd always imagined this was the way "it" was going to happen.

"Thanks," she said gloomily. "I had to check on my father when my mother couldn't."

My legs moved in the direction of Dad's bedroom, and my eyes peeked in, with no backup plan for "it."

He was pulling on his jeans. No "it" today. Do you call the doctor when an old person gets up late? Was this an omen or a fluke?

"Do you know what day it is?" he asked me.

I always read the paper cover to cover in the morning, so I answered, with reverence, "Pearl Harbor Day." I knew it mattered that I understood his history. He sat up taller, buoyed by sharing his weight.

"Right," he said. "December 7, 1941, the day that changed history. Roosevelt knew Hawaii was at risk. He had sent the US fleet to Oahu to keep the Japanese out. Everyone thought that was enough. But Japan, Nazi Germany, and Italy combined into an awful weapon. I was still in high school, and we studied the news every day. So many ships and aircraft were damaged and destroyed at Pearl Harbor that it was hard to imagine, and over two thousand people died."

"Now it is a memorial site with museums," I said. "More than a million people go there every year."

"Good," he said. "That's the way it should be."

That seemed to appease him, so I asked how he was doing otherwise.

"Terrrific."

He'd had a really rough stretch the past month. We'd seen a urologist for dribbling, and Dad had started a new prostate medicine. He had somehow managed not to tell me for the next thirty-six hours that he hadn't peed at all, until an unrelated midnight nosebleed took us to the ER. By then we'd had two emergencies, leading to catheters, and multiple trips to the urologist and the ER. If the medicine didn't start to work soon, he would need prostate surgery.

For the next two weeks, I dragged out my elf suit every morning and performed a one-woman Christmas pageant. My

parents firmly held to the treatise of "playing through" any difficult situation. Even though I was doing all the playing now, I
knew it was their modus operandi and that it worked for them.
Through it all, Dad never complained about the tubing and
plastic bag tied to his leg or his potential surgery.

I decorated their home and mine, planned food and gifts,
shopped, and played tic-tac-toe with my lists. Circle that so I
don't forget; cross that off—it's not going to happen; cross off a
few things I've actually accomplished; always more tasks added
than crossed off. I knew someday I would long for this: my parents alive, Christmas festivities, the holiday routine. I might
even miss having too much to do. My human condition

Chapter 43

....

After Christmas, my plumber friend was scrounging for work, so I decided the time was right to take on making a walk-in shower for my parents. The landlord okayed the idea, on the condition that I agreed to reinstall a tub when my parents were finished with the apartment. Mom and Dad didn't need to know that, or ponder what *finished* meant.

Gary began demolition of the old bathtub December 30, relegating me to plumber's helper. I completely trusted his work, but there was troubleshooting, prep, and running across the street with saw blades or coffee. New Year's Eve blew in abnormally cold, but I ran over with coffee for Gary in just a sweatshirt, not intending to stay.

I found him out back, kneeling over the water shut-off, which was buried a foot deep in a four-inch tube, firmly entombed in the concrete patio floor.

"I can't get my hand all the way down this tube to reach the handle. I might have broken it trying to turn it with pliers. I can't get the water shut off in the bathtub. Can you try?"

I squatted down and put my hand in up to my elbow. "It just spins, Gary. It's not tightening down at all."

"Push down hard to see if the threads will grab," he suggested.

I tried, but my right hand was worthless because of my shoulder weakness, and I'm not strong left-handed.

"I can't get it. Maybe we'll have to shut off the well," I said.

He drew an algebraic equation in the air, like a teacher on a chalkboard, and recited, "One broken faucet under concrete, plus one plumber, multiplied by twelve apartments, minus one holiday, divided by no water for three days, equals . . ."

He grimly shook his head and tried again to scrunch his hand into the tube. It never occurred to me that something might happen that he couldn't quickly resolve. He was my Mr. Fix-It, always miraculously repairing everything for me. I squeaked out, "Is there anything I can do?"

"Pray." Having never heard those words from him in twenty-five years of repairs, I knew we were in troubled waters. I really didn't want to try to locate the landlord or tell the tenants they had no water on New Year's Eve if we had to shut down the pump.

I turned around and stumbled the few feet to the edge of the cliff. As I lifted my face up to pray, the azure sky and glassine lake transported me into a cathedral. A ripple glimmered as an eagle dove for a fish, its mate circling nearby. The angels were easy to access; the primal beauty intensified the depth of my prayer.

"I guess I should call the landlord" came out of my mouth. I dialed my cell phone, dreading bothering him on New Year's Eve. He answered on the first ring, said that particular shutoff for my parents' unit was long since broken, and directed me to another one. *Thank you. Thank you, all my guardian angels.*

The next morning, I schlepped my Christmas Past upstairs and strewed it all over our guest room to sort and pack. Dad called at noon and asked what he could do to help me—code for *Get me out of here. Your mother is in a bad mood.* He'd been having angina attacks and hadn't been looking well at all, so I was willing to do whatever he needed. I left the mess in the guest room and loaded Dad and the dog into Precious to exchange and return Christmas failures and pick up a few groceries. Even though he was out of breath and looked more gaunt every day, he assured me he felt fine. I shepherded him back into his apartment, anticipating my couch, a sandwich, and a cup of tea as my next stop.

I ran into Gary in my parents' hallway with his phone to his ear. "I was just calling you," he said. "We need to decide on the shower walls."

I followed him into the tiny bathroom. "What are our choices?" I asked, hoping I didn't have to drive to the home stores and study sheets of vinyl to answer that question.

"I checked everywhere this morning. The best quality and easiest to work with are plain white. I think your mother wanted a color, though."

"Whatever you think is best is what we should use. Thank you for checking it out."

He closed the door and whispered, "How long do these walls need to last? Should we be doing tile?"

I said, "I don't know. Maybe it has to last only about five years, but right now I'm not expecting Dad to live five weeks. I'm going to call his cardiologist as soon as I get home." My father was withering before my eyes and sucking on nitroglycerin like breath mints. He'd aged ten years in two days. He had appointments scheduled with various specialists, but maybe not soon enough.

I opened the bathroom door quickly, relieved the wall decision was over, and fell into Dad doing his best Dakota-dog imitation. He asked what the problem was and how could he help.

"No problem, Dad. Gary is just getting ready to buy the vinyl for the walls and had a couple questions." I was too tired to review it with him.

"What color are the walls going to be?" my mother demanded. Her acute hearing received every conversation held anywhere in the apartment, so I knew she'd heard the discussion.

I wasn't far enough out the door to pretend I hadn't heard her. "White," I answered.

"Harrumph" accompanied that blasted indignant face she could turn on at will. "I want a color," she demanded. "And I want some of that broccoli soup you made. Why did you give all those mixed nuts to Gary? I wanted some."

Though it didn't happen often anymore, her entitlement monster had been rearing its ugly head lately. She was probably as frightened about Dad's wilting appearance and angina attacks as I was.

Mom had reversed the baby monitor Dad had used to keep tabs on her after her fall, so she now kept surveillance on him all night. At least they were taking turns being critically ill. I called two pharmacists, asking if Dad's new prostate medicine could cause angina; both said no. I called the urologist, who agreed with the pharmacists. I called the cardiologist, who moved up Dad's appointment but had no advice on the prostate medicine. I researched the web—nothing. I called around to other involved practitioners, and the consensus was to resume his antianxiety medicine.

I worked out my twitching tension preparing my house for funeral guests, anticipating the worst. I spent the nights flailing around, waiting for the phone to ring, and accepting my fate, convincing myself I could handle "it" and that this was the normal course of events. "It" was out of my hands.

Dad and I had another midnight rendezvous to remove the catheter and return to the urologist for one last "voiding trial" before pronouncing him permanently pee-less. Dad couldn't remember anything about previous catheter removals, although we had done them together twice in the last month. I made a joke about my role as plumber's friend with his paraphernalia, and with Gary, but he didn't get it.

I changed my tune that night and told the angels I couldn't take it. This was not the way "it" should happen. *Please figure out a better way, much later; I'm not ready.*

Even though we had removed his catheter at midnight, the next day Dad uncharacteristically forgot we were going to the urologist to determine whether the new medicine had done the trick. He shoved his arms into a jacket and climbed into the car without shaving or combing his hair. He failed the urological test, which sentenced him to the catheter until prostate surgery was feasible but freed him from the new medicine, now pointless.

I reviewed the appointment results with Mom and covertly passed her a piece of paper detailing Dad's memory gaps. She wrote back, *I'll call you when he's taking a nap.* We both knew telling Dad would only make him worry. Mom and I talked later and hoped it was just stress, but I said I'd call his cardiologist and neurologist. He'd had enough heart attacks and strokes that we had to take it seriously.

The very next day, after having not taken just one dose of that prostate medicine, he began blooming. By the following day, he was standing up straight, chipper and alert. No more angina attacks. It was disappointing that he wasn't off the catheter, but if he could have urinated naturally, he would have remained on the deleterious medicine. I remorsefully remembered that when all this had started, Dad's proposed treatment had been to go off that medicine, which everyone had pooh-poohed.

When I walked over to the apartment to check on everything, Gary was leaning over the kitchen sink with a flashlight, faucet parts scattered across the counters.

"Your mother asked me to fix this faucet. Do you see a short, fat screw anywhere?" he asked me.

I started scanning the detritus, furious with my mother for taking Gary away from the shower project.

He whispered, "The walls I wanted are out of stock; it would take six weeks and extra shipping costs to get them."

I crawled around on the floor with a flashlight, searching for the lost screw and my patience. I handed Gary the screw; the patience was nowhere to be found. Mom was distracted, talking to her sister on the phone, so I quietly asked him, "What should we do about the walls? We can't wait six weeks." I didn't want Mom's input, so I put my finger to my lips in a *shh*.

"We'll just have to use tile board, and I'll caulk the living daylights out of it. They come in patterns. What do you want?"

I told Gary to get whatever he thought was the easiest tile-board pattern to install and not to worry about what it looked like. He chose a beautiful, soft, bluish-gray faux tile, with a pretty border pattern. Mom would have chosen it and could now safely shower in Technicolor.

Both of my parents expressed extreme gratitude that I had figured out how to get the shower accomplished. They had worried that they would either fall getting in and out of the tub or have to move to a retirement facility. Their independence was still keeping them strong, despite the frequent alterations and compromises. They never considered the shower as a signpost of what they couldn't do; to them it was simply an improvement, a sensible remodeling, like adding a closet or a shelf.

Not to me, though.

Chapter 44

....

Late February offered a tease of spring, so I took Mica out to play. I was on my hands and knees, alternately weeding and throwing her ball, intent on Being in the Moment. It was warm enough for just a light jacket; the sun smiled in and out of wispy clouds. The Steller's jay we interrupted was musically chastising us, and robins were trilling their telephone calls. Tree buds were thickening with promise. The neighbor's dog wasn't yapping; the local kids were all in school. Bliss.

It should have been a premonition.

My telephone shrilled in tune with the birds, caller ID warning personal 911, or maybe a cute e-mail to read. That personal 911 had taken us to the ER seventeen times in the past few months, and not because we weren't seeing doctors enough during regular office hours. We went for chest pains at ten at night that had started at eight in the morning but that my parents hadn't wanted to bother me with; we went for accidents in which the catheter bag pulled loose, fell, or clogged; we went for unstoppable bleeding from various orifices and wounds. They knew us well in the ER, and we never had to wait long anymore. Thankfully, Dad hadn't experienced any more memory-loss episodes since he'd gone off the prostate medicine.

Mom asked how I was, and I responded, "A little tired, but okay."

"You know what Grampa always said about being tired in the spring, don't you?" she teased.

"No, what?"

"He said, 'Spring, when the iron in your blood turns to lead in your butt.'"

We laughed about that; then I asked how Dad's catheter was holding up. I was now flushing it daily and trying to secure it with a variety of options. I didn't want Dad to think daily flushing was a hassle, but I had tried to convince the doctor that every other day would be enough, or that possibly he could write orders for a home care nurse, both to no avail.

It wasn't that it was just darn weird to manage a father's catheter. I simply chose not to think about that aspect, knowing it was worse for him. It was complicated, time-consuming, and somewhat pain-inducing. But I agreed with Dad's usual assessment of anything unpleasant: "It just has to be."

Mom said she'd get him so I could ask him myself how he was doing.

"Tom, Trish is on the phone," she yelled, because walking over to his recliner was too hard for her.

Then, a little more loudly, because he often fell asleep in front of the blaring TV, "Tom, Trish is on the phone."

I had recently lulled myself into thinking I was prepared to deal with the inevitable serious health crises. Not that we hadn't had some bad episodes, but there'd been no true life-altering emergencies. Yet.

I soon discovered I was in no way prepared. I'd characterized their medical emergencies as various levels of hurricanes, but the big ones were, in truth, more like earthquakes: no warning, no idea how long they'd last, no ability to predict aftershocks. The earth under my feet groaned and shook.

Agitated now because she considered his deafness a choice, she said, "*Tom*. Pick up the phone."

Now an edge of panic: "*Tom! Trish is on the phone!*"

I heard rustling as she heaved herself out of her chair. "Tom! Tom! Tom!" The phone dropped. My blood pressure surged in shock waves with each "Tom!"

I jammed my feet into shoes, telling Katy we had an emergency, and was grabbing my pack when Mom came back on the line. "He can't talk."

"I'm on my way," I answered, while dialing 911 on my cell.

Dad seemed awake but completely befuddled. He didn't understand questions and spoke gibberish. The paramedics tried to assess him by asking his address and phone number, but I wasn't sure he had ever known them; he always had Mom or me for those details. I suggested asking the day of the week or his wife's name. They finally acknowledged they weren't speaking his language, no matter what they asked, and told me to take him to the ER, informing me that Medicare wouldn't cover transport if he could walk. I was already in the midst of fighting Medicare about a rejected seven-hundred-dollar ambulance charge for carting Mom from the hospital to the nursing home, so I knew a ride could be expensive.

There we were, Dad in a possible stroke, Mom in a panic, and I needing to discuss Medicare fees and the likelihood of a denied ambulance payment. Dad couldn't grasp the concept of walking and had no idea what his cane was for, but I was supposed to drive him. I opted for the ambulance and obsessed about Medicare as a distraction from the scenario playing out in the back of the medic van.

The tech was again asking Dad questions he would never have known the answers to; the date, addresses, and phone numbers weren't relevant to him. I suggested asking my dog's name, but I didn't hear that happen.

When we arrived at the hospital ten minutes later, I went to the back of the truck as they wheeled him out. He burst into tears when he saw me and sobbed, "I can't remember your dog's name."

I was relieved he could speak normally again and hung on to that for hope. "It's Mica, Dad, and don't worry, it's not like it used to be. If you're having another stroke, they can give you a medicine to reverse it." I prayed I wasn't lying and he wouldn't lose faith in me. He had suffered several strokes, one with a long recovery and lingering effects, so the possibility terrified him.

He tearfully struggled, and failed, to remember my name or Katy's. When asked by the doctor who the president was currently, he replied, "Roosevelt." Everyone in the room agreed they wished it were true.

The nurse asked me if he would normally know who was president. I said, "Definitely. He rails against Bush every day and hates the Iraq war."

He went through X-rays, CT scans, and blood work with a blank stare in his eyes and terror tensing his muscles. Then, all at once, the light came back into his eyes, his face relaxed, and he began greeting people as they entered the room. He started humming, and I could see his lips moving.

"How're ya doin', Dad?"

"I'm fine. I'm just remembering all my friends' faces and making sure I know their names. You can go home and get some rest if you want."

We went home together an hour later, bladder infection the only diagnosable problem. What the hell was going on? Was he really okay? Could I unhook my shoulders from my ears?

Chapter 45

....

The cardiologist thought Dad's memory-loss episode might have been a seizure and threw it to the neurologist. The neurologist tossed it around as a possible TIA, and the two doctors bounced that ball back and forth with various tests requiring several trips to medical facilities for lengthy procedures. In the midst of it, there were still groceries to buy, households to maintain, and an ongoing battle to stabilize Dad's catheter bag.

After all the commercial methods for securing the catheter bag failed, I designed a cloth contraption that wouldn't tear up his paper-thin skin or fall off and tear up everything else. I carried my sewing machine over to the apartment for final adjustments and set it up on the dining room table—a strategic error, I realized, when I had no escape from Mom's prattle.

She groused, "I can't put up the St. Patrick's Day window stickers because these windows are too dirty."

We were all more than a little edgy about Dad's condition, so I just let her agitation roll past me.

She squeaked, "Ouch! I need my chair pad!"

I pretended to be concentrating so hard that I couldn't hear her.

"We need that plastic insulation off the big windows." That must have been something she seriously wanted, because she added an extra manipulative twist: "So Dad can see out."

I was still sewing, still not responding.

"Are you going to the grocery store today?"

"No," I answered, with no explanation or further inquiry. What could she possibly need? She had six of everything.

"I dreamed Sylvester Stallone brought me corned beef and cabbage for St. Patrick's Day," she said in a joking tone, but I heard coercion.

I laughed, so she might think that I took it as a joke, while I grumbled in my head: *First I'll stop trying to fix this catheter problem, which has caused more than one race to the ER with profuse and painful bleeding. Then I'll look for your stickers, which could be anywhere from under the bed to the bowels of the garage to the Goodwill. After that, I'll take off the plastic storm windows, wash all the windows, and hang the stickers. Finally, I'll run right out and get an Irish feast.* I didn't have any idea about a chair pad. None of that was making it onto my list.

I kept my mouth shut and the sewing machine running.

Before I left, I asked Mom if she needed anything from the drugstore while I was out the next day for Dad's doctor's appointment.

She shot me a loaded "*no!*"

I had no clue why such a routine question had incurred a hostile response. I pursued my line of questioning, despite the firefight.

I said, "I may not go again until next week, so if you need something, this would be a good time to get it."

"No, I don't need anything," she said, in rifle-shot rhythm: *bang bang bang bang bang bang.*

I could have just played dead, but there was too much gunpowder in the air to ignore. "Okay. I'll just get Dad's prescriptions."

Suddenly she balled her hands into fists, scrunched up her face, turned her eyes down to the table, and squealed, "I

264 While They're Still Here

thought I would get to go to the grocery store." Her whole bit reminded me of a well-rehearsed Shirley Temple tantrum. If she'd been standing, I'm sure she would have stomped her feet.

It was still puzzling, though, because I took her to the store whenever she damn well pleased and she did have a recent food stockpile that ran several hundred dollars. I asked, "Do you want to go Tuesday after Dad's blood test, Wednesday after his ultrasound, or Thursday after your podiatry appointment?"

"Oh. Thursday, I guess. Oh. Okay." She laid down her weapon.

Why did she want to fight me about this? I went home humorously baffled, shaking my head.

My phone pealed an hour later, releasing the commensurate amount of adrenaline. I wished I knew in advance if the call was to report on a cute commercial or a profusely bleeding body part; maybe one ring for cute, two rings for crisis.

Mom said, "I don't need to go to the store. I wanted to buy a ham for Easter, but Dad's blood pressure is too high." Enough said. She wanted contraband, and I was the involuntary sodium cop.

"What about a turkey ham? That's a little lower-salt," I offered.

She paused while retrieving and reloading her gun, then delivered her lines with a potent pout. "No. If I can't have the real thing, I don't want anything." Shirley couldn't have said it better herself.

The next week bulged with appointments and medical tests. I pondered my little life of caregiving in relation to current events. Katy was in New Orleans for follow-up counseling of Hurricane Katrina survivors, the Dalai Lama was in Seattle for a five-day conference on compassion, Desmond Tutu and the Pope were also in the country. Not that I had ever expected to do anything on a grand scale, but I wondered if it mattered that I was doing nothing to benefit the greater good. Here I was, mowing the lawn and trying to keep my parents alive. Too conflicted to decipher a meaning, I just had to trust I was doing the right thing at the right time and would continue to do so as time turned the pages of my life.

Chapter 46

....

Scheduled and unscheduled medical events controlled my time. The urologist was irritated with me, chastising me for delaying prostate surgery. We sparred about the impact of major surgery in the midst of Dad's recent angina attacks, episodes of memory loss, and uncontrollable nosebleeds. Dad and I both left the doctor's office in tears from the doctor's harsh treatment, while I silently decided to find a new physician.

I phoned various friends and resources, each of whom confirmed my assessment of that doctor and recommended a particular different urologist. I called to see if the new doctor would see Dad. After some basic information, the receptionist hesitated. *Here comes the rejection*, I thought. *What will it be? He'd rather not take Dr. So-and-So's patient midstream, or he's decided not to accept any more new patients right now?*

But no, she said, "He decided to work an extra day. Could you come in tomorrow?"

You bet we can. *Thank you, my magic band of miracle workers.* I felt a surge of strength in my weary bones.

The new doctor was personable and knowledgeable and offered medicines and procedures the other doctor hadn't mentioned in three months of almost weekly visits. Hope was a powerful drug, and I could see Dad smiling with more heart. One month later, he was off the catheter.

Dad underwent an MRI in a failed attempt to resolve the TIA-versus-seizure question. Predictably, the gunshot noise of the test sparked a serious wartime PTSD episode that required three hours of unplanned sightseeing afterward to tuck it back in its cave.

He resumed frequent early-morning angina attacks, starting my day with a blast of adrenaline until he reported in. We went to the ER for a couple more memory-loss episodes, which always resolved unaided within a few hours.

I'd been asleep for an hour when the dispatch alarm, sometimes known as a telephone, rang. Dad pleaded, "I've taken three nitroglycerin, and they didn't help. What should I do?" He had a big sign in his room reminding him that if three nitroglycerin tablets didn't resolve the problem, he must call 911.

"I'll be right there." I jumped into my routine: backpack, food, documents, call 911.

This time it was the real thing: a full-fledged heart attack. Dad's own cardiologist was on call in the ER and scheduled an immediate procedure to look at Dad's heart arteries.

After the test, the cardiologist shook his head gravely as he reported to me, "His original bypasses are failing; there is no good choice. Without a stent, he will surely have a fatal heart attack within a month, but the risk of fatal heart attack during the stent insertion is very high. With the stent, if he survives the procedure, he may have a few months, maybe a year. Talk to your family. I think your choices are either go home with likely hospice or try a risky procedure. You decide. I can do it at eight tomorrow morning if you want to go ahead with it."

He drew diagrams and offered plenty of consolation, but the reality loomed. There was one ending to this story, no matter how we told it. The procedure could kill him or buy him a little time. The cardiologist ordered a consultation with a vascular surgeon to determine if anything else was possible.

I lurked in the hospital hall until the consulting vascular surgeon showed up, so I could intercept him before he entered

Dad's room. I didn't need anyone to reveal specific details to Dad; the stress would cause another heart attack on the spot. The vascular surgeon reviewed the chart with me in the corridor and succinctly told me there was no possibility of any surgical procedure Dad could survive. When Dad had his next major heart attack, it would be fatal. If it happened on the operating table, they couldn't fix it. His arteries were shot.

I thanked the surgeon and told him he didn't need to see Dad, that I understood and would tell the family. He said ethically he must see the patient. I cautioned, "Okay, but you can tell him only positive details; if you say anything negative, it's all he'll hear."

He went in, introduced himself, and said, "Tom, we can't do bypass surgery for you."

Dad burst into tears. Sobbing and shaking, he asked, "What will happen to me? Is this it?"

The doctor looked at me, mouthing apologetically, "You were right."

Some guardian angel overtook my brain, and, almost simultaneously, as the whole thing happened, the words came out of my mouth. "No, no, Dad. This is a good thing. It means you don't need to have a big, complicated surgical procedure; you can just have the stent put in the blockage."

Dad reversed his emotions right away. "Oh, thank God. I thought I was just going to die. Can we do it now?" The surgeon reinforced the good news and left, whispering to me, "Sorry."

I went outside to the hospital's meditation garden and phoned Mom, my brother, and my sister, explaining the choices and risks. There was no hesitation from any of them; everyone agreed, without a doubt, it would be Dad's choice to try the procedure even if he actually knew the risks. They also all agreed I shouldn't tell him the risks or prognoses.

I located the cardiologist, informed him of our decision to proceed with the stent, and recounted the bad experience with the surgeon. I begged him to lie, or at least avoid the major headlines, when he saw Dad. He complied, I signed forms, and we were set for eight o'clock the next morning, eagerly looking forward to a repair. At least the patient was.

I'm not saying Dad was oblivious to the seriousness of the situation; he just trusted the doctor and me to handle it the best way. I knew I had to act confident so he would be. I went home for the night with my brain looping: *Do we really have less than fifteen hours of my father's life left?* I wondered what I should be doing but had no answer.

I arrived at six thirty to keep him company. He was in good spirits; he had shaved and combed his hair. Eight o'clock came and went with the pace of twenty-four hours.

A nurse came in to say we were rescheduled for noon. I phoned everyone about the delay so they could save their praying for the right moment. I sat there for three more of Dad's possible last hours. We chatted and listened to music, and he complimented the nurses on their wonderful care. I was still wondering what I *should* be doing but still had no clue, beyond just playing through.

I flipped through TV channels and came across some black-and-white footage of a train. "Here's something about old trains, Dad. Do you want to watch that?"

I knew he couldn't see that far, but he had the speaker by his ear. The narrator mentioned Pittsburgh and the Great Railroad Strike of 1922, catching Dad's attention.

"Is that the strike your dad went out on?" I asked.

"Probably. It was right before I was born. My mother never forgave him. My dad was management, so he didn't have to strike, but he did it out of loyalty to his crew. He was yard master for the *Pee an' Ellie*."

He rolled *Pee an' Ellie* fast off his tongue, all one word. I knew that was the Pittsburgh and Lake Erie Railroad, and usually he would enunciate *P* and *L E*, but he reverted to a childhood pronunciation this time, like when *ellemenohpee* was one letter of the alphabet song.

The TV narrator went on to say the railroad owners were trying to smash the unions and had cut wages and eliminated time and a half for Sundays and holidays. That strike was the biggest walkout in railroad history: four hundred thousand workers.

"No wonder your dad went on strike. Four hundred thousand men struck."

He couldn't fit that number into the impact on his six-member family. "I didn't know about that. All I knew was my mother was mad. Permanently."

He continued, "Railroading was a good job, respectable. But my dad never got his full position back. Whenever work slowed down, he was laid off, and then they called men back to work on a rotating list. If you missed your phone call, they called the next person. We were never allowed to use the phone. My mother guarded it twenty-four hours a day, glaring at it for not ringing.

"My dad was the greatest guy. Everyone loved him. He died too young; his heart gave out."

This wasn't where I wanted his emotions to go, so I was relieved when there was a knock on the door. The attendants strolled in to take him to surgery with a breezy attitude of *oh boy, you're next*! My legs still worked, even with extreme trembling, so I walked along beside him. Should I say something profound and memorable? *No*, I decided, *don't blow it now*. I gave him a quick peck good-bye, they turned left, and I turned right into the waiting area. I fell into a chair, swept up my scattered nerves, and made my calls. Waiting, wondering, worrying, I didn't know what to ask the angels for but settled on health or nothing. I clearly saw Dad's mother, father, and brother protecting him and trusted them to make the right choice.

An hour later, the doctor was walking toward me, still in full scrubs. Did that mean anything?

"He's fine. The procedure went perfectly; he should be back in his room in twenty minutes and go home tomorrow. You can go in and see him now."

I was stunned. All I could do was thank him profusely. He deflected my gratitude, reminding me this was a temporary fix, just buying time. I assured him we were grateful for every hour he gave us.

I called my mother first. She answered, "Is this a happy ring or a sad ring?"

"Happy," I said, and filled her in. It was more than we had dared to hope.

Dad looked great and was busy thanking everyone and asked them to call the doctor back in. He took the doctor's hand and said, "A doctor can have all the technology in the world, but it has to be in the right hands. Thank you." Everyone teared up.

I told Dad on the way to his room that he had some very effective guardian angels, and he replied, without hesitation, "My mother, my father, and my brother."

We had never discussed his guardian angels before.

Chapter 47

Late afternoon, I was shoving the last of the Christmas decorations back into the closet when Katy came in, saying, "Who would have thought your dad would still be fishing in the Christmas pond three and a half years after that stent surgery? He defies all the odds."

"I know. It *is* amazing; three and a half years ago, we thought he had a few months at most. They said he would live less than a year after that stent procedure. His cardiologist loves him." All his doctors loved him. They treated him with kindness and me with respect. Dad was a walking miracle, and each doctor listened carefully to all my observations and concerns.

Congratulating me, Katy said, "Nine Christmases here in Washington so far with your folks. You did a great job. Everyone had a good time. Too bad your sister couldn't make it."

"She's loving every minute she spends as a new grandmother. It keeps her pretty busy."

I shut the closet door and went in to run a bath. I sank deep down into lavender-scented Epsom salts in my claw-foot tub. I'd been looking forward to this all day as a reward for having successfully orchestrated another Christmas with my parents. My house was clean, and, once again, everything was packed up, except the memories. Mom wouldn't want their decorations put away for another week.

Each year when I decorated their apartment for Christmas I could feel my parents'—and my own—comfort in the routine: This goes on the chandelier; that goes on the mantel; Dad parks here (like Dakota) and holds the lights while I wind them around the tree. The continuity temporarily assured us of their longevity, swatting away the ever-present foreboding that this could and would change.

I never dreamed we would have anything near a decade with them living across the street. As they inched toward ninety, each new ailment or condition weighed more heavily on their accumulated physical deterioration, but they were still alert and living on their own. Like any full-time caregiver, I was utterly exhausted, fueled only by my love for them.

I slid down to neck-depth bubbles, breathed in the lavender, and sighed.

Brrrring, went my phone. Seeing who it was, I quickly dried my hands and picked it up. I hadn't said hello yet when my mother whispered, in a frightened *whoosh*, "A bat just bit me on the foot. Hurry. I don't want your father to try to catch it."

Katy and I flew across the street, and Katy trapped the disgusting little beast in a towel. We took it outside and stuffed it in a big coffee can with a tight lid. I added duct tape to the closure—lots of it.

Even though it was four in the afternoon during the holiday week between Christmas and New Year's, as I dialed the health department, I held a faint hope that they might be open. The receptionist patched in the head doctor, who instructed us to take the varmint to Animal Services as quickly as possible and said they would send it on the six o'clock bus to Seattle for testing. After two days, we'd know the test results.

Lots of congratulations went to Katy for having caught it. Without the bat to test, my mother would have needed shots just in case it might be rabid, even though there was a less than 5 percent chance of that.

Over the next two days, I fielded many phone calls from various health department officials trying to figure out how it had happened and troubleshooting how to prevent it from happening again. I really thought I had hermetically sealed the apartment from mice and bats. When I suggested the possibility that the cat had brought it in from the screened porch, a new hairball of worry took over: If the bat proved to be rabid, by law the cat would have to get shots and be quarantined in a designated facility for six months. Even though everyone speculated that the bat was not rabid, through every discussion there was an underlying question: *Are your parents safe there?*

Friday at four in the afternoon, the health department doctor stunned me with the unexpected news: The bat was positive for rabies. I couldn't tell Mom and Dad this over the phone; I needed to be there to reassure them and help them get ready to go to the ER.

Mom was stirring something on the stove, and Dad was coming down the hall. "Hi," he said. "You come over for supper? Your mother made some great soup and a pie."

"Well, no. I have some rotten news." They both stared into me. As they aged, bad news hit them harder. I didn't keep them waiting. "The darn bat was rabid."

Mom flopped into her chair. "Oh no. What does that mean? Shots?"

"Yes. And right away. Dad has to get them, too, just in case he was exposed. The health department doctor said we have to go to the ER right now. She already called them so they would be ready."

I watched their cogs grind and shift away from wanting to protest and toward accepting their fate with grace, just as they always did.

As soon as I signed in, the head doctor of the ER ushered us to an exam room. He cleaned Mom's wound and gave her several shots in her foot and in her arm and gave Dad two in his arm. I watched my parents wince during the shots, but they never complained and expressed their appreciation for the care. There was a lot of brouhaha, with nurses (many of whom knew us from our frequent ER visits) coming in and out to find out about the rabid-bat bite. The attention and a good story temporarily quelled the repulsion and embarrassment I knew my mother felt.

While we were in the ER, the health department doctor called me again, this time about the cat. I went out into the hall to talk. We had previously discussed the cat's advanced age and antisocial behavior. The doctor wanted to reaffirm that the cat never went outside and never socialized with visitors. I explained that no one ever saw the cat; in its eleven years in Florida, my mom's next-door neighbor, a frequent visitor, had never seen it once. In nine years here, no one had ever seen it. Tillie was terrified of everyone except my mother and my brother, but she loved them with a kitten-like passion. The cat came out of hiding at night when no one was around and allowed Dad to play with her. Under those circumstances, and because of Tillie's age, the state veterinary authorities would permit her to stay home for now, quarantined to Mom's bedroom. I needed to get Tillie's rabies shot tomorrow and had to be careful not to touch her myself, or I'd have to get shots, too.

On the way home from the hospital, I began to present this new predicament to Mom and Dad with all the positive spin I could muster. "Six o'clock Friday night, and people are still helping us. The health department doctor called again. She had just talked to the state veterinarian, who said Tillie needs her rabies shot tomorrow." Their sullen silence stopped me from putting words to caging the cat, finding a vet on a Saturday that was also New Year's Eve, or the six-month quarantine. We'd all had enough for one day.

I found a veterinary clinic that sympathized with and understood the seriousness of my dilemma. Once again, my parents successfully captured and contained the cat, she got her shots, and we returned her to her hiding place under Mom's bed within two hours. I explained how lucky we were that Tillie could be quarantined at home. I moved the cat food and litter pan into Mom's bedroom, knowing we weren't really feeling lucky about anything.

I hoped that was the end of this emergency, but by now I had given up trying to feel prepared for the future. Who would have ever anticipated a rabid-bat bite? What I held on to, though, was all the unexpected help I'd received: the head of the health department talking to me while she was away on vacation; the head of the ER taking care of my parents personally and figuring out a treatment plan to have the home health nurse administer the rest of their shots; a veterinary clinic calling in its doctor, who had her rabies shots, to treat Tillie; the doctor negotiating with the state authorities for Tillie to be quarantined at home. Each of those people had given me their personal cell phone number. Their kindness and support went a long way toward easing my stress.

Chapter 48

In mid-January, I plunged in the yardstick outside the patio doors, where Mom could snap a photo. I supposed it was evident that it was the deepest snow we'd had, since I was up to my knees, but I thought the yardstick photo would be cute in next year's Christmas-card collage. Mom said, "Okay. I think I have it. Come and check."

I brushed the snow off my clothes and the dog and joined them at the table. From there, the vista was spectacular, everything glistening white under a clear blue sky. We were all mesmerized and happy in their snug cocoon, swaddled in fifteen inches of snow.

I looked at the photo. "Excellent. Look how you framed it just right with the railroad tracks and the mountain."

It was a grace moment. No one was bleeding, vomiting, or having urinary problems, at least not any they were revealing. They'd had three of their five scheduled rounds of rabies shots, and both had recovered from terrible bouts of a norovirus. Mom was planning a cake, and Dad wanted help cleaning out a file cabinet.

Then—*crack*—a rifle shot made us all jump. I recognized the ominous sound of a large tree limb snapping off. Before

278 | While They're Still Here

Dad could think of possible frightening causes for the noise, I said, "Uh-oh. That was a tree limb breaking in the woods because of the heavy snow. You'll be fine here, though—no trees overhead."

"You go on home, then," Mom warned me, her eyes worried but her voice calm, trying not to alarm Dad.

Daylight the next morning unveiled a worse scene than any previous storms. Huge limbs, some thirty feet long, were crisscrossing our yard, a few engulfing Precious like camouflage. I couldn't get across the street to my folks for twenty-four hours because limbs and trees were still crashing down and it was just too dangerous. We had phones, thanks to underground lines, but no electricity. Several more inches of snow were predicted.

Our storm behavior was well practiced but didn't factor in the blight of aging. In the last year, my parents' daily needs had exceeded my abilities. We had begun using their home health insurance for housekeeping and bathing, and we frequently had a home health nurse onboard for whichever medical problems percolated to the surface, most recently for the norovirus and rabies shots. Meals on Wheels provided nutritious food and a daily visitor. I had wound through a complicated screening process for more extensive home services through Medicaid, but when they qualified, Mom refused; she would not accept welfare. I was flattened by that decision but still thought it was her right.

At sixty, I felt my storm resilience wearing thin, and my parents had almost none. Mom hibernated in her bed again; Dad shuffled between his chair and bed. I started a fire, but it was only fifty-some degrees in the apartment and the fire wasn't going to help much. After the usual tension about using his oxygen near the fireplace, Dad once again reluctantly consented. I knew I should take them to a motel, but we couldn't get out. A downed tree had blocked our road. Again.

By the time the road was cleared, two days later, all the available motels were full. Nobody had power, including most

of the motels. Men with chain saws were roaming the neighbor-
hoods, looking for work. We hired a crew, and they were cutting
and piling wood and hauling mountains of debris. We lost our
entire backyard barrier of several forty-foot-tall evergreen trees;
their destruction completely exposed the house behind us and
smashed our huge arbor.

On day three, my parents' apartment was still fifty-some
degrees and we were all out of energy just from trying to stay
warm.

Then Dad accidently got himself a warm bed.

"Your dad fell putting a log on the fire, and he can't get
up." Mom's warning voice on the phone wasn't quite as calm or
confident as it had been in the past.

"I'll be right there. Wrap some blankets around him if
you can."

"I already did. I stuck his oxygen on him, too. I think we'll
need 911."

On my way over, I quickly paid a neighbor to shovel the
ramp and a path for a gurney. There were now four inches of
solid ice under fifteen inches of snow.

While the medics assessed him, I realized I had to go to
the hospital in the medic van and then stay there with Dad, and
that Mom couldn't manage at home alone. I called her weekly
caregiver, who said she could get there in her jeep, would take
food over, and would stay for several hours every day. Blessings

By day five, lots of people had power restored, although
the power company had no prediction for our neighborhood.
I found a handicapped-accessible room at a nearby motel and
arranged for the caregiver to take Mom.

Now I could focus on another problem. Even though Dad
couldn't walk and no one knew why or if he ever would, he was
being released from the hospital in the morning. The hospital
was jammed with patients and short staffed. Many employees
couldn't get to work because of impassable roads.

I would have to hire a transport vehicle to take Dad in a wheelchair to the motel with Mom and get myself a room there to take care of him. Mom's voice lost its last ounce of courage when I explained it all to her, but we both knew it was the only option.

Mom gave me her blessing to take a few large pieces of furniture from their apartment to my house to clear a path for a wheelchair. After Dad was settled in for his last night in the hospital, Katy picked me up in the truck, our only vehicle that could make it down our unplowed road, and we went to my parents' dark apartment at nine thirty to haul furniture. By flashlight we packed a cedar chest, end tables, a coffee table, and the electric piano. We backed into our driveway as far as we could to unload, but the sidewalk was still a foot-deep, tangled mass of branches, snow, and ice.

In the pitch black, I heard an "*ugh!*" as the chest we were carrying lurched.

Katy said, "I'm okay. I slipped, but just keep going."

The lights came on as we reached the door. We cheered and then gasped at the puddles of blood that had dripped from her chin onto the snow and the cedar chest as we shoved it in the house.

I knew I should go check the apartment for anything left on when the power went out, but I hadn't slept in a bed with a dog as a comforter for several nights and headed straight there. At midnight, Katy came into the bedroom with a large wad of oozing red gauze strapped to her chin.

"Sorry to wake you up. I just talked to the doctor. I have to go to the ER and get stitches."

I automatically rolled over to get up to go with her, but she pulled the covers back over me, saying, "I can go by myself. I'll visit your dad if I have to wait too long." We each forced an ironic *ha-ha*.

I was too worn out to have any idea how any of this was going to change, but I knew it had to. I conceded I could no longer keep my parents safe at that apartment.

I buried my face in poodle curls.

Chapter 49

....

The dog and I were barely in the door when Mom asked me, "Would you turn the calendar to February as you go by? Let's get rid of January forever."

"No debate from me about that." I laughed, ripping up the page with a flourish.

Mom was setting a slice of warm apple pie in front of Jenny, their home care nurse.

"Want a piece?" Mom asked me. "We're celebrating getting our last rabies shots. Jenny did a great job. Barely hurt at all."

Jenny gave me a hug and slid her paperwork over so I could sit down.

"How is your physical therapy going?" Jenny asked Dad, as he edged the electric wheelchair to the table.

"Terrrific," he answered, his Tony the Tiger roar more of a wheeze.

She'd been their nurse for years and knew to turn questioning eyes to Mom for elaboration. "Tina's great," Mom explained. "She comes three times a week. He can walk quite a bit with a walker now. He says he's done all this before, so he knows how to do it. Right, Tom?"

"What? Oh, the polio. Six months of making my legs work. I can do it again. As soon as I can get on my bike, I'll get stronger fast. That's what cured me the last time." He sank back in the chair, the mere explanation of the recovery having depleted him.

Jenny reached out and gently squeezed his shoulder, saying, "You guys are amazing. But what a terrible winter you've had."

With an unusual note of resignation in her voice, Mom said to her, "Thanks for getting us through it, especially the flu. We've never been that sick for that long. And both of us at once."

I took a good look at the three of us. We were dingy and frayed, expending all our energy just to be congenial.

I walked Jenny to her car, and she confirmed my assessment, suggesting I look at some of the senior-housing options. She apologized for adding to my burden, but we both knew that if anything was to be done, I had to do it.

I was still the conductor of this train, and I'd better figure out the next route, even if I didn't know how long the trip would be or where it would end.

I secretly began exploring senior residential facilities, but the cost was far beyond anything my parents could afford. I was about to admit defeat, but at the sixth place I called, a woman answered and said, "My name is Sarah. Why don't you just come by and let's talk? I'm available for the next hour. Does your father have VA benefits?"

I answered yes and no to the VA question. Yes, because he had full medical benefits and was in the VA's catastrophically disabled category. No, because I had called the number on the VA brochure for financial aid and had been told unequivocally that he didn't qualify. That sure wasn't the way I had read the brochure, but each of my questions had backfired and received a resounding *no*.

I drove right over to see Sarah, taking my parents' tax returns, as requested. This was a new senior residence, just five minutes away from my house. It was bright, cheerful, airy, clean, and tastefully decorated, like a nice hotel. Sarah reviewed the requirements in the VA brochure and assured me Dad would qualify for the largest subsidy, which would cover half their rent. I was skeptical, but she insisted there were many current residents in similar circumstances. I also learned that if Mom had accepted Medicaid home care when I had wanted her to, this new residential arrangement would have been complicated, if not impossible. Divine intervention at its best.

Sarah showed me available two-bedroom apartments, which were very large, each with high ceilings, good carpeting, bright rooms with big windows, a balcony, and a full kitchen. Pets were allowed. She called the American Legion just down the street, and the gentleman who helped with VA applications said he could see me in ten minutes. It could take months for the application approval, but Sarah said the facility would defer half the rent until then. My parents could move in as soon as I could get them ready.

Get them ready? I hadn't even brought it up with them yet!

I dropped off some groceries to Mom and released the tiniest test balloon possible, asking her, "How are you doing here after the bat episode?"

Reluctantly, she answered, "Honestly? I can't sleep. I look in every corner, wondering if something is there."

Okay, here was my opening. "Do you want me to explore other apartments?"

"Oh, would you? I was afraid to ask."

The train started chugging. In the midst of running errands and shopping with Dad the next day, I relayed to him my conversation with Mom about moving.

"What do you think we should do?" he asked.

"I'm not sure. But maybe it's time to find something safer. Someplace where the power doesn't go out every time the wind blows."

"Right." He was quiet, and I knew he was remembering the winter. "I'll do whatever you want. You always make the best decisions."

"Thanks. I'll just start looking around to see what's available. There's no hurry."

"When's the next storm coming?" he teased.

We *happened* to pass by the new facility on our way home. "Let's check this place out," I said, as if it were a spontaneous decision.

I slowly unloaded him, his walker, and the dog, explaining the senior-residence concept. I showed him where to push the automatic door opener, and we entered the cheery foyer. It was a big, open space with a reception desk, a large living room, and archways to the dining rooms.

"This is really nice" was all he got out before the staff greeted us and residents started fussing over my well-behaved standard poodle—always a good conversation starter. We met other dogs, talked to residents, got the lowdown on exercise classes, and checked out the dining rooms. Dad loved every square inch of it and was ready to move in. I made an appointment with Sarah for Mom for the following day, not really knowing if I could persuade her. On the way home, Dad insisted he would convince or coerce Mom to move, acknowledging that neither of them could even manage the ramp at their apartment very well anymore.

We bustled into the apartment with our packages, and I started putting the cat food away while Mom plied tricks out of her granddog with illegal treats. Dad headed for the bathroom, giving me time alone with Mom. I casually reported our excursion, just like I always did when we arrived home. "Got Dad's blood test, picked up your prescription, went to the pet store, looked at an apartment."

She was trying to be casual, too, saying, "Oh?"

I described it and showed her the photos on my phone, ending, "I know this doesn't seem like what you had in mind, but please just go look. I promise I won't ask you to move anywhere you don't want to live."

She grudgingly agreed just as Dad sat down at the table with glowing reports of the facility and declared he was going. He told her that they took residents to the store and the doctor and that there were nurses on staff, and emphasized, "It would take all that pressure off her." He nodded toward me. "It would be nice to have backup if we need it."

As grateful as I was for his acknowledgment, I also knew transportation could be a negative feature to my mother; she wanted me with her when she went out. I reassured her that I would continue to take care of them exactly as I was now; this was just a safety net.

The next day, Mom dressed up and accompanied me to the appointment as if attending a funeral. She selected an apartment with all the exuberance of choosing a coffin and unexpectedly signed a lease, albeit like final arrangements.

We settled in the car, and I needed debriefing. I had no idea what was in her head. "Well?"

"It's just so . . . so . . ." She started weeping, which was rare; stoicism was much more familiar at a time like this. She hadn't given me enough information to help her in any way, so I just waited. She wiped her tears and said, "Final."

"Um, like a rite of passage into the next phase?"

"Exactly. We'll have to admit we're old."

"I agree; that *is* a shock," I replied with all honesty.

That made her laugh a little, and then she said, "It's too fancy. I don't have anything to wear. Did you see those ladies with their suits and jewelry and salon hairstyles?"

This was not what I had anticipated to top her list of concerns, but I went with it. "You know you were still the prettiest one in the place." She granted me a half smile because it was true. Despite her weight, she was still very pretty and still put stock in her appearance. Every morning she fixed her hair and put on a bit of makeup, and she always looked nice when we went out, but I knew she would need an assortment of dressier blouses and jackets to keep up with the ladies.

"I will get you all the clothes you want, and you have beautiful jewelry that you never have a chance to wear. Your hair is full, wavy, and not even gray. There's a hair salon right on the premises. Aside from that, do you think you could live there?"

"Well, my electric wheelchair would work better there for either one of us if we needed it, wouldn't it? And it would go right on their van. Your dad would be safer and happier there; he could roam all day inside that place and make friends. He needs that. But you've worked so hard on our apartment with the shower and the ramp and the screened porch; I hate to make more work for you."

At the time, I had no idea how much work it was going to be. The VA application was over one hundred pages and took a full week to complete. It required official documents on everything from Mom's divorce decree in 1951 to lengthy evaluations by all their doctors and specialists.

Moving day was set for mid-March, and Sarah kindly gave me the keys to the new apartment two weeks early so I could move little by little beforehand. At the old apartment, I packed glassware, a Currier & Ives dinner service for a small fleet, books and knickknacks, and hauled it all to my house. Mom said she was glad to be rid of it—it just looked like dusting to her now. The new apartment was as large as their current one, so they could take whatever they wanted, but we all knew this was an opportunity to start clearing out.

I shopped for clothes for Mom, and she was ecstatic about my bargain hunting. She ordered shoes from catalogs and stocked up on makeup at the drugstore, and I cut her hair. I bought new bedspreads, sheets, and tablecloths and replaced anything else that she mentioned looked even slightly tattered.

The Friday before the scheduled move, I went to the new apartment to get myself squared away.

I had a big tablet divided into columns for Saturday, Sunday, Monday, and Tuesday. I had already moved in anything I could carry and fit in the car, so I crossed off *set up the kitchen* and *hang pictures*. My brother had his rabies shots and would arrive on Sunday to move Tillie to my house. Tillie could not go to the new apartment yet because of the rabies quarantine restrictions. She would live in my guest room for the time being; my brother would stay awhile to ease the transition, and I would wear gloves to manage the cat after he left.

Studying my list, I checked off the biggest worry by calling the mover one last time to confirm the details. Almost everything would be moved on Monday; Mom and Dad would be left with the basics for one overnight. I had tagged everything that was going on day one, including the entire contents of their garage to my garage. I planned that Monday night I would arrange the new apartment so I could focus on their personal needs once they were there on Tuesday. It felt hard and eerily familiar as I compared it with leaving Florida. At least we didn't have to catch a plane.

Satisfied that all was in order, around five o'clock I was leaving the facility when the new director waved me into her office. Without so much as a "how do you do," she said, "Your parents have to go into our assisted-living wing. I've called their insurance, and it will be covered."

I was momentarily confounded but then assumed it was a simple misunderstanding. I'd seen the assisted-living quarters, and there was no way my mother was going to live in a tiny, one-bedroom dorm with no kitchen. None of this was ringing true to me. I knew the strict HIPAA laws dictated that this person had no access to my parents' home health policy, and I knew for sure that policy did not cover rent. I'd explored that option already. I responded with what I considered a fair and polite argument, not wanting to burn bridges, because I was positive this was an error. But she was unbending and then wielded the fatal blow: The VA deferral for half the rent was against company policy and would not be part of the contract.

"Let me talk to Sarah," I demanded.

"Sarah was temporary. She no longer works for the company."

That was that. End of conversation. This person didn't give a hoot that we had a contract, that I'd paid the first month's rent and moved things in, or that the movers were scheduled for Monday. I left feeling as if I'd been hit by a train.

I needed a new plan before I told my parents the old plan had been derailed disastrously. Now that I knew Dad would get a retroactive VA subsidy in about a year, I visited the local facilities that I had originally considered too expensive. Not one of them was willing to defer half the rent until the subsidy came through. They also cautioned me that if I figured out a way to pay the full rent for a year, Dad would be disqualified from the VA subsidy. Although I assumed it was futile, I decided to go to another establishment owned by the same corporation that was giving me trouble.

When I described my predicament, the man I met with showed me an apartment my parents could move right into on Monday, although he could not assure me of the deferral for half the rent until the VA money came through. I gathered from things he'd said that he was an administrator who had some clout with headquarters. I pressed my case about how wrong this was, since all the documents had been signed weeks ago and I was already moving them in. He was a kind man and took pity on me. I waited a few hours while he made calls, including to the corporate attorney. Finally, he happily announced we were back in the original facility, with our signed contract and VA deferral intact.

It had been a rough twenty-four hours, and not part of my carefully planned list, but I didn't have time to be properly indignant. I drew arrows on Saturday's long list, moving the tasks to an already full Sunday.

Chip arrived, his charming presence calming us all. On schedule, he moved the cat to my house and the movers completed everything exactly as planned for day one. The next morning, I deposited my folks at my house, assigning my brother, Chris, and Dianna rotating supervision disguised as visiting. The movers hauled everything remaining, and Katy and I set up bedside commodes for emergencies; a shower seat; a toilet-seat riser; apnea equipment; oxygen; wheelchairs; hospital beds (with overhead grab bars for Mom); and lights, lights, lights. They liked a lamp on every table and lights strategically placed, to leave on all night because of Dad's poor vision and occasional befuddlement.

That occasional befuddlement was a growing worry. In addition to episodes of disorientation, my father had a new neurologic disorder causing a lack of differentiation between dreams and real life. I had no idea how relocating would affect his grasp on reality. I arranged his room exactly like his other room. TV, telephone, lights, magnifying reader—everything was identical. Mom's room also needed to be recreated because of her limited range of motion.

Satisfied I was ready, I picked them up from my house and we headed over. I knew they were nervous, and I hated my role. They probably knew I was nervous and hated their roles, too. But we were all determined to play our best parts to help each other through. We'd had a lot of practice at that.

I unlocked the door, and Mom guided her walker in. "Oh my God," she exclaimed.

The dog and I were stuck behind Dad, who had his walker wedged in the doorframe, so I couldn't tell what she meant. Was she happy, or was there a dead body sprawled on the floor?

We finally all scooted in, and she said to Dad, "Tom, can you believe what she's done? It's all set up. It's beautiful.

It looks like we've always lived here, except it's not covered in cat hair yet."

Dad looked bewildered, and Mom calmly oriented him, "Look, here are the hooks for our coats, and there's your chair in front of the TV, just like always. The bathroom is right here."

"That was a long walk. I have to sit down," Mom said, as she headed to her Command Post. Katy and Chip came in the door, loaded with our favorite Subway sandwiches. "Just make yourselves at home," Mom greeted them, spinning the lazy Susan in front of her like a roulette wheel. "Everything is right where it always was, so you shouldn't have any trouble finding anything."

It felt so familiar and looked so good, even spacious, because of the open layout, ceiling height, and windows. I had cozied it up just the way they liked It, leaving a small pile of things for Mom to arrange to put her mark on the décor.

For several nights, we had family dinners with Chip in the main dining room, with lots of drop-by welcomes and introductions. Mom proudly presented her husband, the NCR service manager; their son, now a successful, professional animal communicator; and their daughter, the retired dental hygienist. Each resident had some little tidbit in common to lead to conversation.

I went over every morning to attend exercise class with Dad and walked him around the building to help him get his bearings. The first night that Chip and I didn't go over for dinner, Dad went by himself, and Mom produced flimsy excuses for staying behind.

After Dad had gone to dinner by himself three nights, I became concerned. I wanted Mom to have the built-in physical activity and social interaction. She was finally on a pain medication that worked and seemed more able to walk than she had been for months. I asked her why she wasn't going down to dinner.

She was prepared for this challenge and issued her defense: "I'm a better cook. I don't want to get dressed up every day. It's too far to walk. It's—"

Dad interrupted her, "We're paying for that food with our rent. You *are* going."

She made a face and went to her room. I left not knowing whether she was never coming out or getting dressed for dinner. This was between them now.

Chapter 50

....

The next morning, when I was helping Dad get ready for exercise class, he joked, "We created a monster. I missed the baseball game last night because your mother stayed so late in the dining room."

"Good news and bad news, huh?" We laughed about that as I walked him to his chair in exercise class. I parked his walker with all the others, then headed back up to the apartment to sort out his medications for the week.

There was a woman at the apartment door, ready to knock. I said, "Hi, I'm Trish, Marg and Tom's daughter. Can I help you with something?"

"Well, I want to meet your mother. I'm Mary, the new director. Evidently, your mother had the dining room in stitches until nine thirty last night."

"Oh, new director?" I asked, probably a little too enthusiastically.

"Yes. I understand you had some trouble with the last one. Can we start fresh?"

"You bet. My parents know nothing of what she did to me. I'm happy to forget that nightmare."

As I opened the door, an elderly woman came bustling out. "Oh, hi, I'm Evelyn. You must be Trish," she said. "I'm late for exercise class, but I wanted to make sure Marg was going down to dinner tonight. We had a ball last night."

"I'll save your seats," she called to Mom, as she rushed out the door.

"I guess I haven't lost my touch," Mom said with a shy grin after Mary remarked about what a welcome addition she was to the dining room.

"My mother was always the neighborhood hostess. She's a people magnet," I said.

Mary said, "Last night she had her table laughing all through dinner and dessert. Afterward, other residents pushed their tables up to hers, drank coffee, and gabbed long after the kitchen staff went home."

Soon residents were dropping by the apartment to visit, often bringing a book or a recipe. A group of regulars started arriving at the dining room early to reserve "Marg's table" for supper. One day when I was at the apartment, a neighbor came to the door and asked if she could get on a waiting list to sit at Mom's table in the dining room.

There was social pressure on Mom to attend events and to join the crowd for lunch. The only thing she consented to was church once a month and supper every night. Dad walked and visited, enjoyed events and concerts, and went to exercise class Monday through Friday.

Mom's new friend Evelyn was up and about from six in the morning, when she walked her dog a mile or so, until closing time, whenever that was. She popped in during the day, bringing in all the current news and gossip, providing a conduit to the community. By the time Mom went down to dinner, she knew who had moved in, who'd gone to the hospital, and who was going to California for two weeks.

Mary had everything running smoothly and kept a watchful eye on her flock. I trusted her completely to help us through any complexity. Even though my parents were safe, I still had to attend to their daily needs, and there were plenty of those: finances, pills, groceries, appointments, home care personnel, wounds, and electronics failures. It was better to have my eyes on them, assessing them every day, than to get a phone call about a crisis I could have prevented.

The cat was released from quarantine at my house and snuggled right into Mom's bed as a surprise on Mother's Day. Tillie also had her own quarters, since Mom had selected this particular apartment so the huge walk-in closet off her bedroom could be Tillie's room. The reclusive cat had a cozy hideaway nest, a litter pan, food, water, and grass in Mom's closet. I added a barrier to the balcony so she could safely go outside, and she had her big climbing tree in the window.

She seemed to settle in, but a month later, Tillie began screaming relentlessly. There was no consoling her. My brother said he would talk to Tillie to find out what was wrong. Chip had earned a bona fide reputation as an animal communicator and had a full-time business resolving animal behavioral problems and finding lost pets. He reported that Tillie told him there was a vibrating noise in the apartment that she could not tolerate. Mom was at her wits' end—the earsplitting screaming was keeping her awake all night so I carted Tillie and all her accoutrements back to my guest room for a respite while we resolved the problem. In the process of rearranging Mom's closet, I discovered a rattling, wheezing air vent—a disturbance that would have made me scream, too, if I'd tried to sleep by it.

We needed to decide what to do with Tillie. Mom hated to admit it, but she was all out of energy to take care of a cat, even if we could abate the offending vibration from the air vent. Tillie couldn't live permanently at my house because she was afraid of Mica, even though Mica loved cats. In our family, pets' needs were a high priority, and we all wanted to take our time and do right by Tillie. I canceled our scheduled houseguests and settled into our familiar routine, with the cat occupying the guest room.

Then she started screaming at my house.

It was like a baby wailing uncontrollably: gut-wrenching, heartbreaking, and nerve-shattering. She showed no obvious signs of being physically ill, and taking her to the doctor was so stressful to her that I considered it a last resort.

Chip offered to come and get Tillie and take her home, but he couldn't make the trip until he recovered from back surgery. In the meantime, he said, he would communicate with Tillie to find out what was the matter. A few days later, he told me that she missed playing. I was so flustered that I was willing to try anything.

I sat on the bed in my guest room, reading a book, and flicked a catnip mouse on a string over the edge. In a few minutes, there came a *thwap* at the mouse. Soon Tillie was out from under the bed, batting and lunging after the toy. Her screaming stopped, and we played several times a day, until she ended up on my lap.

My brother still couldn't travel, so his lovely and loving wife, Jonquil, also an animal communicator, made the trip to retrieve Tillie. After a few days visiting with my parents, Jonquil bundled Tillie into a small carrier and rode off in the airport van, undaunted about flying a twenty-year-old cat in the airplane cabin cross-country.

I went over to the apartment to provide a distraction while Jonquil and Tillie were in the air. Dad was in his room, getting ready for exercise class. Mom was at the table, looking worried, but I knew she'd be in suspended animation until the plane landed. I told her Jonquil had called after they'd boarded and that they'd had a private room for their security check-in.

"It sounds like she just charmed everyone into helping her with the cat." I laughed, trying to ease Mom's mind.

"Good. Just like Jonquil. What a blessing," she said, but she did not seem relieved.

After a moment, she said quietly, "Did your father seem right when Jonquil was here? He seems really distant to me lately. He used to have an off day now and then, when he'd be a little rummy, but it's getting worse."

"I noticed that, too," I agreed. "At his birthday party, he'd talk if someone spoke right to him; otherwise, his head drooped to his chest and he drifted into a daze."

"Do you think he's depressed? Had another stroke? Or is this just what eighty-nine looks like?"

I trusted her assessments and level of concern, answering, "I really don't know. We see the cardiologist and neurologist next week. I'll check it out."

"Be subtle," she cautioned. "Don't worry him, or it will be worse."

The phone rang, and she gave me a thumbs-up. I went into Dad's room, where he was on the edge of the bed, with one pant leg on and his head hanging down.

"Jonquil and Tillie made it. Chip's on the phone."

"Good. Can you help me? It takes me so long to get dressed, I'm going to be late for class. I have to rest after every damn leg and sock and shoe. I don't think I'm going to like eighty-nine very much."

"I could get a helper to come in every morning to get you up and at 'em. Lots of people here do that."

"I hope to God I never have to resort to that," he grumbled.

Over the next two weeks, we saw his GP, neurologist, cardiologist, pulmonologist, and urologist, but there was nothing obvious to change. There was some speculation about weakness from postpolio syndrome, so we scheduled physical therapy. The physical therapist came three times a week to help

Dad hold his head up and breathe, but he just couldn't do it. It exhausted him.

Despite his gloom about his weakness, which he revealed to me privately, he smiled and was kind to everyone. He loved their new residence and every person he met. Everyone took care of him under the auspices of friendship. The exercise teacher saved the chair next to him for Dad, and another person always walked with Dad to the lobby for the social and snack hour. But as soon as we were alone, he retreated. Daily life depleted his energy, and the morning's fresh supply was dwindling. It occurred to me that now that Mom was happy and settled, maybe he realized he could let go.

On Thanksgiving, I pulled his chair and a tray in front of my big TV and he sullenly watched a game. We had the usual crowd, and he was pleasant if someone engaged him directly, but then he just shut down. It was so unlike him, but I had no explanation or treatment.

Was he giving up and letting go?

Chapter 51

....

"Your dad fell. The nurses are already here; the medics are on their way." My mother was using her modulated, state-the-facts-and-you'll-get-through-it voice, as she had done all my life when alerting me to crises and tragedies. Whether it was about tornadoes, the Twin Towers, assassinations, floods, or sick or dying relatives, her mother instinct compelled her to prepare me and guide my way with strength and faith.

I arrived at the apartment in five minutes flat, and after years of emergencies I wasn't panicked until I saw Dad's whole leg twisted in an alarmingly unnatural position. Within hours, he underwent surgery for a broken hip. The next day, the surgeon declared it repaired and estimated he'd be home in three or four days, then said I should take Dad in to the doctor's office the next week for a follow-up. That seemed unlikely to me, but I held on to that prognosis with both hands and cheerfully passed it along to everyone. I concealed my suspicion that my father's engaging smile, healthy complexion, and full head of wavy, black-and-silver hair didn't accurately portray his debilitated condition for the doctor's assessment.

Mom let Chip know that Dad was in the hospital but told him not to worry. Chip still couldn't travel, and we didn't want him to feel any regret about that. I stayed at the hospital and called Mom with frequent updates; she kept everyone else informed. She talked to Dad on the phone but confessed to me that she couldn't bear to see him in a hospital bed. I didn't pressure her to visit, trusting her to gauge her own and Dad's emotions.

Dad began hallucinating, entranced by "Tillie" as a kitten scampering in midair all over the room. He laughed and described her antics, sometimes playing with other kittens. When he grew tired of her, he asked me to put her in the closet. I pretended to catch her out of midair and made a bed in the closet for her. Then, a few minutes later, he said, "The cat got out. Look at her! That Tillie loves to play."

Because of the hallucinations, the doctor took him off opiates. The third day, nurses tried to get him up to walk. He couldn't maneuver himself, even with three nurses helping. When they asked him how he felt, he would say only, "Terrrific," then look to me to provide the medical answer, but I had no idea. He thought describing his condition was complaining, so we had no idea of his level of pain. I explained to the nurses his possible weakness from postpolio syndrome, and that it had taken a long time for him to walk the previous winter after his fall.

Without explanation, he was moved from the orthopedic floor to the geriatric floor. It was dark and sedate, and the hall by the room next door was filled with crying people. I plastered on my sympathy smile when I passed them.

Dad's hallucinations mutated into terror-filled thrashing and shrieking anytime he was not talking with or listening intently to someone. His hallucinations and anxiety were now, the hospital staff believed, the result of a stroke or a common reaction to anesthetic in the very elderly—common enough to have a name: postoperative cognitive dysfunction. Not even a hint of a prognosis was given.

We still couldn't tell how much pain he was in; he said he had zero pain when he was lying still, and we couldn't get him to move enough to see how much pain he would have if he tried to walk. He was out of control anytime he was unengaged for a few seconds, panicking, pulling out his IV, and trying to remove his catheter.

The nurses described the legal and technical process of restraining him, and we all agreed it was too aggressive. They brought a recliner and pillows so I could be right next to him, level with his bed. I calmed him down and covered his hands with socks. After a minute, he would yank them off, but as soon as I said, "Let's leave those on, because when you fall asleep, you try to pull out your catheter," he slid them back on with complete awareness. Then, if I didn't engage with him for a few seconds, it happened all over again.

He wanted his watch, keys, and wallet and was furious with me when I said I'd sent them home with Katy. I told him I'd have her bring them back, but he wanted them Right Now. He started stretching his arms and swiping at the air, trying to grab something. When I asked what he needed, he pointed toward the ceiling and said he couldn't reach his wallet, keys, and watch and asked me to get them. I reached for each item, sliding the "watch" on his wrist, putting his "keys" and "wallet" in the appropriate "pockets," and putting my heart back in my chest.

Where was he getting ready to go?

Chapter 52

....

I was completely unnerved and needed some sleep. The nurses agreed to check Dad frequently while I slept on a mat in the physical therapy room down the hall. A nurse woke me in an hour, saying he was hysterical and crying. When he saw me, he squalled, "What's happening to me?"

I found my lying voice and calmly and casually reassured him, "Oh, it's just what happens sometimes after general anesthetic. It takes time for it to get out of your bloodstream. Let's play cards." Katy had brought games to occupy him, so we played Old Maid and Go Fish. Still, he was okay only if I was talking directly to him. The minute I stopped, he drifted. His hallucinations ranged from tormented, frenzied combat against a fierce demon assailant to a perfect pantomime of eating a hamburger. He repeatedly picked his keys, watch, and wallet out of the air and frequently laughed at Tillie and a half dozen kittens rolling and tumbling near the ceiling.

When he abruptly gasped as if he were choking, a nurse responded to my call button, then unhurriedly fastened on an oxygen mask. To me, every gasp was quicksand and she seemed to be proceeding in unconcerned slow motion. Oxygen helped for a day, but then anytime I wasn't talking to him, he sank into a pleading hallucination, imploring a force unseen by me, *Help me—I want to go home.* The nurses never saw this distress because he was fine as soon as anyone appeared. I had to leave him alone long enough to thrust the nurses into action, but it was the worst thing I had ever experienced. I can still see him searching for me as I left the room. I was his tether. But I hadn't slept in nine days and had no reserves. I had to have help, and the nurses had no evidence to support my claims that he could not be left alone even for a few minutes.

Finally the nurses heard him wail, "Help me" and activated an emergency code, bringing an army of nurses and equipment within seconds. They assessed him, aspirated fluids, and ordered more medications. Everyone found ways to avoid answering my questions about what was happening.

It hit me that they knew he was dying, and probably had known for some time. I called Katy, who came immediately and stayed with Dad while I found his nurse. I managed to make my voice ask, "Is he dying?" She stared at me for too long. "Is he dying?" I had to ask again.

"I'm not able to answer that question. All I can do is ask you if you want to keep him comfortable. I'm so sorry."

Now *I* was staring too long. She repeated, "Do you want to keep him comfortable?"

Finally, I answered, "Of course." Was there any other way to answer that question?

With a penetrating look, she asked, "Do you understand what I'm saying?"

I was completely divided. My brain understood exactly what she was saying, but my heart was pounding, *No, no, no— the doctor said he would go home.* The nurse reconfirmed what was happening, with a few more oblique disclosures, but I knew I was holding the information as just that—information. It hadn't crossed into reality. For fifty years he hadn't died when doctors had predicted he would.

A friend who had been an ER nurse for decades stopped in to see us. With her I could ask the hard questions and trust her for the truth.

"Is he dying?"

"Yes," she analyzed without hesitation.

"How long? A week? A day?" I asked.

Her answer staggered me: A few hours, a day at most; do the morphine and keep him comfortable.

After I had one more cryptic confirmation with his nurse, the morphine was solemnly administered and his face relaxed for the first time in ten days.

I called Mom. "They think he's going."

"Tonight?"

"Probably. Maybe tomorrow."

After a long pause while I heard her rustling for the tissue box, she said, "I had a complete sense of calm a few minutes ago, and I knew he was at peace. Thank you for being there with him."

"Do you want Chris or Dianna to bring you to the hospital?"

I waited while we both cried; then she answered faintly, "I just don't think I can. I don't want to remember him that way. Is that okay? Do you need me there?"

"No. We're okay. I trust you to make the best decision for yourself. Dad would, too."

She thanked me as we both did our best to talk through the tears. She said she'd been trying to reach Chip and Jonquil all night but hadn't gotten any answer.

I also hadn't been able to reach Chip for several hours, which was more than unusual; it had never happened before. When we had spoken the previous day, my report had been grim but had not passed into any foreboding that Dad might die.

Chris and Dianna came and said hello to Dad but meant good-bye. He held their hands tight, then began fading. After they left, nurses suggested Katy and I go get coffee so they could tidy everything. When we returned, the lights were dimmed, all the equipment was gone, and he was sleeping sweetly, breathing gently, with the covers smoothed and folded under his arms.

At eleven thirty that evening, my phone shrilled into our pall: Jonquil returning my call at last. It was two thirty in the morning their time, and she sounded stressed, so I asked her what was going on. She whispered, "Tillie is dying, and we are helping her cross over." In a hushed revelation, I uttered that Dad was dying also. We were both stunned into silence; the spiritual relevance was too potent to reduce to words. After we reverently and briefly offered each other condolences, she said she would prepare my brother and we hung up, both dazed.

Around midnight, I fell asleep in my chair by Dad's bed, dreaming of him ice skating away from me with his brother, Nelson, in Andrews' Hollow. I had been in Andrews' Hollow with Dad in the summers, walking beside the trickling creek through the spectacular, deep gorge, and I knew it was his favorite place in all the world.

Katy woke me up, whispering, "I think he's going."

Just like that, it was over. A few easy breaths, a peaceful countenance into heaven.

Mom answered her phone with a quavering "hello."

"He's gone," I answered, in the same shaky voice. "It was very peaceful."

"Oh, honey, are you okay?" she sobbed.

"About as well as you. I'm fine and I'm awful. Just sad. Should I come there?"

"Evelyn is with me. You can go home if you want to. Get some sleep."

Neither of us could bear more talking just then, so I said I'd see her in the morning. Katy and I left the hospital empty-handed and empty-hearted at one thirty in the morning. Being empty was fine; I didn't want to feel anything at the time but sleep. I knew there were things that had to be done, but surely the hard part was over.

Dad's horoscope that morning in the local newspaper said, *Find a child and go ice skating.* I knew he had.

Chapter 53

....

When the dog and I arrived at the retirement facility at our usual time of eight in the morning, the director pulled me into a hug. After sincere condolences, she tried to break her bad news to me gently, but there was no soft landing for this. Dad's VA payments would end immediately, and I would have to reapply for VA widow's benefits for Mom. Mary said she'd been on the phone for the last half hour, fighting for a continued 50 percent deferral until the widow's benefits came through, but the administration just wouldn't allow it. It was December 9, and Mom had to be out of that apartment by December 31 or pay in full.

I lurched out of Mary's office in a dazed despondency, envisioning my mother living at my house after she had been so happy here.

"Wait! I do have one idea," Mary called out to me.

I turned the dog around and went back to her office with barely a brain to listen or think.

"We have one studio apartment available. Come on, let's go look at it." She grabbed her keys and my arm and led me down the hall a few steps. "It's right here, close to everything."

It was on the first floor, had a full kitchen, and was close enough to the dining room that Mom wouldn't have long halls to negotiate—all strong persuaders for my mother. As we viewed the apartment and Mary discussed the cost, I estimated that Mom's Social Security and pension would pay half. I'd just bite the bullet and figure out the rest, trusting the VA would come through eventually.

Mica and I rode the elevator up to Mom's, bracing for the unknown. My mother was brave, but everyone must have a breaking point. Was losing Dad her final blow?

She was up, dressed, and drinking coffee at her Command Post with Evelyn. After dog greetings and treats, I reported the events from the hospital, embellishing every spiritual and upbeat iota, omitting the distress. They wanted the details of the invisible cat playing in the air, so I painted that as an uplifting story. It was an uplifting story, but he had died, after all, and spinning the story took more energy than I wanted to spend.

After Evelyn left, Mom chewed her lip and said, "Well, what now? Am I out on the street?"

I hadn't considered that she would plunge her plight right into destitution. But we had all been spooked for decades about her income if Dad died first.

"Not quite. How would you feel about moving into a smaller apartment here?"

"Can I?" she asked with skepticism. I nodded an affirmative, and she went on, "This one is too big. Just getting from my bedroom to the bathroom is a hike. I'd really like to be on the first floor. I worry constantly that I'll be stuck here in a fire. I only wanted to be up here so Tillie couldn't accidently get outside."

I described the location and explained it was just a studio, but with a kitchen.

"All night I've been worried sick that I'd have to move in with you and ruin your life. Can you survive moving me one last time?" she asked with a crooked smile.

The possibility of staying here in any fashion was deliverance to her. I did not discuss the details of the money, other than that her income and VA benefits would cover it. There was no point in having her worry about it.

She wanted to see the apartment, so we went right down. She loved it. She determined her exact Command Post placement by the window, where she could monitor the main entrance to see everyone's comings and goings. We planned furniture, TV, and picture arrangement. She signed papers in Mary's office, and we went back upstairs.

She plopped in her spot and started drawing a diagram for furniture while I made lunch.

"What do you think about trading tables?" she asked. "You take this big one"—she rapped her knuckles on hers—"and I'll use yours."

"That's pure genius. Mine looks exactly like yours, only smaller. That's why I bought it years ago."

I was setting our sandwiches on the table just after noon when her phone rang. After checking caller ID, she held it out to me, her voice and hands shaking. "Your brother. Can you tell him?"

After a dispirited "how are you," he found his modulated, state-the-facts-and-you'll-get-through-it voice and mourned that Tillie had just passed. It took a while for me to find any voice at all, but then I feebly muttered that Dad had died just after midnight.

They had gone exactly twelve hours apart. Chip and I were both depleted and didn't need to verbally console each other or dissect the significance of the entwined departures. Our hearts were cradled together in understanding.

I hung up the phone and told Mom that Tillie had just died.

Grasping the meaning immediately, she said, "Your brother always said he sent that cat out West with us for protection. She alerted me about things burning on the stove and woke me many

310 | While They're Still Here

times when Dad was having a problem. She was completely noc-
turnal, like Chip, and Dad played with her at night when he
watched the late news. I woke up to catnip mice and toys all over
the floor. She loved to play. Chip was her one true love, though."

As we talked about Tillie, I broke under the weight of
Chip's sorrow. The dog comforted me in her usual way: paws
reaching up, eyes searching mine, her head of soft poodle curls
my soul's cushion. Our pets had always smoothed our paths—
and apparently also the path to heaven.

Chapter 54

....

I must have been in a daze while moving Mom, because it seemed that all of a sudden, January 1, there she was at her Command Post, in the midst of all her usual trappings but with a slightly different backdrop out the window. I vaguely remembered Chris, Dianna, and Katy sliding everything in and out of the elevator while I organized and set it up, and Carolyn hiring strong boys to move the heavy stuff. I knew we had left the old apartment open for residents and staff to take what they wanted, then donated the remainder. I knew every nook and cranny of my house was stuffed with the unneededs, but the process was just a distant nightmare buried under a new one-hundred-page VA application.

"Isn't this the best?" Mom swooped her arms around, as if showing off a new car. "Everything right at my fingertips. No long walking anywhere." She was distracted by activity out the window. "Oh, there's Evelyn back from the store. I gave her money for Hershey's Kisses. I can't keep the candy dish full, with all the company I have."

"How are you?" she asked, then noticed Mica rummaging around aimlessly. "The dog missing Grampa already?"

"I think she is. I'll have to ask Chip to tell her what's happened. But not yet. He's got his own grief."

She teared up. "It *is* sad. But Dad was getting so unhappy with his struggles. And I realize now I was really stressed, watching and waiting for disasters. You must have been, too."

I agreed, saying, "He was worth every minute of it, but it was so hard. The worst part was that I wasn't able to fix him anymore. That was frustrating."

We were quiet as the dog went back and forth between us, giving and seeking comfort.

Mom broke the silence. "I'm so glad to be out of that big apartment. Thank you for that. Those last few days, I kept waiting for your dad to come out of his room with a cute story or something bleeding. Equal chance of either." She lightened the mood, as always.

"Any New Year's resolutions?" she asked. "Not that you need anything more on a to-do list."

"No, not really. You?"

"Well, I think I do have one, but I might need your help."

I nodded, and she continued, "I want to bake and cook for the gang here. I keep bragging about my cooking, and I want to prove it. What do you think?"

"Brilliant. I'd love to do that with you." We both knew she'd be the brains and I'd be the legs.

She rubbed her hands together, then pulled out her iPad. "Jeannie just sent me this cake recipe. I can't get it to print, though."

I fussed with the printer while she babbled her ideas. "I want to take desserts to the dining room and maybe once a week have people in for dinners. Can you get me a really good cut of beef? Can I afford groceries?"

I knew she wasn't joyous and giddy; she was occupying her mind and time to chase away the shadows. She was teaching me coping skills by example. *Do something. Do anything. Make a list. Have a project. Involve your friends.*

The printer whirred out the recipe, and she opened her ever-present notebook to add the ingredients to her grocery list.

"Yes, you can definitely afford groceries," I answered definitively, without really knowing if it was true. "Well, at least until people start lining up at your door; then you may have to start charging."

We laughed, and I left with a long grocery list.

My mother held people close with every remaining resource she had, and it usually involved food. Carolyn had spent every Tuesday for months having lunch and teaching Mom how to use her iPad. Now Mom could swap recipes by e-mail, Facebook, Skype, phone, and snail mail. She didn't dwell on all the things she couldn't do; she focused on what she could do. And she taught me.

We baked her first New Year's resolution a few days later. I pulled the chocolate cake out of the oven while Mom sorted through a box of old photos. I'd hung a big bulletin board in the kitchen, and we planned to fill it with photos, articles, and anything of interest to her guests. So far it held sympathy cards and Dad's death announcement, which we'd sent to seventy-five of their friends and relatives.

She broke the silence: "This is the first day of my life that I woke up not worried about anything. How can I ever thank you for that?"

I went over and sat at my spot at the table. "I'm so happy to hear that. That's all the thanks I need. But what do you mean?"

"Well, I love it here. I'm not worried about bills or not being able to manage things. A nurse comes running if I push that red button. You have taken the most amazing care of us, and now me."

She didn't seem finished, so I waited.

"I think worrying made me edgier than I realized. I'm sorry about that," she said with sincerity.

"I don't harbor any bad feelings about anything. I always trust we are all doing the best we can."

"Your father taught you that. He always gave everyone the benefit of the doubt. You couldn't even say he gave everyone a second chance; he gave everyone as many chances as they needed."

I smiled an agreement with a gulp.

"I guess if I worry about anything, it's you," she said softly.

"But I'm fine. I'm healthy and have no financial problems."

"I know. And I'm so proud of you for that. But I'm worried about you missing your dad—he was your buddy your whole life—and how you're going to be when, you know, when I'm gone. You have some losses ahead of you." She made a sidelong glance toward the aging poodle.

"You've set a darn good example for dealing with hardship and loss. And gave me a nice, strong gene pool."

That seemed to satisfy her. "Oh, here," she said, handing me snapshots. "Get these adorable pictures of Chip and Dewey on the wall. And here he is, talking to Pookie when they were both about seventeen. That was one gorgeous cat. We never doubted that Chip could talk to animals, even as a child, did we?"

I agreed wholeheartedly and tried rearranging things to make room on the board.

"Maybe stack the sympathy cards over here, since there are so many," she said. "But leave Dad's announcement; thanks for doing such a sweet job with that. Everyone loved the photos and the poem."

For the next week, she sorted photos and I labeled them. She could instantly name all fifteen people in a tiny, grainy family reunion picture who were all dead long before I was born. But she didn't just name them—I watched her conjure their essences and visit their memories. We loaded the bulletin board with her grandmothers, parents, sisters, aunts, uncles, and cousins; each photo was greeted affectionately and produced a story.

All our pets were represented, usually with Chip. All our homes were lined up on the bulletin board in chronological order. She walked through each house while holding the photos, then lovingly tended their gardens in her mind's eye. Her first-place ribbon from the county fair for Best Apple Use featured prominently; she considered it a crowning achievement. We posted the photo of the grade-school class where she had volunteered as a reading aide, and the principal's thank-you letter. We tucked in newspaper articles, drawings, cartoons—anything and everything she'd saved that might spark a story as a friend walked by it.

She pointed to a box, saying, "I don't know if I want to look in that one. That's all the baby books, isn't it? You three kids and Paul?"

"Yes. It was in the cedar chest. You don't have to look. I'll just put it back."

"The bad part about having a good memory is never forgetting anything. I can see Paul's beautiful little face as clear as day. I remember on the morning of his funeral sitting in front of my makeup mirror, putting on lipstick, and wondering how I could look the same, when I would never be the same. Your dad just cried and cried."

"I've thought about Paul a lot and wondered what he'd look like now. I picture him looking like Nelson or Dad. Sometimes I feel like I see him out of the corner of my eye."

"He *would* look like them, because he looked exactly like you. Maybe he's your guardian angel. Although I always figured your dad's father was your guardian angel; he loved you so much."

I was basking in that thought while she sorted the last of the photos.

After I tacked up the last picture, we admired the arrangement.

"Beautiful," she said. "But there is one odd thing about having all those photos right there that I'm not sure I should tell you."

"Oh, go ahead. Now I'm curious."

"Well, a heck of a lot of those people and pets are dead, and I've really missed them—especially my parents."

I didn't think that was the whole revelation, so I waited through a long pause while she read my face.

She decided I could handle what she wanted to say, and continued, "Now, instead of missing them, though, I look at their pictures and hear Grampa cheer, 'Yippee damn,' because I'll be seeing them soon. They don't feel as far away. It doesn't feel morbid; it feels good."

Ah, teaching me, teaching me. I'm going to miss her, but she won't be far away.

"I love that!" I said honestly. "Thanks for that perspective. But don't be in too much of a hurry, okay?"

She laughed and said she had a few more cakes to bake before she was done.

I went home with my head and heart overflowing with her inspiration and love. My computer now sat on my mother's table in my dining room, and every day I made notes on my family to add to my writing, seemingly buoyed by vibrational spirits radiating from the oak.

I used the names and dates on the photos to begin a family tree on Ancestry.com and posted the photos online for my cousins. Mom also knew all the people in Dad's old photos, so the branches of the family tree were laden with pictures and information. I was quickly and thoroughly hooked on genealogy. More and more relatives gathered around the table every time I went online.

One day, I received a message through Ancestry's member services, asking about Margaret, in reference to Mom's first husband. I responded and discovered Fritz's daughter from another marriage.

I took my computer over the next day to show Mom the growing family tree and told her about Fritz's daughter. "Do you want to communicate?"

She froze. This was untrodden territory. She didn't want to violate the memory of Dad so soon after he died. Breathlessly, she asked, "What do you think I should do?"

"Whatever you want, really. There's nothing to lose by saying hello."

She was already reaching for her iPad. "Give me that e-mail address."

Chapter 55

....

Four gray heads had bowed for grace and now were gushing over Mom's roast beef, browned potatoes, and dark, rich gravy. I was washing up pans and enjoying their conversation. One mentioned she'd been married four times, and Mom asked her which husband she'd be with in heaven.

Mom had already asked several people this question; Chris's comic response was her favorite so far: "All of them—that's why they call it heaven."

Tonight's response was good, too. "None of them—that's why they call it heaven."

They all had a good laugh, but this question deeply perplexed Mom. She had fallen in love with Fritz with a vulnerable teenage heart and was reconnecting with those feelings through photos his daughter had e-mailed. Mom had recently read the latest releases of books about people's experiences in heaven and was a firm believer. She loved both of her husbands, though, and didn't want to hurt their feelings.

Thankfully, the next person Mom asked the husband-in-heaven question laid the problem to rest. Jenny, her home health nurse, quickly convinced Mom that God would make the best decision for her; Mom could just leave it to fate and faith.

Mom frequently took treats to the dining room and had her friends in often for dinner, and after several months, her cooking and baking reputation wafted through the place like the aromas it created. People were raving about her roast beef, crispy oven-baked chicken, meat loaf and mashed potatoes, and scalloped potatoes and ham, and making requests. We baked cheesecakes, fruit pies, brownies, and all kinds of cookies and cakes. For St. Patrick's Day, in addition to cabbage rolls and sauerkraut, she had Googled and researched authentic Reuben sandwiches and had Dianna and Chris over for taste testing. All this activity required a lot of grocery shopping on my part, but I was a willing conspirator. I had needed to be occupied this first year without Dad, too.

Now Mom was working on her voice. One of the ladies had heard her singing at the Easter church service, and there was no denying her talent. Mom had chosen two dozen favorite patriotic songs and hymns, and I made twenty copies of sheet music for a booklet I named "Sing-Along with Margaret." One of her friends was a magnificent pianist, and tonight, after their Memorial Day dinner, we'd have the big reveal of the songbook.

I came into the group dining room carrying the music booklets while Mom's latest chocolate cake concoction was being devoured. I passed the booklets around, and each person started humming or singing his or her own favorite, creating a spontaneous chorus. Eventually they channeled their excitement into moving the tables and steering their walkers to the piano. I had slipped Mom's pianist friend a preview copy so she could practice in her apartment. She did a brief scales warm-up, then started a gorgeous, full-keyboard rendition of "America the Beautiful." She waved a signal to start singing because no one wanted to interrupt her music. They began singing shyly but quickly found their stride, their Memorial Day passion so expressively American and so beautiful.

They interspersed the patriotic songs with familiar hymns, many not needing the song sheets for words. My mother was radiant, her spectacular soprano growing stronger with each selection. The music and voices uplifting her in companionship were her generational soul mates—patriots with a shared history. What more could I ever hope for her?

By eight thirty, I realized they could go on way past my bedtime, so I gathered up the dog and the cake pan and got ready to leave, waiting until I caught Mom's eye.

I smiled and waved good-bye to her, and she blew me a kiss. I went home and sat at her table with a heart full of memories to write.

Epilogue

....

My mother is gone now but lived all of her last days joyously, surrounded by friends, family, and faith. After she was diagnosed with terminal cancer, her hospice nurses, caregivers, and chaplain all felt they gained more strength from her than they gave. I cared for her through her last breath, and she continued to mother me until the end. Here is her farewell letter, sent to seventy-five people.

May 2014
Dear Friends and Family,

Well, hello! Here it is, May already. I've baked nuthin from New Years, Valentine's Day, St. Patrick's Day, and Easter. I've made pies, candy, brownies, and some dynamite Reuben sandwiches. I've researched, downloaded, printed, and practiced recipes! High tech!

So while I'm still enjoying life here at my apartment, I want you to know I have signed up for hospice. There isn't a known time frame for me, but hospice has so much to offer in the way of care and comfort that it seemed like the right thing to do. And rather than try to tell you one at a time, or take the risk of accidentally not telling you,

I'm sending you this note. I hope you accept it with my best intentions in mind.

I came up with this idea because Trish mentioned how awful it would be for her to tell someone I was gone if he or she didn't even know I was going. I suggested she just say, "Oh, Mom is away on an extended vacation, visiting long-lost relatives and friends."

And, honestly, that is how I feel. I have deep faith that I am going to a beautiful place to be reunited with loved ones.

That is not to say that I'm not going to miss you, each and every one of you. As you all know, I have a good memory and I am filled with joyful scenes of the past. Elyria, Cumberland, Englewood, Washington, and all points in between are very vivid to me. You are in my thoughts more than you can imagine. I have a wall of photos in my kitchen; if you hear me saying, "Hi!" to you, I probably am. When you think of how much I care about you, multiply it by one hundred and you might come close.

With much love,
Marg

Acknowledgments

....

I never dreamed I'd be writing this; for that, I thank Katy, who set me on this unexpected writing path that I have loved.

Thanks to my intrepid band of support—Katy, Chris, Dianna, and Carolyn—for caring for my parents in whatever way they needed. I couldn't have done any of this without each one of you. From the beginning, many decades ago, my parents loved you as I do: as family. You are my greatest blessing. My life, my parents' lives, and this book blossomed from your nourishment.

I thank all my relatives for keeping our family memories vibrant, reading chapters, and encouraging my writing. I treasure their comments. My cousins Robbie and Ann reviewed the manuscript with educators' eyes, offering important contributions. My mother's sister, my beloved aunt Judy, helped with memories and editing. My cousin Marcia, my anchor since childhood, encouraged, comforted, and inspired me. My brother-in-law, John, skillfully helps Katy manage my website. I give my boundless thanks and love to all my cherished relatives.

I thank my brother for "Holy shit, Sister—your writing is passionate and brilliant." I originally wrote these stories for my family, and Chip's encouragement tipped the balance toward publishing. I thank his wife, Jonquil, for her devotion to our family, for her editing, and for propping up the empty spot in my heart.

Thanks to Ali and Diane, dear friends of thirty years, for their thorough reading, and to Rosalie for an outsider's perspective. Their kind words made my heart sing when I needed it. Katy, Chris, and Dianna lived the daily story, read and reread, and bolstered me through years of writing.

Thanks to Jessica Morrell for considering my early paragraphs relevant. Thanks to Annie Tucker, Karen Parkin, and Jennifer Munro, editors, who guided me through transforming my words into a book.

Thanks to my final proofreaders: Cynthia, Jeanne, Carolyn, Marcia, Sonya, and Amber. Their enthusiasm and editing helped calm my last-minute publishing worries.

Thanks to all the friends, neighbors, medical personnel, caregivers, and strangers who rallied and came to my parents' aid with generosity and grace. It really does take a village.

About the Author

Trish Williams grew up in Elyria, Ohio, surrounded by relatives and friends, then spent a few unforgettable years in Cumberland, Maryland. A retired dental hygienist, she lives in Olympia, Washington, where she has enjoyed gardening, crafting, tracing genealogy, reading, caring for pets, and visiting with friends on the same parcel of paradise since 1977. She lives with her spouse, Katy Murray. Trish would love to hear from you and can be reached through her website: www.patriciawilliamsbook.com.

Selected Titles from She Writes Press

She Writes Press is an independent publishing company founded to serve women writers everywhere. Visit us at www.shewritespress.com.

Don't Leave Yet: How My Mother's Alzheimer's Opened My Heart by Constance Hanstedt. $16.95, 978-1-63152-952-8. The chronicle of Hanstedt's journey toward independence, self-assurance, and connectedness as she cares for her mother, who is rapidly losing her own identity to the early stage of Alzheimer's.

The Space Between: A Memoir of Mother-Daughter Love at the End of Life by Virginia A. Simpson. $16.95, 978-1-63152-049-5. When a life-threatening illness makes it necessary for Virginia Simpson's mother, Ruth, to come live with her, Simpson struggles to heal their relationship before Ruth dies.

Scattering Ashes: A Memoir of Letting Go by Joan Rough. $16.95, 978-1-63152-095-2. A daughter's chronicle of what happens when she invites her alcoholic and emotionally abusive mother to move in with her in hopes of helping her through the final stages of life—and her dream of mending their tattered relationship fails miserably.

Green Nails and Other Acts of Rebellion: Life After Loss by Elaine Soloway. $16.95, 978-1-63152-919-1. An honest, often humorous account of the joys and pains of caregiving for a loved one with a debilitating illness.

Role Reversal: How to Take Care of Yourself and Your Aging Parents by Iris Waichler. $16.95, 978-1-63152-091-4. A comprehensive guide for the 45 million people currently taking care of family members who need assistance because of health-related problems.

Falling Together: How to Find Balance, Joy, and Meaningful Change When Your Life Seems to be Falling Apart by Donna Cardillo. $16.95, 978-1-63152-077-8. A funny, big-hearted self-help memoir that tackles divorce, caregiving, burnout, major illness, fears, and low self-esteem—and explores the renewal that comes when we are able to meet these challenges with courage.